India-European Union Trade Prospects and Impact of Euro

About the book ...

European Union (EU) is the concrete expression of the common desire of the sovereign nations of Europe to work and live together. As an advanced form of multi-sectoral integration, its competence extends to the economy, industry, politics, and citizens' rights of the Member States. The EU is India's largest trading partner, accounting for about one-third of both India's exports and imports. However, India's share in the EU's imports and exports is less than 1 per cent.

This book provides a detailed description of the evolution and the present working of EU with a view to understand its impact on India's foreign trade. More precisely, the book focuses on the impact of developments in the EU on India's exports to it.

About the author ...

Dr. Vibha Mathur is Head of the Department of Commerce, Jesus and Mary College, University of Delhi. She is a product of the University of Delhi and did her research work for M.Phil. and Ph.D. degrees at the prestigious Department of Commerce, Delhi School of Economics, University of Delhi. Her specialisation in India's trade relations with European countries has attracted considerable attention from academicians and policymakers.

India-European Union Trade Prospects and Impact of Euro

Vibha Mathur

Indian Tax Institute
Delhi **India**

First Edition 1999

For details of our other publications, please contact

Indian Tax Institute
34, Gujranwala Town, Part-2
Delhi - 110 033 INDIA

Tel.: 7138192, 7247805 Fax: +91-11-7464774

Email : indiatax@del2.vsnl.net.in

Website : http://www.nexusindia.com/indtax

First Edition 1999

ISBN: 81-87046-07-4

Published by Indian Tax Institute and printed at D.K. Fine Art Press (P) Ltd., Delhi-110 052

PRINTED IN INDIA

Key to Numeration

1 lakh = 0.1 million
10 lakh = 1.0 million
1 crore =10.0 million
100 crore = 1.0 billion

Exchange Rate

The unit of currency in India is Indian Rupee.
As on 23.2.1999

1 US Dollar = 42 Rupees (Approximately)
1 UK Pound = 69 Rupees (Approximately)

Fiscal Year

Fiscal year in India runs from April 1 to March 31 of the following year.

Contents

EUROPEAN UNION
DELEGATION OF THE EUROPEAN COMMISSION
IN INDIA
The Ambassador
Head of Delegation

FOREWORD

As we stand on the threshold of the 21st century, we should perhaps look at what the European Union has achieved over the past few years and decades. If the clock were to be stopped today and objective judgement were to be passed on the European Union as it has developed since its foundation in 1957, I am convinced that it would be viewed primarily as an unparalleled experiment in economic integration driven by the dynamic effects of converging transnational market forces. The European Union's single market, by far the largest single market in the world, was established on the back of a remarkable and comprehensive removal of national regulations and restrictions, frontier controls, and sheer red tape. It has given way to economies of scale and a significant increase in competitive pressures as companies jostle to trade on a level playing field with 370 million potential consumers - rising to around half a billion consumers as the European Union enlargement to Central and Eastern Europe proceeds.

Dr. Vibha Mathur has succeeded in giving us an eminently readable account of the economic developments in the European Union and its impact on India's trade and industry. She traces the evolution of the European Union, the functioning of its different institutions and the process of European integration. Against this background, the author discusses in-depth EU-India trade relations, which is the prime focus of the publication.

The analysis convincingly demonstrates that, following the creation of the Single European Market, India's exports to the Union, in absolute terms, have increased. This seems to be the initial impact and over a period the growth rate is likely to pick up. However, in order to improve India's exports to the European Union broad strategies are recommended at three levels, namely, firm specific, industry specific and country specific.

65, Golf Links. New Delhi - 110003 INDIA Telephones : 4629237, 4629238 Fax : 4629206
email: eudelind@giasdl01.vsnl.net.in

In a comprehensive coverage of EU-India trade relations, the prominence given to the new European currency, the Euro and its implications for India, are timely. The introduction of the Euro on 1st January 1999 was an historic step towards European integration. On that date, the national currencies of 11 European countries became denominations of a single currency - the Euro and the Eurosystem (composed of the European Central Bank and the 11 national Central Banks of the participating European Union Member States) assumed responsibility for the monetary policy of the Euro area.

I am sure that this book will be found useful by industry, government, academicians and students of economics.

Michael Barrie McGeever
Ambassador and Head of Delegation
of the European Commission in India

Preface

Pursuant to the Treaty of Rome (March 25, 1957), the European Economic Community (EEC) was set up with the primary objective 'to establish, within the framework of an economic union, a common market providing for healthy competition and having characteristics similar to those of an internal market.' From July 1, 1968, all customs duties and quotas in the trade between EEC member countries were abolished to move towards a common market with equality of competition as a condition. Following the principle of destination, exports to member countries became entirely tax-free, and imports from countries within the community began to be treated in the same way as domestic production destined for home consumption. The concept of a vast single market, unhampered by internal frontiers, was at the core of the objectives set in the Treaty of Rome.

The present work is an attempt to understand the working of the EEC, now known as the European Union (EU). The impact of the developments in the EU on India's trade relations with it forms the focus of the study. The chapter scheme of the book is as follows.

Chapter 1 is the introductory chapter. Chapter 2 traces the origin and evolution of European Union over the years and describes its present institutional framework. Chapter 3 is devoted to the objectives laid down in the Act, targets set and achievements made. Chapter 4 surveys Indo-EU trade relations, examining in detail India's exports to and imports from EU. Chapter 5 provides an a priori analysis of the impact of European unification on India's foreign trade. Chapter 6 examines the impact of Euro on India's trade with EU. Chapter 7 contains conclusions of the study.

Delhi
26.2.1999

Vibha Mathur

List of Tables

India-European Union Trade Prospects and Impact of Euro

Chapter 1

Introduction

European history pertaining to Medieval period is replete with dreams and aspirations of rulers, clergymen, thinkers and philosophers conjuring the picture of an enlarged and unified Europe, going far beyond the territory of one's own. In the given situation of those times, the concept of European unity was, however, pursued with means that gave rise to conflict and wars, sowing seeds of bitterness, rivalry and disintegration as opposed to friendship, co-operation and unification. By the time the seventeenth century came to a close, several changes had occurred in the structural layers of power in different principalities and kingdoms and the concept of a continental integration had started taking a different shape. Intellectuals and the Quakers, with humanistic approach and belief in universal brotherhood, had come out with a proposition that an unified Europe can possibly emerge if an institution in the nature of European Senate, consisting of representatives of rulers, can be created [1].

During the eighteenth and nineteenth centuries, while here and there individuals did keep on arguing about the desirability of creating unified Europe, the idea that caught the imagination of principalities and kingdoms in that period was the urgency of consolidation and integration at home rather than across the continent; examples thereof being zollverin - a German Customs Union - and the adoption of the concept of a single unified state encompassing different principalities and administrative units of Italy. However, a more significant development that took place during this period was the emergence of ambition on the part of almost each and every important European power to acquire and expand colonial empires overseas. This naturally diverted their attention from the goal of European integration to that of colonial expansion, which in turn invariably led to rivalries and intercine wars. During this phase, while occasionally some individuals [2] did advocate the need for forging unity at the continental level, the atmosphere was not really conducive to pursuing this goal even in this loosest possible form. Thus, the concept of continental unity got completely eclipsed under the shadow of overseas colonial expansion and ambitions.

During the first half of the present century, two world wars erupted, each one of them originating from rivalries among the European powers themselves. Both these wars, in particular the second one, resulted in inflicting heavy costs, gigantic devastation and immense human suffering on all those who were involved in the wars, including the European countries [3] constituting the main war theatre. A painful realisation emerged from these tragedies : unless the Europeans do make sincere attempts to forge strong co-operative links among them on the one hand and their governments do adopt a political system in which the latter would be effectively responsible to the governed, history would keep on repeating itself.

As the second world war was drawing to its termination stage, the Allied powers were concurrently busy preparing blue prints of multilateral institutions that could possibly play an effective role in minimising the intensity of factors that in the past had given rise to flares and conflicts. There, thus, emerged charters for setting up United Nations, World Bank, International Monetary Fund (IMF) and other similar organisations. In addition, the United States came out with a large package of assistance - the Marshall Plan - with a view to helping the West European countries in the task of reconstructing their war-ravaged economies. On the security front, initiatives taken by US government eventually resulted in the creation of North Atlantic Treaty Organisation (NATO). All these developments inspired the creation of a few other institutions, two important ones being: (i) Organisation for European Economic Co-operation (OEEC) and (ii) European Payments Union (EPU). These institutions did help in bringing concerned countries closer to each other and in that sense made a significant contribution towards creating an atmosphere and an urge among the Europeans for taking steps for European integration.

While the second world war was still on, there were some leaders in the resistance movement who were applying their mind to the problem of avoiding future wars. Among them were two proponents of European Unity: Altiero Spinelli of Italy and Jean Monnet of France [4]. They were of the view that unless steps are taken to promote in the post-war Europe democratic ideals as opposed to totalitarianism and also to curb national antagonism, the objective of avoiding future wars would never be achieved. In their view, what was needed was interaction and co-operation among European powers at all levels and joint action by them in certain selected areas so that eventually European integration materialises.

After the cessation of the war, it was Sir Winston Churchill, who, in as early as September 1946, emphasised the desirability of European countries, and in particular France and Germany, making determined efforts for creating "the European family and building for that purpose a kind of United States of Europe". Gradually, the idea of forging unity among Western European countries started catching on. At the Hague Congress held in 1948, in which Paul Heri Spaak played a significant role, the desirability of creating a supranational institution, superimposed on a European Federation, was discussed in a general way and a feeling emerged that nothing worthwhile would be accomplished without taking brick-by-brick steps for creating European unity. Consultations among West European countries that followed resulted in a decision to create that nothing worthwhile would be accomplished without taking brick-by-brick steps for creating European unity. Consultations among West European countries that followed resulted in a decision to create a ministerial council called Council of Europe - which came into being in May 1949 and initially consisted of ten countries: Belgium, Denmark, France, Italy, Ireland, Luxembourg, the Netherlands, Norway, Sweden and the U.K. Later on, some other countries - Greece, Turkey, Iceland, Germany and Austria also joined. But this organisation turned out to be more of an inter-governmental consultative forum that a foundation-stone for European integration [5].

Conflicts had ravaged the continent of Europe during the first half of this century, and at the end of the Second World War, there emerged a broad vision of a new united Europe which would transcend national antagonisms [6].

This vision was shared by many statesmen across the continent. Among them, Mr. Robert Schuman, the then French foreign minister, who in concurrence with German Chancellor Konrad Adenauer, in a declaration on May 9, 1950, proposed the pooling of the coal and steel industries of France and the Federal Republic of Germany. Responding to this appeal, six European countries - Belgium, France, Germany, Italy, Luxembourg and the Netherlands - came together to sign the Treaty of Paris, establishing the European Coal and Steel Community. The foundations of the European Union were, thus, truly and firmly laid as clearly envisaged in the Preamble to the Treaty of Paris.

European integration has developed in several stages and various forms. In 1957, these six nations signed the Treaties of Rome to create the European Economic Community (EEC) and the European Atomic Energy Community (EURATOM); EEC entered into force from January 1, 1958.

Initially the European Community (EC), which now is known as European Union (EU), was conceived mainly to promote common policies in the pursuit of economic and monetary union among the member states, involving the creation of a common free trade zone and a customs union. In 1962, the Common Agricultural Policy was adopted establishing a single market and common prices for most agricultural products.

The Union's institutional framework comprising the European Parliament, the European Commission, the Council of Ministers and the Court of Justice takes care of the legislative, executive, decision-making and judicial aspects of its work.

Over the years and considering the rapid development of exchanges and industrial development, neighbouring countries joined the successful Union - Denmark, Ireland and the United Kingdom in 1973, Greece in 1981, and Spain and Portugal in 1986. On January 1, 1995, Austria, Finland and Sweden also became members, taking the membership from 12 to 15.

In February 1986, the 12 member countries of the Union signed the Single Act, committing themselves to the creation of a single market with free movement of goods, capital, services and labour across national frontiers by 1992. On January 1, 1993, the Single Market was formally launched, removing internal frontiers for 12 separate national markets.

A significant landmark in the process of European integration was the signing of the Treaty of European Union on February 7, 1992, at Maastricht in the Netherlands. The Treaty came into force on November 1, 1993, after it was ratified by the 12 member states, and the European Community was renamed the European Union (EU).

The objectives of the Treaty were : a common European currency by 1999, at the latest; rights for European citizens; new powers for the EU in some areas, such as consumer protection, public health, visa policy, trans-European transport, telecommunication, education, culture etc. and the introduction of a common foreign and security policy. Euro, Europe's new currency, as scheduled was launched on January 1, 1999 opening new and varied opportunities for India's foreign trade.

The Union is today the world's biggest free trade area, offering the largest market in the industrialised world with a population of nearly 370 million people. It is also the world's biggest importer of agricultural products.

India's association with the European Union dates back to over 30 years, when the six-member Union was barely four years old. India was among the first developing countries to establish diplomatic relations with the European Union.

EU is India's largest trading partner accounting for Rs. 32,910 crore for exports and Rs. 38,082 crore for imports in 1997-98.

The EU remains India's largest trading partner, accounting for nearly 30 per cent of both imports and exports. At the same time, trade with India represents only around 1 per cent of total EU trade.

Main sectors of India's exports to EU are: ready-made garments (13 per cent of total exports to EU in 1997-98), leather and its products including footwear (11 per cent), gems and jewellery (11.33 per cent), agro-based goods (9.8 per cent), chemical material and its products (7 per cent) and engineering goods (5.4 per cent).

India's main imports from EU are : gems and jewellery (representing 31 per cent of total imports in 1997-98 from EU), capital goods (25 per cent), iron and steel (5 per cent), and chemical material and products (6 per cent).

India is the second largest beneficiary of the EU's Generalised System of Preferences (GSP). Under the new GSP scheme that came into place from January 1, 1995, and ran up to 1998, India continued to enjoy preferential access to EU markets.

Under the Textiles Agreement negotiated in the Uruguay Round, the EU and India have concluded a new bilateral textiles agreement which came into effect on January 1, 1995. The EU, which will be phasing out all Quantitative restrictions in the next few years, has increased the quotas allocated to India and will provide greater flexibility in the implementation of the regime. India will eliminate some Balance of Payments restrictions imposed on the import of textile products and will bind some tariffs.

The EU and India grant each other Most Favoured Nation (MFN) treatment in their trade relations. Moreover, under the new Co-operation Agreement, both parties have agreed to consult each other, at the earliest opportunity, on any specific issue which may arise in connection with the bilateral trade.

In the scenario of growing co-operation and friendship, India and the European Union, the world's two largest democratic entities, can look forward to a real working partnership based on mutual interest in the years ahead.

Notes

1. Prof. Hans A. Schmitt of Tulane University, North Orleans, has argued this aspect in his research study entitled *"The Path to European Union : From the Marshall Plan to the Common Market 1962"*, some important instances quoted in that publication being:

(i) "Richard Zouche, a professor at oxford contended in 1650 that local governors should be allowed to by-pass their rulers and send embassies to peace congress that proposed to discuss matters concerning their province"

(ii) "In 1693, William Penn (in a paper entitled *"An Essay towards the Present and Future Peace of Europe by the Establishment of a European Dyet, Parliament and Estates"*) called for a European Parliament, not a democratic gathering but an institution representing people rather than princes. John Bellers, his co-religionist wished to divide Europe into one hundred constituencies, each to send one representative a European Senate"

2. The following paragraph taken from Prof. Hans A Schmitt's research study, referred to earlier, makes a mention of selected individuals who did espouse the cause of setting up institutions which would have led to countries in the European continent coming closer to each other.

"The champions of continental union toiled on, but in obscurity. For a time in the 1860's, they found an eminent sponsor in Napoleon III, who was ever willing to outdo his uncle without taking his risks. Under his benevolent patronage, a "League for Peace and Freedom" was founded and at its first meeting in 1869, Victor Hugo eulogised the "United States of Europe". Before the year was out, a German Edward Loewenthal, had founded the "League for the Union of Europe...".

3. National Conference on *"European Union : Now and Beyond - A Backgrounder"*; PHD Chamber of Commerce and Industry; February 9, 1995.

4. According to EU publication entitled *"European in Ten Lessons"*, Altiero Spinelli's view was that the best method of attaining European unity would be to follow federalist model under which while there would be co-operation between European nations at all levels - local, regional and national, each federation unit would continue to have its own autonomy. Jean Monnet's view, on the other hand, was that in selected areas there should be not only joint action but indeed even transfer of sovereignty from national to continental level. The integration model that has finally emerged in the form of European is indeed a mixture of the two approaches.

5. Prof. Hans A. Schmitt in his research study, referred to earlier, points out that from the very beginning there was difference of opinion between the French and the British about the precise objective of this institution. The French took the view that this Council would be in the nature of a political union between the signatory nations whereas the British view was that this organisation would facilitate common action between separate and independent states.

6. *"The European Union and India - A Partnership for Progress"*; European Union publication; March, 1995.

Chapter 2

Origin and Growth of the European Community

Economic development of a nation is largely affected by a number of economic and non-economic factors. Among the economic determinants of growth, expansion of trade occupies an important place. The historical experience of a few advanced nations too has clearly demonstrated how foreign trade can be an engine of growth. The economic progress of most of the present industrially advanced countries of the world like U.S.A., France, U.K. etc. is attributable to their ever-expanding external trade. Trade, hence, has been rightly termed as *an engine of growth*, *an activator of change* and *a barometer of economic progress*.

The European Union [1] and the democratic independent India, both were born out of the turmoil of the World War-II aftermath. It was in September 1946 that Winston Churchill, the then Prime Minister of Britain, called upon the people of Europe to raise the banner of reconciliation and peace and at the same period, Mahatma Gandhi was urging national reconciliation, unity and peace.

Thus, both India and the European Union had a vocation to replace confrontation with co-operation and to speak the language of unity in diversity. India's relationship with Europe stretches beyond the days of the Greco-Roman Empire in Europe and the advent of Islam in India. There is a long history of cross-fertilisation of ideas, mutual impact of culture and exchange of goods between the two major entities of the 'Old World'. And yet, in another sense, both the Republic of India and the European Community are young entrants to the world polity. It was only after Independence that India began to build upon its 'older ties' with Europe. In the pursuit of its policy to diversify and deepen the country's external relations, India was the first developing country to accredit its diplomatic mission to the Union in 1962. Before giving a detailed background about the trade relations between India and EU, a brief historical background about the European Union is necessary.

2.1 Earliest Attempts at European Union

The basic idea of European integration is very old; primeval examples of such movements can be found as early as in the 15th century. Although, those ancient and vague suggestions had little in common with the modern concept of European integration, they do prove how deep the roots of European movements for unification lie.

Historically, they can be appreciated as being the initiators of the basic principle.

Indeed, the very first signs of "European" feeling were connected more often with religion than with economy. Furthermore, in the 15th century, of course, the concept of the World did not stretch much further than Europe and suggestions for the creation of some form of international government could be understood as an early attempt at intra-European co-operation. Thus, the Councillor Movement of Jean Gerson could be judged as the earliest timid proposal for the co-ordination of European proposals. Though, his main attempt was undoubtedly directed more towards the reorganisation of the Roman Catholic Church and did not go into many of the technical details, yet he thought that the best way to deal with European problems was to create an international government.

The first real proposal for European Union before 20th century came only in the 17th century, when the famous 'Grand Design' was introduced by the Duke of Sully. The Duke, who was the chief advisor to king Henry of France and one of the most brilliant minds of his epoque, suggested that the fifteen Christian kingdoms of Europe should unify under a General Council of Europe.

The "Grand Design" was the model for the scheme for a "European State" which was proposed by John Bellers, and it provided the basic idea for the Abb de Saint-Pierre when he advocated the creation of a permanent alliance between all the sovereign nations of Europe. His plan, which was called "Project of Perpetual Peace", was aimed mainly at the maintenance of peace in Europe.

During the 18th and 19th centuries, the idea of European Union was advocated mainly by Philosophers such as Kant, Bentham and Rousseaue, who based their proposals on the realisation of perpetual peace in Europe and consequently in the whole world. At the end of the 19th century, the idea of a "Unified States of Europe" became increasingly popular, though politicians and statesmen directly connected with the realisation of such a distant dream, still considered it as a desirable but highly impracticable idea definitely more connected with humanitarian, religious, and peace-loving ideals than with any solid proposals to solve political or economic problems. The necessity for a European or even a World Federation had occurred rather to philosophers and religious thinkers, probably because of the theoretical obviousness of such propositions.

2.2 Pan-European Union Movement

One of the most significant step towards European integration in the first half of the 20th century was the founding of the "Pan-European Union". Although the movement, which was directed by an ardent apostle of European unification, Count Coundenhove Kalergi received little, if any, official support from the European governments, the enthusiasm of its advocates had a noticeable influence over the members of several international organisations such as the League of Nations, as well as over various parliamentary groups in European countries. The Pan-European Union was founded in 1923 and from the beginning of its existence, it persistently advocated the creation of a political and economic federation. Count Kalergi, the founder of the Union, recommended the convocation of a Pan-European Conference as a positive, first step towards the realisation of a "Pan-Europe" in successive stages.

Hence, it can be concluded that attempts to unify Europe date back to the 17th century when the first famous "Grand Design" was introduced. Other attempts to unify Europe also include military invasions of Napoleon and Hitler, who tried to impose unity by force. Other important movements which took place in the 19th century were the Kalergi and Pan-European movement.

It can, therefore, be stated that the European ideal was unknown to all but philosophers and visionaries until it crystallised into a political concept and became the long-term goal of the Members States of the European Union [2].

The notion of United States of Europe was part of the humanist pacifist dream which was shattered by the conflicts which brought destruction to the European Continent in the first half of the century. The classic argument for creating a political unit in Europe rested on the need to preserve peace in traditionally bellicose part of the World. At both the intellectual and emotional levels there has been a constant interplay between the opposing force of nationalism on the one hand and, on the other, the desire to create an organisation which would express the enduring sense of common history, culture, ideas and experiences in Europe and which would be able to resolve antagonisms in a non-war like manner [3].

2.3 Various Movements Towards European Unity

One of the main sources of the newly revived enthusiasm for European Union sprung from the psychological effects of the second world war. The disastrous experience of the war clearly demonstrated that national states were no longer effective as political defence organisations [4].

There was no doubt that economic reasons, such as the acceleration of technical progress, the introduction of automation and methods of mass production, the increasing importance of intra-European trade, etc., clearly pointed towards a new system based on closer European collaboration. Nonetheless, the horrible experience of the War was still the principal ideological factor that encouraged the popular acceptance of the idea of a unified European economic and political system. Thus, the real history of European economic integration started with the end of the second world war.

The economic background of this period was by no means favourable for the undertaking of such an ambitious project. European recovery started slowly and hesitantly in 1945 and 1946. The next year, 1947, brought further disappointments, in fact, it was described as a crisis year. It was certainly an unlucky year for European agriculture, which was accompanied by growing deficits in the balance of payments and serious inflationary pressures in most of the countries with an undesirable effect on industrial output and internal and external stability. There was a growing realisation of the need for European collaboration, if not even for integration. Statesmen, economists and important personalities supported publicly the idea of the European brotherhood and co-operation. As early as in November 1945, Winston Churchill advocated a "United States of Europe" which would unify the continent at a level never experienced since the fall of the Roman Empire. The popular support for European unity, partly as a result of his speeches which had attracted great attention all over Europe, had been more or less captured. In January 1947, the United Europe Committee was created which held its first meeting in London on 14th May 1947. The main objective of the United Europe Committee was to encourage European movements and to organise public support for European unity.

By the end of 1947, the European leaders were fully convinced of the necessity for urgent and efficient unification. In December 1947, an important step was taken towards closer co-operation by the formation of the "European Movement". It was composed of the "European Union of Federalists", "the United Europe Movement", "The European League for Economic Co-operation", "British United European Committee" and "The Socialist Movement for a United States of Europe" which would unify the continent.

2.4 Congress of Europe

The various national movements in favour of a United Europe organised their first big international conference at Hague in May 1948. Hence, the first concrete step towards European co-operation in the economic sphere was taken in 1948 with the setting up of the Organisation for European Economic co-operation (OEEC) whose functions were to distribute Marshall Aid funds, to co-ordinate investment programmes and to resuscitate intra-European trade [5]. In the previous year, a customs union between Belgium, the Netherlands and Luxembourg - BENELUX - was formed; in the years following, many other steps were taken towards the economic integration of those three countries. Partly in reaction to these moves, Russia and the Eastern European countries set up the Council for Mutual Economic Assistance - Comecon - in January, 1949; broadly speaking 'Comecon' has been much less integrated than the European Economic Community [6]. Within the limited sphere of reviving trade between the European Countries after the war, the OEEC was very successful. Its first step was a programme of trade liberalisation, but after a certain stage it was found that trade could not be expanded further without setting up credit facilities and making payments multilateral. Both these functions were performed by the European Payments Union, set up in 1950. Actual European integration began when Belgium, France, Germany, Italy, Luxembourg and the Netherlands, in 1951, signed the treaty establishing the European Coal and Steel Community (ECSC). The primary object of the Union was to set up common markets in coal, iron-ore, scrap and steel, and by early 1953 most of them were in being. But its larger aim was to lay the basis for some form of European Federation. The British refused to join it.

The movement towards integration was, for a time, halted by a quarrel over defence, sparked off by the Korean war. In 1950, the U.S. proposed the rearmament of Germany within NATO, but the French refused to allow Germany to re-establish an army and to become a member of NATO, whereas the Germans would not rearm under joint European control.

A Treaty setting up a European Defence Community was signed in May 1952 by the 'Six', the British again refusing to join. At the same time, the 'Six' made detailed proposals for a European Political Community with a directly elected Parliament Community. In 1954, the Communists and Gaullists combined in the chamber to reject French membership of the European Defence Community. A variety of feelings lay behind this coalition. Fear of a new German army, anxiety lest the French economy become a casualty in any closer integration, resentment against the threat to French sovereignty - these combined effectively with the Stalinism of the extreme left.

A new organisation, Western European Union, was set up to control the strength of military forces and armaments and in this Britain was associated with the 'Six'. After the failures of the plans for the Defence and Political Communities, the 'European' decided that their next move should be in the economic and not in the political field and that it should take the form of a supra-national institution. This move was based on the experience of existing European institutions; the working of the OEEC showed the limitations to purely inter-governmental action and the success of the European Coal and Steel Community showed the scope for supra-national organisations.

2.5 Formation of the European Community

On the 27th May 1952, the inherent dynamism of the new-born Europe prompted plans for two new communities - the European Defence Community (EDC) based on a treaty signed by the 'Six' [7], on the same day and a European Polity Community. The EDC was conceived as a means of bolstering the Atlantic Alliance, the aim was to integrate the armed forces of Europe.

The ministers of the 'Six' called to prepare a plan for a political Community. However, on 30th August, 1954, the French National Assembly rejected the plan outright. In the meeting at Messina, at the beginning of June 1955, the foreign ministers of the 'Six' announced that they intended to continue the attempt to establish a United Europe so as to preserve Europe's role in the World, restore its influence and prestige and steadily increase the standard of living of its people.

In February 1957, the Council of the Organisation for European Economic Co-operation (OEEC) began negotiations for the establishment of a free trade area. At the same time then, there were two separate series of negotiations - one culminated in the Treaty of Rome signed by the Six on March 25, 1957 and the other in the formation of the European Free Trade Association (EFTA) on May 3, 1960. The Rome Treaties establishing the European Economic Community (EEC) and the European Atomic Energy Community (EURATOM), together with the Paris Treaty, establishing the European Coal and Steel Community (ECSC), formed constitution of the European Union. The EEC and EURATOM treaties entered into force on January 1, 1958.

Thus, all three European Communities - the EEC, ECSC and EURATOM - had the common aim of political union, and common methods of bringing this about the removal of market barriers, the formulation of common policy and the formation of the habit of looking at problems from an international point of view. The European Economic Community naturally had the widest scope: it set out, first to establish a customs union (or a common market in goods) with no internal barriers to trade and a common external tariff and commercial policy and secondly, to abolish all obstacles to the movement of people and capital within the Union.

In the words of the preamble of the Treaty of Rome, the European Community was to "lay the foundation of an ever closer union among the people of Europe and by pooling resources was to preserve and strengthen peace and liberty" [8].

2.6 Enlargement of the European Union

2.6.1 First Expansion of the Union

The United Kingdom originally refused to play any part in the ECSC and the EEC [9]. It was a founding member of the seven-country European Free Trade Association (EFTA), which was set up in 1960. Britain soon realised that it could not make its political influence felt through EFTA.

Denmark also saw the European Union as a free access to a common market, with its food production being three times the requirement of its population. Ireland too saw entry into Union as a chance to boost its economic growth. At this time, the need was felt for the unification of the EEC proposal. The time was ripe for the countries to apply for membership.

So, on August 9, 1961, Britain made its first formal application for full membership to the Union. On November 9 and 10, 1961, the representatives of the six governments of the member states held a meeting in Brussels with the British delegation led by Lord Privy Seal, who had been appointed by the British government to conduct negotiations on the accession of the U.K. to the Union.

On August 10, 1961, the Danish government requested the opening of the negotiations with a view to Denmark's accession. The government of Ireland applied for an accession to the European Union on July 31, 1961. However, the British application was turned down by the French in 1963. In 1967, Britain applied again and once again, the attempt floundered against French reservation.

The negotiations for the accession of the United Kingdom and three other countries (Denmark, Ireland and Norway) proved to be long and arduous [10]. After being suspended twice, they finally led to the Treaty of Accession which was signed in Brussels in January, 1972.

After a referendum in Norway had rejected the idea of membership, the first enlargement took effect on January 1, 1973, and increased the Union from Six to Nine Member States.

2.6.2 Second Enlargement

The Second enlargement involved three Mediterranean countries which applied in 1975 and 1977 after the restoration of democracy. The Hellenic government made a formal application to join the European Union on 12th June, 1975. Greece became the 10th member of the Union on January 1, 1981.

2.6.3 Third Enlargement

The Kingdom of Spain and Portuguese Republic applied for membership on 28th July and 28th March 1977 respectively. Negotiations for their accession began on 17th October 1978 with Portugal and on 6th February 1979 with Spain [11].

Their accession raised several difficulties and it took six years of negotiations to solve them. The Treaties between the 10 Member States and Spain and Portugal providing for Spanish and Portuguese accession were signed in Lisbon and Madrid on 12th June, 1985. The Treaties were verified by the Parliaments of the Member States and the applicant countries. Spain and Portugal duly became the eleventh and twelfth members of the Union on 1st January 1986.

2.6.4 Fourth Enlargement

The most recent enlargement of the European Union took place on January 1, 1995 when Austria, Sweden and Finland became members of the Union [12]. These three countries signed the Treaty of Accession at the European Council summit in Corfu held from June 24 to 25, 1994.

Austria had applied for membership to the Union on July 17, 1989; Sweden had applied on July 1, 1991 and Finland had applied on March 18, 1992. Subsequent to the signing of the Treaty Accession, national referenda held in Austria, Finland and Sweden had ratified the decision to join the EU.

Austria voted positively on June 12, 1994 with a landslide majority of 66.58 percent. The Finish referendum result on October 16 showed 57 percent 'yes' votes against 43 percent adverse votes. The Swedish referendum on November 13, 1994 showed 52.2 percent for the Union and 46.9 percent against.

Norway had also applied for its membership in early 1993 to the European Union. Norway had made two previous requests to join the European Union (1962 and 1967), together with the United Kingdom, Ireland and the Kingdom of Denmark on which the Commission expressed its opinion in 1967 and 1969 [13].

The Norwegian government suffered a setback in its bid to join when the Norwegians rejected EU membership in the referendum held on November 28, 1994. The voting was 52.5 percent against and 46 percent in favour.

2.6.5 Proposed Enlargement of the Union

As seen above, the Union has been enlarged four times since its foundation and its membership has risen from six to fifteen in January, 1995. It is now on the threshold of a series of enlargements which could bring its membership to 20 by the year 2000 and even more in the early years of the 21st century.

EU has received applications for membership from the Mediterranean countries and Central and Eastern Europe; with these applications EU is set to expand further. Turkey, Cyprus and Malta are among the Mediterranean countries which have applied for membership. On April 14, 1987, Turkey applied to join the EU; Cyprus applied on July 4, 1990 and Malta applied on July 16, 1990.

The Commission's opinion on Turkish membership was that economic dislocation would be too great - the emphasis was on the realisation of the customs union. Malta and Cyprus are expected to be included in the next phase of enlargement. In Central and Eastern Europe, the EU has concluded association agreements, known as 'Europe Agreements' with Poland, Hungary, the Czech and Slovak Republics, Bulgaria and Romania, creating closer economic and political links. The 'Europe Agreement' with Poland and Hungary came into force on February 1, 1994. The remaining four have been signed but are awaiting final ratification. The Copenhagen summit in June 1993, explicitly recognised the eventual goal of membership for these countries when they could satisfy the economic and political conditions required. To aid the process of integration and convergence in these countries, the Commission has launched pre-accession strategy. This involves deepening the relationship, creating the appropriate legal and institutional environment enhancing trade, aiding in the development of macro-economic and reform policies and reforming the EU assistance through the Phare programme.

Hungary and Poland submitted their membership applications on March 31 and April 4, 1994 respectively. Negotiations for 'Europe agreement' are now underway with Slovania and Baltic states; negotiations are expected to start in 1995. The EU has already concluded Free Trade Agreements (FTA) with the Baltic states on July 18, 1994 and has a long-term plan to prepare them for subsequent accession.

Of the EFTA countries, Iceland and Liechtenstien have not formally applied for EU membership. Switzerland's application in 1992 for membership of the EU has been put on hold due to the rejection of the EEA (European Economic Area) through a referendum on December 6, 1992. However, the Swiss government has expressed an opinion that its long-term political goal is to join the EU.

On June 22, 1995, Romania applied to join EU. Slovak Republic applied for EU membership closely after Romania, i.e. June 27, 1995. On 27th October, 1995, Latvia applied to join EU. On 28th November 1995 Estonia applied to join EU. On December 8, 1995 Lithuania applied for EU membership and immediately after this Bulgaria applied for EU membership on December 14, 1995. On January 17, 1996 Czech Republic applied to join EU. On June 10, 1996 Slovenia applied to join EU.

In mid-1997, concerning the countries of Central and Eastern Europe, the Commission presented in its opinions an objective analysis, in the light of the criteria laid down by the Copenhagen European Council. The Commission considered that none of them fully satisfied all the criteria at present. However, nine countries satisfied the political conditions while certain countries had made sufficient progress towards satisfying the economic conditions and those related to the other obligations of membership.

In the light of its analysis, and in accordance with their respective merit, the Commission considered that Hungary, Poland, Estonia, the Czech Republic and Slovenia could be in a position to satisfy all the conditions of membership in the medium term if they maintained and strongly sustained their efforts of preparation.

In the case of above mentioned countries listed by the Commission, it was stated that they presented the characteristics of a democracy with stable institutions guaranteeing the rule of law, human rights and respect for and protection of minorities. It could be regarded as a functioning market economy and should be able to cope with competitive pressure and market forces within the Union in the medium term.

However, they would be able in the medium term to participate fully in the single market, provided that these countries continued their efforts on transposition of the acquis, and intensified work on its implementation.

Hence, with so many applications for membership on the table or expected in the near future, the Union has no choice but to move further along the road to a Union based on the federalist philosophy. Unless it can strengthen its structures and rationalise decision making to combine efficiency with democracy, the Union cannot hope to develop into a genuine union. On the contrary, it will be faced with the prospect of dilution or paralysis. Greater Europe, stretching from the Mediterranean to the Arctic circle, will only develop into an organised power if it is built around a stable nucleus capable of speaking and acting as one.

To conclude, it can be stated that the disappearance of East-West antagonism is a triumph for the European spirit, which Europeans need now more than ever as they embark on building a new continent with 15 member countries having an area of 2,794 thousand sq. kms., a population of 369.6 millions and gross domestic product of 5,805 thousand million PPS.

2.6.6 Economic Growth and Gradual Recovery of the Union

The GDP (Gross Domestic Product) of the European Union was 0.9 percent higher in the second quarter of 1994 as compared with the first quarter. According to the Bureau of Statistics, Eurostat, it was the

"Strongest growth" registered for some years. The comparable figure for 1993 was 0.3 percent, which was itself a great improvement over the previous quarter when the figure was negative (-0.7 percent). According to Eurostat, the EU's GDP rose by 2.1 percent from the first quarter of 1993 to the first quarter of 1994.

Indeed, in 1994, the rate of growth had been positive in all 12 member states. The strongest growth was in Italy (+1.4 percent), followed by Britain (+1.2 percent) and then France and the Netherlands (each +1.4 percent). In comparison, the United States' rate was equal to the overall EU figure (+0.9 percent) while Canada's was higher (+1.6 percent) and Japan's was negative (-0.4 percent).

2.6.7 Key Dates in European Integration

Following are the key dates in European integration.

April 18, 1951: the 'Six' signed the Treaty establishing the European Coal and Steel Community (ECSC) in Paris.

May 27, 1952: The Treaty establishing the European Defence Community (EDC) was signed in Paris.

June 1-2, 1955: The Foreign Ministers of the 'Six', met in Messina and decided to extend European integration to all branches of the economy.

March 25, 1957: The Treaties establishing the European Economic Community and the European Atomic Energy Community were signed in Rome.

July 30, 1962: The Common Agricultural Policy (CAP) was set.

July 1, 1968: Remaining customs duties in intra-community trade in manufactured goods were abolished 18 months ahead of schedule and the Common External Tariff (CET) were introduced.

January 1, 1973: Denmark, Ireland and the U.K. joined the Union

Table 2.1: Basic Demographics of the 15 Member States

Country	Area ('000 sq. km.)	Population (Millions)	Gross Domestic Product ('000 Million pps*)
Austria	84	7.9	136.2
Belgium	31	10.1	172.3
Denmark	43	5.2	88.5
Finland	337	5.1	68.4
France	544	57.6	1,015.3
Germany	357	81.2	1,357.1
Greece	132	10.4	81.7
Ireland	70	3.6	44.6
Italy	301	57.1	960.6
Luxembourg	3	0.4	8.4
Netherlands	41	15.3	248.1
Portugal	92	9.9	91.1
Spain	505	39.1	475.9
Sweden	450	8.7	134.9
U.K.	244	58.0	922.0

*PPS : Purchasing Power Standard - a common unit representing an identical volume of goods and services for each country.

Table 2.2: Basic Demographics of the Applicant Countries of Central and Eastern Europe

Country	Area ('000 sq. kms.)	Population (Millions)	GDP ('000 Million PPS)
Hungary	93	10.2	64.6
Poland	313	38.6	203.3
Romania	238	22.7	94.3
Slovak Rep.	49	5.4	38.0
Latvia	65	2.5	7.9
Estonia	45	1.5	5.9
Lithuania	65	3.7	15.3
Bulgaria	111	8.4	35.4
Czech Rep.	79	10.2	97.2
Slovenia	20	2.0	20.1
CE - 10	1078	105.3	582.0

Source: European Commission Document entitled "*Agenda 2000 - The Challenge of Enlargement*".

December 9-10, 1974: At the Paris Summit, the Community's Heads of State or Government decided to meet three times a year as the European Council gave the go-ahead for direct elections to the European Parliament and agreed to set up the European Regional Development Fund (ERDF).

July 6-7, 1978: At the Bremen European Council, France and the Federal Republic of Germany presented a scheme for closer monetary co-operation (the European Monetary System) to replace the currency 'snake'.

March 13, 1979: The European Monetary System (EMS) started operating.

June 7-10, 1979: The first direct elections to the European Parliament were held.

February 28, 1984: The 'Espirit' programme for research and development in information technology was adopted.

January 1, 1986: Spain and Portugal joined the Union.

February 17-18, 1986: The Single European Act was signed in Luxembourg.

May 29, 1990: The Agreement establishing the European Bank for Reconstruction and Development was signed in Paris.

October 21, 1991: The Agreement creating a European Economic Area (EEA) was signed by the Union and the EFTA countries.

February 7, 1992: The Treaty on European Union (EU) was signed in Maastricht.

January 1, 1995: Austria, Finland and Sweden joined the EU.

January 9, 1995: Austria joins EMS.

June 12, 1995: EU signs Association Agreement with Estonia, Latvia and Lithuania.

June 27, 1995: Slovak Republic applies to join EU.

October 27, 1995: Latvia applies to join EU.

November 28, 1995: Estonia applies to join EU.

December 8, 1995: Lithuania applies to join EU.

December 14, 1995: Bulgaria applies to join EU.

January 17, 1996: Czech Republic applies to join EU.

March 29, 1996: Intergovernmental Conference on revision of Maastricht Treaty formally opens in Turin.

June 10, 1996: Slovenia applies to join EU.

October 14, 1996: Finland joins EMS.

November 24, 1996: Italy rejoins the EMS exchange rate system.

June 16-17, 1997: Amsterdam Treaty signed by EU.

2.7 Legal Framework of the Union

What sets the Union apart from more traditional international organisations is its unique institutional structure. The founding fathers believed that economic integration and its control should not be left in the hands of the member states. Instead, the treaties set up an institutional system enabling the Union in the areas assigned to it to enact legislation that is equally binding on all its members.

In accepting the Treaties of Paris and Rome, Member States relinquish a measure of sovereignty to independent institutions representing national and shared interests. The institutions complement one another, each having a part to play in the decision making process [14].

Hence, it can be stated that the task of achieving the aims of the three Communities - the European Coal and Steel Community (ECSC), the

European Economic Community (EEC) and the European Atomic Energy Community (EURATOM) - rests with the following institutions:

- the European Parliament
- the Council
- the Commission
- the Court of Justice

They are assisted by the following bodies:

- the Economic and Social Committee (ESC)
- the Court of Auditors
- the European Investment Bank (EIB).

The functions and their respective roles are briefly discussed in the following paragraphs.

2.7.1 European Parliament

It provides a democratic forum for debate. It has a watch-dog function and also plays a part in the legislative process. Although its powers are more limited than those of Parliaments in Parliamentary democracies, the European Parliament has a say in Union legislation and the budget and is the Union's supervisory body.

It can, therefore, be said that parliament is the drawing force and watch-dog and enjoys significant budgetary powers and is becoming increasingly involved in the adoption of European laws.

2.7.1.1 New European Parliament : The Fourth Since 1979: Elections for a new European Parliament (EP) were held in the 12 member states of the European Union on June 9 and 12, 1994. It was for the fourth time - following June 1979, 1984 and 1989 - that the citizens of the Union had voted for a new Parliament.

The Act of September 20, 1976 provided for the election of members of the European Parliament through direct universal suffrage. There was no uniform electoral system - each member state applied its own electoral law for the election to the European Parliament also.

A recent innovation has been the European Council directive of December 6, 1993 on the right to vote and eligibility for election to the Parliament which enables European citizens to vote and be candidates in their country of residence.

Another notable change is the increase in the number of Parliamentary seats from 518 to 624 after accession of Austria, Finland and Sweden on January 1, 1995. This new total and its distribution were decided at the Edinburgh European Council meeting on December 11 and 12, 1992. The Council also took account of German unification and the further enlargement with three member countries.

Its legislative powers have been strengthened by the 1992 Treaty on European Union which introduces a co-decision procedure in a number of important areas, giving the Parliament in conjunction with the Council, the power to adopt regulations and directives on an equal footing.

The Parliament has ambitious plans for its future role. It has drawn up a draft constitution which aims at establishing a new balance of power between the three EU institutions - the Parliament, the Commission and the Council.

Under the proposal, Members of European Parliament (MEPs) would join the European council in defining the guidelines of EU policy, adopt laws jointly with the Council, elect the European Commission's President and table a vote of confidence in the Commission. The Parliament has also recommended that the Western European Union (WEU), the future military arm of the 12-nation Union, be absorbed into the European Union in order to organise a foreign and defence policy.

The Parliament also plays an important role, through its Committee on petitions, in redressing the grievances of the citizens of the Union. There are many examples of how the Parliament has helped ordinary citizens. These include cases such as harassment in the delivery of driving licences, failure to reimburse medical expenses, non-payment of unemployment benefits and discrimination based on nationality.

The Parliament is headed by a Bureau composed of the President and 14 Vice-Presidents elected by the members. Ordinary sessions of the European Parliament (one week a month except in August) are held in Strasburg, but some extraordinary sessions are held in Brussels. Its secretariat is in Luxembourg and its 18 Committees, which prepare the work of the plenary sessions, meet in Brussels. The term of Presidency is two and a half years.

2.7.1.2 Composition of European Parliament:

		Changed	Old
Austria	-	21	(-)
Belgium	-	25	(24)
Denmark	-	16	(16)
France	-	87	(81)
Germany	-	99	(81)
Greece	-	25	(24)
Ireland	-	15	(15)
Italy	-	87	(81)
Luxembourg	-	6	(.6)
Netherlands	-	31	(25)
Portugal	-	25	(24)
Spain	-	64	(60)
Sweden	-	22	(-)
U.K.	-	87	(81)
Finland	-	16	(-)
New Composition		**626**	**518**

(as in 1998)

In the previous Parliament, the 518 seats were distributed among eight political groups, of which four contested the June elections in 1994 on common programmes and campaigns as well as on common logos. These were the Christian Democrats, Socialists, Liberals and the Greens.

2.7.1.3 Role and Functioning of Parliament: The composition of Parliament makes it a fully integrated Union institution. The Commission is answerable to Parliament and Parliament alone guarantees its independence. Parliament, thus, keeps constant watch on the Commission's doings, making sure that it faithfully represents the Community interest, ready at any time to call it to order if it gives the impression of yielding to the lobbying of governments. Parliament shares the legislative function with the Council; it has a hand in the drafting of directives and regulations, proposing amendments which it invites the Commission to take into account. The Single Act which amended the Treaties, established a procedure with two readings in Parliament and two in Council known as the Co-operation Procedure, it gives Parliament a bigger say in wide range of policy areas, notably the Single Market [15].

The Maastricht Treaty strengthens Parliament's hand even further by granting it powers of co-decision in specific areas: the free movement of workers, the single market, education, research, the environment, trans-European networks, health, culture and consumer protection. If the Council and Parliament are unable to agree on a Community regulation or directive, a compromise has to be found by a special Conciliation Committee, on which both institutions are equally represented. Parliament has also been given the right to approve the Commission prior to its appointment.

But there is a long way to go before Parliament has full legislative powers. The inter-governmental conference to review the Maastricht is of particular significance for parliament's institutional position in that the agenda includes a review of the co-decision procedure.

Besides the above stated powers, Parliament has also the power to dismiss the Commission by a vote of censure supported by a two third majority of members - a power it has yet to use.

2.7.1.4 Budgetary Powers: When the Council decided to give the Community, financial resources of its own, the Member States agreed to amend the treaties to increase Parliament's budgetary powers. Two Treaties were concluded for this purpose - one on 22nd April, 1970 (effective from January 1, 1977), the other on July 22, 1975 (effective from June 1977). Parliament's budgetary powers cover the institutions' administrative costs and, above all, certain operational expenditure (Social fund, Regional fund, Research and Energy, Industrial Policy etc.).

Parliament has the right to reject the budget as a whole: this it did for the first time on 13th December 1979, a few months after direct elections, when it threw out the draft of 1980 budget placed before it by the Council. Parliament also rejected the 1985 general budget as well as a supplementary budget in 1982.

Backed by the democratic legitimacy deriving from its election by direct universal suffrage and taking full advantage of all the possibilities it has to play a part in the Community's legislative process, the European Parliament expects the move towards political union to produce wider reforms which will increase its role in Community decision making.

2.7.2 European Council

In December 1974, the Heads of State or Government, meeting in Paris, took two major decisions. Firstly, they agreed that the European Parliament should be directly elected by universal suffrage (though it took five years before direct elections were actually held). Secondly, they decided to meet regularly within a 'European Council' with their Foreign Ministers and the President and one of the Vice-Presidents of the Commission. The decision came into effect immediately, the first European Council being held in March 1975 in Dublin. Subsequently, the existence of the European Council was formally enshrined in the Single European Act in 1986.

2.7.2.1 Composition of the Council: The Council is made up of representatives of the Governments of the Member States. When the Ministers for Foreign Affairs meet, it is called the 'General Council' and deals with major political questions.

Since 1975, there have been regular meetings of the European Council. The Presidency of the Council is held by each Member State in turn, in alphabetical order, for six months.

2.7.2.2 Council Presidency: A significant institutional change in recent years (i.e. in the early 1990s) has been the bigger role played by the Council Presidency. It is a development which can be attributed, firstly, to practical needs resulting from the more complex operation in an enlarged Community of a body with representatives from nine, then 10 and 12 and now 15 countries, plus the Commission and, secondly, to political factors resulting from the excessive insistence on unanimity (and the consequent need for compromises which may bear little relation to the Commission proposal) and from the way the European Council rotates.

Under Article 145 of the EEC Treaty, the Council is responsible for co-ordinating the general economic policies of the Member States. But as the Community's competence increases, so does the range of Council activities. The Council, which represents the Member States, adopts Community legislation (regulations, directives and decisions). Article 148 of the EEC Treaty distinguishes between decisions adopted unanimously, by a simple majority and by a qualified majority. Before the accession of new members on January 1995, the Qualified majority was 54 votes out of a total of 76. As from January 1, 1995 the votes are distributed as follows:

Austria	4
Belgium	5
Denmark	3
France	10
Finland	3
Germany	10
Greece	5
Ireland	3
Italy	10
Luxembourg	2
The Netherlands	5
Portugal	5
Spain	8
Sweden	4
U.K.	10
Total	**87**

Qualified Majority - 60 votes.

Most decisions are taken by a Qualified majority. Unanimity is only required on issues of fundamental importance such as the accession of a new member state, amendments to the Treaties or the launching of a new common policy.

It was its first Presidency as a United Country and its first since the entry into force of the Treaty of Maastricht in which the German government played a major role. The two major aims of the German Presidency were to promote European integration and to strengthen the trans-Atlantic partnership.

2.7.3 The Commission

The Commission is another key institution of the Community. The Commission is responsible for both proposing and implementing Community's policy. It is the driving force behind the European Union, manages the common policies, implements the budget and directs the administration.

A single Commission for all three Communities (the ECSC, the EEC and EURATOM) was created when the Treaty merging the executives entered into force on July 1, 1967.

2.7.3.1 Composition of the Commission : As from January 1, 1995 the Commission has 20 members as proposed by Mr. Jacques Santer, the new President-elect of the European Commission, who took over from Mr. Jacques Delors on January 1, 1995. The 20-member Commission replaces the old one with 17 members. Following is a break up of its membership:

Country	**Members**
Austria	1
Belgium	1
Denmark	1
France	2
Finland	1
Germany	2
Greece	1
Ireland	1
Italy	2
Luxembourg	1
The Netherlands	1
Portugal	1
Spain	2
Sweden	1
U.K.	2
Total	**20**

From 1995, the Commission's President term in office has been raised from 4 to 5 years, bringing it into line with the European Parliament.

Parliament will be consulted before the Member States appoint the President of the Commission; the appointment will have to be approved by the Parliament before being appointed by mutual agreement of the governments of the Member States [16].

In carrying out their duties, Members of the Commission are obliged to be completely independent of their national governments and act only in the interests of the Union; only Parliament has the right to pass a motion of censure. Each Member of the Commission has special responsibility for one or more policy areas but decisions are taken on the basis of collective responsibility.

The Commission is first and foremost the guardian of the Treaties. It is an impartial body which sees to it that Treaty provisions and Union's decisions are correctly applied.

It can initiate infringement proceedings against any Member State and may, if necessary, refer matters to the Court of Justice. It can also impose fines on individuals or companies, notably when they act in breach of the Union's competition rules.

2.7.3.2 Powers of the Commission : The Commission is the guardian of the treaties and sees to it that both their provisions and those adopted by the Union's institutions are properly implemented. The Commission is the executive body of the European Union by virtue of the executive powers conferred on it by the Treaties and by the Council, it:

- adopts implementing regulations for provisions of the Treaties and adopted by the Council for implementing the various Union policies;

- applies the rules of the Treaties to individual cases involving governments or individuals.

- Administers the 'safeguard clause' under which, in exceptional cases for a limited period, exemptions of the rules of the Treaties may be granted.

- Administers Union funds and the European Social Fund (ESF), the European Agricultural Guidance Guarantee Fund (EAGGF), the European Regional Development Fund (ERDF), and the European Development Fund (EDF).

- Negotiates, on behalf of the Union agreements, any matter falling within Union's field of competence particularly trade agreements and represents the Union in international organisations (GATT, OECD, ILO).

The Commission is assisted in its tasks by a large number of special Committees: advisory committees, management committees and regulatory committees, which are composed of representatives of the Member States governments.

2.7.4 Court of Justice

2.7.4.1 Composition: The Court of Justice is the supreme judicial authority of the Union- an independent body which ensures that Union law is applied in a uniform manner. It is the final arbiter of Union law.

The Court consists of 15 judges and 9 Advocates-General appointed by common accord of the governments of the Member States. They hold office for a renewable term of six years. After every three years there is a partial replacement of the Court's membership, affecting six or seven judges and three Advocates-General. Currently, there is one Judge per Member State. The independence of the Judges is guaranteed by the statute; they are irremovable and their deliberations are secret. They select one of their members to be President who directs the work of the Court for three years. The Advocates-General are likewise appointed at the discretion of the governments. Their function, according to the Treaties, is 'acting with complete impartiality and independence to make, in open court, reasoned submissions on cases brought before the Court in order to assist the Court in the performance of the tasks assigned to it.

The Court sits in plenary session for its most important tasks. Most actions are referred to chambers set up within the Court.

A Court of First Instance, attached to the Court of Justice, was set up in 1989. It has 15 members appointed for a renewable term of six years by common accord of the governments of the Member States. There is a partial replacement of the Court of First Instance after every three years. There is currently one judge per member state. The Court of First Instance sits in the chambers composed of three or four Judges; for important matters it may sit in plenary session. Both the Court of Justice and the Court of First Instance are based in Luxembourg [17].

2.7.4.2 Powers and Functions: The Court ensures that the law is observant in the interpretation and application of the Treaties. It may, at the request of a Union institution, a Member State or an individual directly concerned, annul an Act by the Council or Commission if is found to be incompatible with the Treaties. The Court has two main functions:

- To check the laws enacted by the Union institutions for compatibility with the Treaties (a matter may be brought before the Court by one of the institutions, by a Member State or by members of the public if they consider that their rights have been violated).

- To give its opinion on the correct interpretation or the validity of Union provisions when requested to do so by a national court. If a question of this kind is raised in a case before a court or tribunal against whose decision there is no appeal, the Court of Justice must be asked to give a preliminary ruling.

As stated previously, in addition to the above mentioned institutions, following bodies have also been set up to assist the institutions:

2.7.5 Economic and Social Committee (ESC)

The Economic and Social Committee provides institutional representation for the various categories of economic and social activity: employers, workers and interest groups covering the other forms of activity, including agriculture, transport, commerce, crafts, the professions, small businesses, consumer affairs, protection of the environment and co-operatives are all represented on the Committee.

The Committee has 222 members drawn from the most representative national organisations; they are appointed in a personal capacity (after consulting the Commission) for a term of four year.

2.7.5.1 Composition of ESC (as in 1998):

Country	Members
Austria	12
Belgium	12
Denmark	9
France	24

Finland	9
Germany	24
Greece	12
Ireland	9
Italy	24
Luxembourg	6
The Netherlands	12
Portugal	12
Spain	21
Sweden	12
U.K.	24
Total	**222**

2.7.5.2 Role of ESC: The Committee brings together different economic and social interest groups with the united aim of building the European Union. It is an institutional task which ensures that the Commission, the Council and the European Parliament are aware of the points of view of the various economic and social categories on the current priorities of the Union. It has nine specialist sections and must be consulted by the Commission and the Council before certain decisions can be taken. It may also, either on request or on its own initiative, issue opinions on all aspects of Union legislation. Its role is, therefore, that of consultant to the political decision makers.

The activities of the Committee have increased steadily (from seven opinions in 1968 to nearly 180 in 1989). The Single European Act has increased the involvement of the Committee in the drafting of texts relating to completion of the Single Market. The role of the Committee is destined to increase further with the advent of the Single Market and of Economic and Monetary Union in that it will be responsible for ensuring that those involved in business and commerce and the two sides of industry play a part in the implementation of major ventures and in progress towards European Union in general.

2.7.6 Court of Auditors

The Court of Auditors was set up by the Treaty of 22nd July, 1975 and held its constituent meeting in Luxembourg (its provisional headquarters) on 25th October, 1977. The Court took over from the EEC and EURATOM Audit Board and from the ECSC Auditor as the body-in-charge of external auditing of Union's general budget and the ECSC's operating budget. Internal auditing is still a matter for each institution's financial controller.

In setting up the court, the governments and institutions (particularly Parliament) showed that they wanted a qualitative change in the style of budgetary auditing, given the steady increase in the size of the Union's budget.

2.7.6.1 Work of the Court of Auditors: The main task of the Court is to examine the accounts of all revenue and expenditure of the European Union and of all organisations set up by the Union. It investigates whether all revenue has been received and all expenditure incurred in a lawful and regular manner and whether the financial management has been sound. Audits are based on records forwarded by the Union institutions or by auditors sent to inspect certain departments of institutions or governments or organisations receiving Union funding. Audits may be carried out not only in Member States but also in non-member countries receiving Union aid, such as ACP (African Caribbean and pacific) States receiving support from the European Development Fund.

At the end of each financial year, the Court draws up a report on its work. This is published in the official journal with the institution's replies to its observations. In addition to this, it produces a large number of special reports on individual and sometimes major issues (e.g. the operation of the EAGGF's Guarantee section or food aid to developing countries).

Parliament, which had attached enormous importance to the establishment of Court of Auditors, makes full use of the opportunities offered by the Court's investigatory powers, opinions and annual report to reinforce its own control over Union's expenditure and give full weight to its annual decision granting a discharge in respect of implementation of the Union's budget.

2.7.7 European Investment Bank (EIB)

The European Investment Bank (EIB) was founded in 1958, by the Treaty of Rome establishing the European Economic Community, as the means of financing capital investment and promoting the balanced development of the Union.

2.7.7.1 Organisation of EIB: The EIB, based in Luxembourg, is administered by :

- A Board of Governors consisting of ministers designated by the Member States, which lays down general directives on the Bank's credit policy.

- A Board of Directors consisting of 22 administrators and 12 deputies appointed for a renewable five-year term of office by the Board of Governors on the basis of nominations by the Member States and the Commission. It directs the general administration of the Bank and takes major decisions on the granting and raising of loans, the fixing of lending rates, etc.

- A Management Committee consisting of a President and 6 Vice-Presidents appointed for a renewable six-year term of office by the Board of Governors. It controls all current operations, drafts loan agreements and implements the decisions of the Board of Directors.

The EIB's capital, subscribed by the 15 Member States of the European Union, has been raised several times by the Board of Governors and was doubled in 1990. The capital of the EIB, subscribed by the member states, has since January 1, 1995 amounted to ECU 62 billion. According to its statute, the aggregate outstanding amount of loans and credits may not exceed 250 per cent of the capital.

2.7.7.2 Role of EIB: As an autonomous institution of the Union, the EIB is responsible for granting loans and issuing guarantees to finance capital projects consistent with the aims of Union's economic policy. Within the Union it finances investment whose purpose is to :

- Improve transport & telecommunication infrastructure of benefit to the Union.

- Foster the economic advancement of less favoured regions.

- Make industry more competitive at international level, particularly by promoting state of the art technologies and small medium-sized businesses.

- Protect the environment and improve the quality of life: town planning, water supply and treatment, pollution control, waste management, soil protection etc.

- Secure energy supply.

Outside the Union, the EIB helps to implement Union's development policy under the Lome Conventions (69 African, Caribbean and Pacific States) and financial agreements with 12 Mediterranean countries. Since 1989, it has extended its activities in assisting the economic recovery of Hungary, Poland and other countries of Central and Eastern Europe, particularly by investing in transport, telecommunication and energy.

The EIB raises virtually all the resources needed to finance its lending by tapping the capital markets, chiefly in the form of fixed-rate borrowings. Its excellent credit rating enables it to obtain the most favourable conditions available, the benefits of which are then passed on to the recipients of its loans.

2.7.7.3 Key Role of EIB in European Integration: The European Investment Bank, set up to finance trans-European infrastructure networks and other industrial projects, has played a key role in promoting European integration. Most significantly, it has brought to the European Union its ability to borrow a substantial volume of long-term funds and its project appraisal expertise. Owing to its "triple A" credit rating, it is able to raise a considerable volume of funds on the finest possible terms.

Since it was set up, the activities of the EIB have expanded considerably. In 1993, lending by the EIB continued to surge ahead, totalling ECU 19.6 billion - compared to ECU 17.0 billion in the previous year.

The Bank has played a key role in helping sustain the level of economic activity in the Union's poorest Member States. In addition to its contribution in favour of the EU's economic and social cohesion programme, the EIB has played an important role in financing trans-European networks in telecommunication, transport and energy.

Outside the Union, the Bank is also playing a role in implementing the Union's Co-operation policy in favour of non-Member countries. This encompasses the ACP states signatories to the Lome Convention, those Mediterranean countries which had concluded association or co-operation agreement with the EU, 10 Central and Eastern European countries and the Asian and Latin American countries which signed co-operation agreements with the EU.

Summing up its achievements, the Bank's President, Sir Brian Unwin stated that the operations of European Investment Bank had increased, both inside and outside the European Union and at the request of successive European Councils, it had played a key role in the Union's economic recovery programme and, in particular, the financing of trans-European networks.

The institutions of the Union are, thus, empowered to bring in full scale 'European laws', directly enforceable in all Member States and capable of producing radical changes in the sectors concerned. To give an example, the great corpus of 'European laws' on agriculture, promulgated from 1962 onwards, is comparable in scope to the corpus of rules contained in the ECSC Treaty. Moreover, the guidelines laid down by the Heads of State or Government of the Nine at the summit conferences in Hague in 1969 and Paris in 1972, and subsequently reiterated, require the institutions to draw up common policies in fields not strictly provided for in the Treaties. The Single Act puts the final stamp on Union's action in several fields such as social policy, research and technology, environmental and monetary policy.

2.7.8 Committee of the Regions

The Committee of the Regions[18] is the European Union's youngest institution whose birth reflects Member States strong desire not only to respect regional and local identities and prerogatives but also to involve them in the development and implementation of EU policies.

2.7.8.1 Guardian of Subsidiarity: Created as a consultative body by the treaty on EU, the Committee has emerged as a strong guardian of the principle of subsidiarity since its first session in March 1994; composed of about half regional and half local authority representatives.

2.7.8.2 Composition of the Committee of the Regions: It comprises of 222 members who are elected officials from the levels of government closest to the citizen.

Country	**Members**
Austria	12
Belgium	12
Denmark	9
France	24
Finland	9
Germany	24
Greece	12
Ireland	9
Italy	24
Luxembourg	6
The Netherlands	12
Portugal	12
Spain	21
Sweden	12
U.K.	24
Total	**222**

The treaty requires this committee to be consulted on matters relating to trans-European networks, public health, education, youth, culture and economic and social cohesion.

The committee has also established a Special Commission on Institutional Affairs, which is responsible for contributing to the debate on the reform of the EU institutions.

In its brief existence, the committee has already grappled with a wide range of issues including guidelines for a trans-European airport network, the development of rural tourism etc. A constant theme running through its opinions is the need to involve the regions and localities much more closely in the design and implementation of policies.

2.7.9 Conclusion

The European Union is unique. It is the concrete expression of the common desire of the sovereign nations of Europe to work and live together. The Union, as we know it today, is a monument to the dedication of the early pioneers. The history of Europe is not just a history of wars, as it has been for several generations nor of diversion and outside dominance, for Europe has always been a place of peaceful encounter and mutual exchange between people too and this shared experience lies as much at the root of European integration as the realisation that a Union is more than the sum of its members.

The Union is an advanced form of multisectoral integration, its competence extending to the economy, industry, politics, citizens' rights and foreign policy. The Treaty of Paris establishing the European Coal and Steel Community (1951), the Treaties of Rome establishing the European Economic Community and the European Atomic Energy Community (1957), the Single European Act (1986) and the Maastricht European Union Treaty (1992) form the constitutional basis of the Union binding its Member States more firmly than any conventional agreement between sovereign states.

To sum up, it can be stated that the European Union as in 1998, embraces more than 370 million people, stretches from the Mediterranean to the Arctic Circle and has 15 Member States with the inclusion of three new Member countries viz. Austria, Sweden and Finland. Though rich in diversity, the Union countries share certain common values. By entering into partnership, their aim is to promote democracy, peace, prosperity and a fairer distribution of wealth.

Notes

1. A significant landmark in the process of European integration was the signing of the Treaty of European Union on February 7, 1992, at Maastricht in the Netherlands. The Treaty came into force on November 1, 1993 after it was ratified by twelve Member States and the European Community was renamed European Union.

2. Pascal Fontaine: *"Europe in Ten Lessons"*: A European Documentation Series; office for official publications of the European communities, Luxembourg; 1992.

3. ALI-MEL-AGRAA, "*The Economics of the European Community*; Philip Allan Publishers Ltd.; 1982.

4. Seymour E. Harris: *"The European Recovery Programme"*; Harvard University Press; 1948.

5. Dharma Kumar: *"India and the European Economic Community"*; Asia Publishing House; 1966.

6. 'Comecon' was formed by Bulgaria, Hungary, the then East Germany, Poland, Romania, the erstwhile U.S.S.R. and Checkoslovakia.

7. 'Six' members were: former Federal Republic of Germany, France, Italy, Belgium, the Netherlands and Luxembourg.

8. ALI-MEL-AGRAA: *"The Economics of the European Community"*; Heritage Publishers; 1981.

9. *"Europe in Figures"*; Eurostat, Third edition; office for official publications of the European Community; 1993.

10. *"Europe in Figures"*; Eurostat, Third Edition; office for official publications of the European Community; 1993.

11. 'EC'; Bulletin of the European Community; Supplement 1, 1986; pp. 7-8

12. *"European Union News"*; Newsletter of the European Commission in India; published by Francine Henrich for the Delegation of the European Commission in India; Vol. 6, No. 5, December, 1994.

13. *"The Challenge of Enlargement - Commission's Opinion on Norway's Application for Membership"*; Bulletin of the European Communities; Supplement 2/293.

14. Pascal Fontaine; 'Europe in Ten Lessons'; European Documentation Series; office for official publications in Luxembourg; 1992.

15. 'Europe in Figures'; Eurostat, Third edition; office for official publications of the European Community; 1993.

16. *"The Institutions of the Community"*; European Documentation Series; Office for official publications of the European Communities; Luxembourg; 1997.

17. *"The Institutions of the European Community"*; European Documentation series; Office for official publications of the European Community, Luxembourg; 1997.

18. "Europe from A to Z, Guide to European Integration"; Werner Weidenfeld, Wolfgang Wessels; Luxembourg: office for official publications of the European Communities; 1997.

Chapter 3

European Unification : Targets and Achievements

3.1 Evolution of European Unification

The founders of European Union were inspired by three ideals: peace, prosperity and stability. The first objective of peace has been a complete success till now.

Some major economic achievements have also taken place since the signing of Treaty of Rome in 1957. The common Agricultural policy, for instance, which transformed the European Union from a net importer into a net exporter of certain key agricultural products was a major achievement [1]. Another major achievement was the establishment of customs union which put an end to import duties and import quotas between the Union members.

However, the process of unification has always gone hand-in-hand with alternating periods of Euro-pessimism and Euro-optimism. The signing of the Treaty in 1957 heralded a period of great optimism.

The concept of a vast single market, unhampered by internal frontiers, was at the very core of the objective set in the Rome Treaty in 1957. In the Treaty also, the major stress was on the elimination of barriers which divided Europe to ensure the economic and social progress of their countries [2].

After the signing of the Treaty in 1957, success in certain fields was achieved. The economy grew in size and the customs union seemed to bear fruit. The years from 1960 to 1967 were golden years of economic growth combined with an inferiority complex vis-a-vis the United States.

In the early 1970s, Europe began to regain its self-confidence. In 1971, the EU's regained confidence took concrete shape in an undertaking to achieve a new monetary union within ten years. But in the mid-70s, events took a turn for the worse. The oil crisis shattered the economic boom, lessening the bright prospects for the future. Japan and the United States appeared to have a tight grip on things than the European Union. An era of Euro-pessimism, thus, set in the mid-70s.

This situation lasted until the late 1970s when the American economy started to falter. Inflation in the United States was at a record high, the economy was slowing down and the dollar was plummeting. In contrast, the European economy enjoyed two relatively good years in 1978 and 1979.

The establishment of the European Monetary System (EMS) and the first direct elections for the European Parliament marked two important steps towards European integration. But the new sense of confidence, unfortunately, was short-lived. The second oil-crisis in 1979-80 plunged the world into a new recession. Japan and the United States, however, soon bounced back out of the crisis.

At the beginning of the 1980s, Europe slumped into a long period of stagnation. The gap with the United States and Japan seemed unbridgeable and the Member States were more remote from Brussels than ever. Euro-pessimism reigned supreme. It was not until the mid-1980s that things took a turn for the better when the European leaders decided to tackle the problems jointly. It had become clear that in the fifteen years after the creation of the customs union, nothing had been done to realise the aims of the Treaty of Rome and achieve a target that could put the EU back in the race with Japan and the United States: a genuine European Market [3].

The markets of the Member States were still working as separate units and the economies of scale, which an integrated market could bring about, were not in sight in the mid-1980s. Free circulation of goods or services within the Union was being hampered in view of the various border controls, differing technical standards and nationally oriented public procurement policies.

The Union GDP, which grew at a rate of 5.1 per cent between 1958 and 1973, dropped to 2.2 per cent between 1973 and 1980 during the oil-crisis and further down to 1.8 per cent after 1980. The initial dynamism with which the Union had started appeared to have been exhausted and Europe was slowly receding from the forefront among the industrialised countries, giving way to Japan and the United States in terms of economic advancement, employment and new technologies. Therefore, some radical changes were required to get the EU back into the race.

In the early 1980's, however, the mood began to change and there emerged a growing realisation that a fresh concerted attempt had to be made to create a single economic framework [4]. At the heart of this renewed impetus was the recognition that unless it could make full use of the potentially vast single market that the then twelve member states constitute, the Union would continue to lose ground and markets to its main competitors.

3.2 White Paper of 1985

The initiative for the Single Market Programme came from Jacques Delors, the former French finance minister, who became the president of the European Commission in January 1985. Delors deliberately chose the Single market to relaunch the Union after five years of near-immobilism, rather than his alternative projects for EMU on Political Union.

The Brussels summit of March, 1985, asked the European Union Commission to draw up a detailed programme with a specific time-table to achieve a Single Market by 1992. A white paper was drawn up under the direction of the British Commissioner, Lord Cockfield, whose brief included internal market affairs. The Single Market Programme aimed at creating a unified trading block, where the free movement of goods, services, capital and people between Member States was expected to provoke a "Quantum Leap" in economic efficiency and growth [5].

In other words, the Internal Market Programme basically involved the removal of all types, namely, physical, technical and fiscal barriers that acted as impediments to the free movement of people, goods, services and capital between the then twelve Member States of the Union [6].

The necessary measures numbering three hundred, needed to lift these barriers, were all listed in the white paper of the European Commission published in 1991: pp. 24-25 in June, 1985. The white paper envisaged that the various proposals required to complete the internal market should be discussed, adopted and implemented according to a time-table between 1985 and 1992. Subsequently, some of the measures proposed were consolidated and certain others dropped bringing the number to 282.

3.3 Single European Act, 1987

The white paper, on the completion of the internal market, contained a programme setting an objective, putting forward a method and spelling out the instruments. The objective was clear : to create the largest frontier-free market in the world and to increase the Union's competitiveness by stimulating business through competition and economic growth through increased trade. To achieve this objective, an Act commonly known as 'The Single European Act', was entered into force on July 1, 1987 after necessary ratifications. It provided the necessary political impetus and additional legal framework to achieve a Single Internal Market by 1992, although the Treaty of Rome itself had, in 1957, spelt out the objective of establishing a common market in specific terms: "The Community shall have as its task of establishing a common market and progressively approximating the economic policies of Member States to promote throughout the Community a harmonious development of economic activities and a continuous and balanced growth."

The Act replaced the original Treaty requirement for decisions to be taken by unanimity with a qualified majority requirement, as regards, certain measures which have, as their object, the establishment and functioning of the Internal Market..The Single Act not only reinforced the general approach to European Union, but it specified in detail the policies to be followed; they were:

- Firstly, the completion of a large market without frontiers allowing the free movement of people, goods, services, and capital which implied removal of all frontier formalities by January 1, 1993.

- Secondly, the objective was to have structural policies to be pursued at Union level which provided opportunities for all regions, particularly those which were lagging behind.

- Thirdly, the objective was to have total co-operation on research and technology.

- Fourthly, the objective was to have monetary co-operation, i.e., the European Monetary System.

- Another objective, which formed an important part of The Single Act was the social dimension.

- Lastly, the objective of the Act was to have an environment policy.

The four principles to achieve these objectives were :

- To have a policy of co-operation among the countries of European Union along with the policy of more competition among them.

- To remove obstacles for trade, but at the same time, to establish a minimum set of rules, for without these, the market would not be able to function in a balanced manner.

- Another principle was of Diversity. This was necessary because of the differences in the standard of living, in the levels of prosperity and also the different traditions in different countries.

- Lastly, the principle of Subsidiarity. This implied that from the point of view of political effectiveness, one should be able to combine decision-making from the top and from the bottom.

A detailed description of the measures, proposed under the white paper, is given below. The paper classified all the measures under three headings [7]:

- the removal of physical barriers;
- the removal of technical barriers;
- the removal of fiscal barriers.

3.4 Removal of Physical Barriers

The physical barriers, at the frontiers between the Member States, held up both goods and individuals. Physical barriers at the customs post, the immigration controls, the passport, the occasional search of personal baggage, etc., were obvious manifestations of continued division of Union - not the broader and deeper Union as envisaged by the original treaty. The removal of these barriers were to constitute one of the most direct and visual benefit of the Union to its citizens. It would be the first step in the creation of a people's Europe - a positive Europe which can be seen to help people in their daily lives rather than a Europe that appears to be obstructed throughout by rules and regulations.

Frontier controls were not merely a physical constraint but a significant economic constraint. They imposed an unnecessary burden on industry flowing from formalities, transport handling charges to which goods were subjected to whenever they were taken across the frontier, thus, adding to costs and reducing competitiveness. In case of goods, checks were carried out for a number of purposes:

- collection of VAT duties,

- carrying out administrative formalities at border posts,

- monitoring the differing commercial and economic policies in the Member States,

- carrying out veterinary and plant health checks,

- monitoring present restrictions on intra Union transport operations and quotas for hauliers, and

- collecting data for statistical purposes.

Since 1985, the Commission has progressively introduced measures to rationalise and relax checks and controls on people and goods travelling or being transported between the Member States. Some of the measures aimed at removing physical barriers on goods were as follows:

- A single administrative document was introduced which replaced nearly seventy forms for goods transportation across the frontiers,

- All frontier formalities were sought to be removed to improve transit procedure,

- Removal of exit formalities at borders and removal of postal fees for custom presentation,

- Abolition of 'Transit Advice Note',

- Rationalisation of the system of collecting statistics by prescribing easy and harmonised 'Commodity Description System'; and other related procedures.

In the case of individuals, passport controls, the occasional searches of baggage and vehicles and custom checks on purchases were a constant reminder that the Union was divided into distinct sovereign states. There were two basic reasons for such control over the people : Immigration and Tax [8].

Since 1984 an initiative to abolish such control was taken within the scope of the Schengen Agreement among five Member States, namely France, the BENELUX countries and Germany. From November 1990, however, this was also extended to Italy. This agreement provided a valuable experience regarding the development of free circulation of people within the Union.

Other frontier controls related to the application of quotas under International Trade Agreements, e.g., in relation to textiles under the International multifibre arrangement or to automobiles under the bilateral agreements. These controls resulting from national commercial policy measures were justified by Article 115 of the Treaty of Rome.

However, it became apparent that the recourse to Article 115 was occurring less and less: from 1300 Surveillance measures granted in 1987 to only 184 in 1991. Except for the textile sector national restrictions, till mid -year 1991, were applied to only 14 products.

Lastly, among the category of physical barriers, efforts had been in progress since 1990 to remove control over checks on collection of statistics in the industrial, agricultural and commercial sectors. Regarding plant and animal health checks, steps were taken since 1990 to raise the health standards of all member states to the highest level so that there was no need for any restrictions on trade.

Since July 1, 1990, technical checks on vehicles are no longer carried out at frontiers, but within the Member States as part of their overall road safety policy.

3.4.1 Achievements

The Single market became operational on January 1, 1993 and the process of achieving the Single Market, as provided for in the white paper, has been completed. Even though new aspects have been added to the programme set out in the white paper, in particular in the energy field, the Union's activity has, over the last few years (i.e. from 1985-1993), not once deviated from the programme more than 95 per cent of which has been implemented. It was widely accepted that the implementation of the Single Market programme has enhanced market flexibility and improved business opportunities for internal and external suppliers alike. Many long-standing trade barriers among the Member States have been removed and internal border controls have disappeared. Though concerns were expressed that the legal provisions of Article 115 of the EEC Treaty remained on the statute books, the EU representatives confirmed that the Single European Act provided no scope for any internal trade measures against imports from external sources. Previous regional quotas on textiles and clothing have ceased to exist.

Measures relating to the opening-up of markets to flows of products, services and capital from other member states have been made irreversible by the elimination of all administrative checks at intra-Union frontiers. The abolition on 1st January, 1993, of the single administrative document in intra-Union trade and the entry into force of a series of provisions, reorganising tax, veterinary and plant health, safety and statistical controls have made it possible to do away with checks at frontiers [9].

However, considerable slippage has occurred as regards freedom of movement of individuals. Although tax controls have been abolished and the right of establishment and residence recognised, police controls at frontiers remain a fact of life still for the general public.

In other words, freedom of movement for individuals has not yet become a reality. However, individuals do benefit from the dismantling of customs and tax controls at internal frontiers and since their educational qualifications are now being recognised, the Union nationals may now work in any other member state and may even reside in any other Member State regardless of any economic activity.

Despite all this, checks on individuals are still carried out at internal borders, although these have been lightened. The Commission has frequently deplored this situation, particularly to the European Parliament. The Commission hopes that substantial progress will be made in near future under the Schengen agreement.

To sum up, it can be stated that frontier controls were not merely a physical constraint, but also a significant economic constraint and their maintenance perpetuated the costs and disadvantages of a divided market. The removal of most of these barriers has constituted one of the most direct and visible benefits of the Union to its citizens. It is the first step in the creation of a "People's Europe".

3.5 Removal of Technical Barriers

The elimination of frontier controls does not itself create a genuine common market. It would be futile to abolish the obstacles at frontiers and simply to continue with the obstacles within the Member States [10]. These hidden obstacles were created by a host of technical barriers, which hampered the free flow of trade in goods and services and sometimes, also hampered the free movement of people. The measures to remove such barriers are discussed separately in separate areas.

Regarding goods, there were three types of technical barriers:

- The first caused by differences between national industrial standards, e.g., DIN in Germany, Anfor in France, BSI in U.K., etc.

- The second type resulted from differences in national regulations, which were similar to standards but were legally binding.

- The third type of barrier was created by testing and certification procedures which ensured conformity of a product to national rules, regulations or industrial standards.

The various measures proposed in this regard were intended to ensure that if a product found access into one Member States of the Union, then it should be acceptable in all the others [11]. The approach adopted by the Union was to set certain common minimum requirements to the extent of ensuring protection of human health and safety.

For many years, the Union attempted to eliminate these barriers through harmonisation - the adjustment of national regulations to conform to an agreed Union standard. But, unfortunately, this proved to be very difficult and complex and years were spent trying to reach agreement on the technical minutial of a single product or a group of products. Administrative difficulties were exacerbated by the misunderstandings, which have plagued harmonisation efforts since their inception.

The successive judgements of the European Court of Justice facilitated the removal of technical obstacles to trade which harmonisation seemed incapable of eliminating alone. In its new approach to technical harmonisation, outlined in the white paper, the Commission attempted to reconcile a number of conflicting considerations. The new approach sought to meet these requirements in the following ways:

National regulations applicable to production and marketing, which concerned such essential requirements as the protection of health and safety, were still the subject of Union legislation. This legislation, however, laid down mandatory requirements only in the form of general levels of protection, leaving the detailed rules of their practical application to be drawn up by the European standardisation bodies. About two hundred and forty technical committees worked within these bodies on the preparation of such detailed standards in all sectors.

The national rules which did not concern the above stated essential requirements are no longer the subject of Union legislation. They are automatically subjected to mutual recognition, enforceable before the European Court. In this way, unnecessary harmonisation is avoided altogether.

Overall, the new approach leaves much greater scope for flexibility in individual production and marketing methods. It also provides a better balance between the Union harmonisation and national mutual recognition, between the roles of the legislator and the standard bodies, and between the consumer/environment protection and the consumer choice.

Although the new approach has considerably increased the rate of decision-making by the council of ministers, the work-load of the Union standard bodies is very heavy in relation to drawing up standards in respect of essential requirements in the new approach directives and in relation to the public procurement tendering specifications which took place on January 1, 1993.

3.6 Free Movement of People

Movement of citizens of the Union from one Member State to another and taking up employment was largely affected because of lack of mutual recognition of diplomas, vocational training or other professional qualifications.

However, from January 1, 1992, those so far excluded from the free movement of people, students, pensioners and persons of independent means were allowed to settle down wherever they desired in the European Union.

Efforts have been in force since the 1960s to remove obstacles by establishing harmonised national qualifications for a number of specific professions. The Commission's approach towards dismantling such technical barriers has been to make education system of different member countries comparable, to recognise the qualifications through the process of mutual recognition and harmonisation of rules and regulations of residence. The Commission introduced various proposals in this regard:

- Mutual recognition of higher education : diplomas, degrees concerning doctors, lawyers, veterinary doctors, commercial agents, architects etc.

- Recognition of the profession to enable European citizens possessing such qualifications to use professional title corresponding to the regulated profession which he or she professes.

- Strengthening co-operation between industry and training to improve the initial training and updating of skills for those whose employment was affected by technological innovation through various programmes.

3.7 Free Movement of Capital

Since July 1, 1990, the directive completing liberalisation of capital movement has been in force in eight member countries. However, Greece,

Portugal, Spain and Ireland had a transitional period until the end of 1992 in respect of short-term capital movements. This liberalisation corresponded to the implementation of the first phase of monetary union. Such free movement of the capital significantly facilitated business and personnel transaction in the Union. As a result, for example, it shall be possible to open up a bank account anywhere in the Union and to switch unlimited funds from one member state to another.

3.7.1 Financial Services

Financial services is a sector which has a vast potential market and is vital to the efficient working of the whole of the economy. The Single market in financial services is an integral part of creating Europe without frontiers. The liberalisation of financial services had two aspects : Firstly, it involved harmonisation of the rules necessary to guarantee probity and security in the sector to protect users of financial services and to ensure conditions of fair competition for all the institutions involved. Secondly, it is based on the mutual recognition of remaining national rules, acceptance of the principle of 'home-country control' in relation to services to be provided Union-wide, acceptance of a degree of co-operation to facilitate 'home-country control' of services supplied in another Member State and the creation right to supply services from one Member State to another without re-establishing a credit institution in each Member State where the services are to be supplied. Since July 1990, major directives in almost all the sectors, ranging from banking sector to insurance sector, have been adopted.

3.8 Transport

The completion of a true European Union in the field of transport was one of the priorities in the preparation for 1992. Transport represented more than 7 per cent of Union GDP and although, it is by nature a very widely traded service, for long it has paradoxically remained one of the most highly regulated and protected markets in the Union. In the framework of the Single Market, however, the Commission had put forward comprehensive proposals; it had tried to deregulate all modes of transport - road, rail, inland-waterways, marine and air-transport.

One-third of the Union's internal trade and ninety percent of the external trade was carried by sea, but the tonnage of the Union's fleet was halved between 1980-88. To improve the situation arising out of increased competition and protectionism, the Commission took following steps after presenting the white paper:

- In 1986, the council of ministers adopted four regulations proposed by Commission. These provided for freedom of service in the area, thus, abolishing national preferences, application of competition rules to sea transport, allowing imposition of compensatory fines on companies of third countries indulging in unfair charging, and taking counter measures where a third country prevented European companies from having access to freight market.

- In 1989, the European Union submitted a proposal to rectify the economic situation of the European fleet. This measure included a series of steps to reduce operating cost of European ships and increase their competitiveness while, at the same time, improving the monitoring of welfare and safety standards.

Regarding the road transport, the 1992 programme of action in this area included the following measures:

- Introduction of common standards for safety system, and

- harmonisation of taxation.

As regards air transport, the Union intended to create the conditions for improving the international competitiveness of European carriers and giving users of air-transport the benefit of more connections and lower fares in good safety conditions. The following measures were taken:

- A greater flexibility in sharing of capacity and also access to route was introduced. Since October 1989, a range of 60 per cent had substituted for 50 per cent, whereas 50 per cent capacity sharing was often the rule among airlines.

- There was relaxation brought in pricing : carriers were no longer obliged to align their fares with those of their competitors.

- Application of the Union's competition rule to air traffic, with exemptions, was allowed only for agreements indispensable to the coordination of services.

- A coherent civil aviation policy was chalked out; essential questions such as safety measures, air traffic congestion, recognition of diplomas and other qualifications were dealt with.

- A common approach in dealing with countries outside the Union was taken.

Along with these measures, to meet the challenges thrown by 1992 programme, the Commission was further set to improve transport infrastructure in the form of integrating national networks and introducing strict safety measures.

3.9 Telecommunications

The principal objective of the Union in this field was to take full advantage of vast potential of a unified market. The activities were initiated in the following five areas:

- Co-ordination of future development

- Telecommunications

- Creation of a common market for terminals and equipments.

- Development of joint research.

- Promotion of modern telecommunication services and networks in the less favoured regions of the Union.

- Adoption of common position on the international scene [12].

The Union had adopted a two-pronged approach to give European character to the audio-visual sector in the run-up to Europe of 1992. The two-pronged policy is as follows:

- Encouragement to the development of European programme industry so that it can cope with the rising demand and the fierce competition coming from outside parties.

- Meeting the challenge of the new technology by defining common approach to television standards for production and broadcasting.

3.9.1 New Technologies and Services

The rapid changes in information technologies had given rise to a range of new information services. These had potential for considerable cross-border development and the Union had been active in promoting European networks as well as in liberalising the provision of the services and in harmonising the different standards.

In particular, given the importance of telecommunications for implementing the 1992 objective, the Commission had been concerned in liberalising this sector. Thus, in 1987, it published a Green Paper on the development of a common market in telecommunication equipment and services. Subsequently, two basic directives - one on the competition in telecommunications and the other on open network provisions - were noticed to the Member States in July 1990 to guarantee parallelism between liberalisation and harmonisation in this sector.

The general principles of Union's telecommunication policy were to be applied also to satellite communications. With this aim, in November 1990, the Commission adopted a Green discussion Paper on a joint approach to satellite communications.

3.9.2 Achievements

- Harmonisation of technical rules, as provided for in the white paper, has now been completed; initially confined to specific limited areas, it was extended to cover entire sectors such as agricultural and food products, pharmaceutical products and motor vehicles. Harmonisation of essential product safety requirements, backed-up by a policy of certification and the general provisions on product safety and liability for defective products mean that all manufactured products marketed in the Union are now covered.

- With regard to services, the over-all position is positive, though progress between different sectors has been uneven. The problems most commonly encountered by the Commission with regard to services relate to transposition and implementation.

- With regard to transport, since the main priorities have been covered, measures now should also be introduced on freedom to provide special transport services such as the transport of dangerous and perishable goods, taxi services, transport carried out by security firms, transport by ambulance, own-account transport and car-hire. The Commission's attention has also been drawn to the administrative complications involved in the transport of bodies; measures should be taken to relieve families of the burden of formalities to be completed in such circumstances.

- The environment is a key element in the achievement of the internal market; the adoption of high environmental standards at Union level and their uniform application will strengthen the process of convergence and cohesion and remove the fears of many countries against products of other member states, allegedly produced under lax environmental conditions. There are solutions and various important options in connection with these matters. One is the harmonisation of environmental national legislation. Another is the application of the principle of 'conditional equivalence' which means that the various national systems should be made equivalent from the economic point of view.

- The development of cross-frontier activities, the need for firms to be able to take advantage of all the management flexibility afforded to them by the Union dimension, and the need to preserve the public interest from the effects of disorganised competition had prompted the Commission to extend the rules on the operation of the single market to other spheres not initially covered in the white paper, notably telecommunication services, postal services and energy.

With regard to telecommunication services, and along-side its action on the mutual recognition of the approval of telecommunication terminals, the opening-up of public contracts and European standardisation, the Commission is pressing ahead with its work on the opening up of the markets for services by proposing, in parallel with the implementation of the ONP (Open Network Provisions) framework directive, that markets be completely opened up by January 1, 1998.

With regard to postal services, following its Green Paper published in May 1992, the Commission had drawn preliminary conclusions from the wide-ranging consultation process underway.

With regard to energy, the Commission, while applying the Treaty in the normal way to deal with rules and regulations that are incompatible with it and inappropriate conduct on the part of enterprises in the energy sector, has developed a step-by-step approach on electricity, natural gas and hydrocarbons. For instance, it had put forward, in mid-1994, a proposal on the harmonisation of conditions for access to exploration and extraction of hydrocarbons. In the case of gas and electricity, the Commission's approach was geared to three objectives: freedom of movement and freedom of establishment, industrial competitiveness and security of supply. In order to achieve these three objectives, an initial set of measures was adopted on transit and price transparency; a second set of measures on the opening up of markets for large consumers is still before the Council and Parliament, with the objective of abolishing remaining obstacles to strengthen competition, effectiveness and transparency in the Union's energy markets.

3.10 Removal of Fiscal Barriers

Fiscal barriers are the tax related barriers of formalities obstructing the free flow of goods, services, people etc. and causing delays and cost escalation.

The taxman has perhaps the biggest stake in frontier controls; whenever goods are moved from one country to another, they are elaborately documented at the border so that the fiscal authorities can collect the taxes - the VAT and excise duties to which they are entitled [13].

Abolition of frontier controls required that the indirect tax systems and levels do not diverge significantly between member states. The complete removal of border controls after 1992 meant that a new system for collecting indirect taxes had to be devised.

The Single European Act (SEA) noted that the Union would adopt provisions for the harmonisation of the legislation concerning turnover taxes, excise duties and other forms of indirect taxation to the extent that such harmonisation was necessary to ensure the establishment and functioning of the internal market.

It had been suggested that sales and purchases across member states would be treated in exactly the same way as sales and purchases within a single member State. In the case of VAT, exporters would charge the usual positive rate on sale for exports as for domestic transaction and importers would reclaim that as input tax, just as they would for domestic purchases.

The Commission, in 1987, had put forward two proposals for the approximation of the indirect tax rates operating in the Union aimed at reducing tax-induced price differences to a point where they do not themselves constitute an incentive to cross border provisioning.

For VAT, the Commission proposed a two rate system - a standard rate for most of goods and services and reduced rate for basic necessities with the member states free to fix their own rate within a band of 14-20 per cent for standard rate and 4-9 per cent for the reduced rate.

3.10.1 Introduction of the New System

Although member states' authorities had committed themselves to putting in place, by 31st December 1992, a system of collection of VAT and excise duties compatible with the abolition of frontier controls, they decided at the end of 1989 their incapability to adopt the definitive regime outlined above in relation to VAT in time for January, 1993.

They agreed instead to a more flexible approach consisting of a transitional regime for a limited period maintaining taxation in the country of destination but in conditions compatible with the abolition of fiscal barriers.

In addition, member states agreed to :

i) Freeze the divergences in VAT rates and set the standard rate within a bracket to be fixed by 31 December 1991 within the limits of 14 to 20 per cent as proposed by the Commission.

ii) Fix reduced rates for certain essential goods and services by January 1993, within a range of 4 to 9 per cent with the possibility of zero rates for a very limited number of products.

iii) Thirdly, they had the target of abolishing the restrictions on purchases by individuals from January 1993.

Further, harmonisation of rates on savings, abolition of stamp duty, adoption of directives concerning avoidance of double taxation on projects of company in case of mergers, amalgamation, clearing house arrangements were expected to facilitate in dismantling fiscal barriers.

3.10.2 Achievements

By mid-1994, most of the tax controls were abolished and certain forms of double taxation were also eliminated but, at the same time, key proposals like complete elimination of taxation at source on interest and royalty payments were before the Council. The measures taken on indirect taxation, however, need to be completed by the adoption of proposals on the taxation of transport of passengers. However, the most important proposal, whose adoption is a matter of urgency, is that on VAT arrangements applying to second-hand goods, works of art, antiques and collectors' items.

The removal of frontier checks require particular vigilance on the part of the Commission and the member states with regard to some goods that are not subject to harmonisation requirements, in order to ensure that differences in rules and regulations do not result in fraud or in difficulties for consumers.

3.10.3 Conclusions

The legislative framework for an Internal market, as defined in the Commission's White paper of 1985 is almost fully in place. 95 per cent of the checklist of White paper legislation has been adopted and is in the process of being implemented by the EU institutions and member states. Of the 282 White Paper measures, 265 have been adopted by the Council (95 per cent). The transposition in the national legislations is proceeding; 261 White Paper measures have entered into force (90 per cent) of which 219 require national transposition measures. 85 per cent of the total number of necessary transposition measures have been taken. 110 of the 218 measures have been transposed in all 12 member states [14], 28 in 11 member states, 21 in 10 member states, 62 in 9 or fewer (of which 21 in 5 or fewer) member states [15].

An analysis by member states shows that Denmark has taken 94 per cent of the necessary transposition measures followed by U.K. (90 per cent), Italy and Belgium (89 per cent) each. Most delay in transposition are in Ireland (80 per cent), Germany (78 per cent) and Greece (75 per cent). When broken down by sector, it emerges that transposition has been completed or is above average in the areas of freedom of movement of capital, in elimination of physical frontiers (various controls and controls on persons), in financial services (excluding insurance), in elimination of technical barriers, company taxation, VAT and excise duties.

This accomplishment is all the more impressive as the measures which require the greatest adjustment on the part of the member states - the switchover to the "Transitional" VAT regime, the abolition of capital controls, the freedom to provide banking and insurance services throughout the EU, a framework for the liberalisation of public procurement in all sectors including the utility sectors, the liberalisation of air and road transport - have all been successfully negotiated and adopted. The legislative steps which have already been taken constitute the principal elements of the internal market framework and will be sufficient to trigger the bulk of the pro-competitive and resource allocation gains which will flow from internal market completion.

A handful of white paper measures, however, remain on the table, many of which would greatly facilitate the exercise of cross-border activities by economic operators. In particular, progress on proposals relating to the introduction of a Union trade mark, the alleviation of double taxation problems and the creation of a European Company Statute are eagerly awaited by the business community. The Union must also look beyond the White Paper to areas where additional trade barriers have been identified; areas like sectors where the granting of exclusive rights at national level have been identified. The Commission has also tabled proposals or launched discussion on possible forms of liberalisation in voice telephony, energy and postal services. Internal market completion in these sectors has progressed at varying speed and with varying degree of success.

On the whole, the back of the legislative work has been broken. The task of the Union, at present, is to ensure that internal market enabling legislation is properly transposed in all member states. At this stage, 86 per cent of necessary transposition measures have been taken and there is continual improvement on this front. Member States have been less diligent in transposing internal market legislation in the fields of company law, public procurement and financial services possibly because these measures entered into force at a later date and transposition was accorded a lower priority.

However, the task of making the internal market work does not stop at monitoring the rate of transposition. The Commission is currently elaborating its strategic programme for the internal market which is designed to maximise the benefits of the internal market framework for consumers, citizens and enterprises. This involves coherent action on a number of fronts. In particular, the Union must now devote increased attention and resources to the following themes:

- Monitoring the quality, as well as the rate of transposition, and improving the transparency of national transposition measures;

- Ensuring the quality of enforcement by setting up necessary channels for administrative co-operation and developing new instruments for monitoring enforcement;

- Preventing the emergence of new barriers to trade through stringent application of competition policy safeguards, and the reinforcement of early warning systems for the detection and prevention of new regulatory or administrative trade barriers;

- Enforcement can also be improved by imposition of sanctions on recalcitrant member states;

- Empowering businesses and consumers to defend their rights within the internal market by improving access to justice, and ensuring an even interpretation and application of EU law.

- Ongoing monitoring and evaluation of internal market legislation and its impact with a view to up-grading its performance.

In addition, the Union must look at ways of improving the interaction between internal market measures and other Union policies which can make a contribution to the improved functioning of the single market - notably, policies to assist SMEs, Standardisation, Conformity assessment, Competition policy, environmental policy and the common commercial policy.

Internal market enabling legislation, whose impact will be amplified by the strategic programme, creates a legal and administrative environment in which economic operators can develop their activities on a pan-European scale. It allows them to exploit market opportunities or tap resources in other member states. Economic operators are beginning to witness some of the concrete benefits of a single market. For instance,

- Border controls and formalities on cross-border shipments of goods are now a thing of the past.

- Technical harmonising legislation, which was adopted at an early stage of the internal market programme, is eroding technical trade barriers in sectors such as toys, medico-surgical equipment, and pressure-vessels.

- the removal of controls on capital movement has contributed in no small measures to the increased integration of some member states into international capital markets. This in turn has facilitated cross-border investment and eased credit shortages in those member states.

Although the advantages of internal market integration are beginning to filter through, it would be premature to undertake a global assessment of the internal market at this stage. For a start, much internal market has yet to enter into force, or to be transposed into national legislation. Secondly, complementary actions to capitalise fully on the potential of the single market must be implemented in parallel with the legislative framework (e.g. Trans-European Networks, the development of European Standardisation etc.). Last, but not the least, economic operators must become acclimatised to the new legislative environment and learn how to turn legal developments into commercial opportunities.

Nevertheless, there are some preliminary indications that anticipation effects unleashed by the internal market programme have been the catalyst for a revitalisation of corporate strategies and a shake-up of market structures in many industrial and services sectors. Many companies have responded positively to the emerging internal market and this has been reflected in the following trends:

- A surge in the intra-EU foreign direct investment which has been heavily concentrated in those sectors most directly concerned by internal market liberalisation.

- The wave of cross-border mergers and acquisitions which has formed part of the increase in intra-EU FDI.

- Increased interest on the part of third country investors in locating in the Union.

- Indications that the internal market has been accompanied by profound changes in the degree of market integration in banking and insurance markets.

- Marked evolution in the proportion of output from particular sectors which is sold in other Union markets and an increasing share of national consumption which is met by intra-EU imports.

These trends suggest an increasing Europeanisation of companies' sales strategies and increased competitive discipline on domestic incumbents in the markets concerned.

The internal market programme was not constructed in an economic vacuum. The recession in early 1990s, which had been provoked by forces unrelated to the competition of the internal market, had overshadowed the process of adaptation to the emerging single market framework. The depressed state of EU markets obscured the potential market openings created by the internal market. In addition many, particularly, small and medium sized companies did not have the resources or were wary of positioning themselves in order to take advantage of opportunities which lied around the corner. However, there are reasons to believe that the restructuring and investment undertaken during the late 1980s, in anticipation of the internal market, have strengthened the underlying competitiveness of Union industry and services. These latent strengths will provide individual companies with a springboard once economic recovery gets underway. In addition, the internal market has acted as a brake on any temptation on the part of member states to renationalise certain elements of economic, monetary or commercial policy.

The widening of margins for exchange rate fluctuation contains some potential dangers for the operation of the single market, should these new exchange rate arrangements not be managed carefully. In particular, the increased scope for exchange rate fluctuations could disrupt the operation of capital markets, while sudden changes in relation competitiveness provoked by nominal exchange rate fluctuations could generate-demands for safeguard restrictions on cross-border trade. To this extent, a return to greater exchange rate stability represents a pre-condition for the proper functioning of the internal market. Conversely, the internal market programme can promote structural and micro-economic convergence which is needed to sustain further progress towards Economic and Monetary Union.

3.11 Economic and Monetary Union

3.11.1 Background

In as early as 1970, the Werner report, named after the Luxembourg Prime Minister, put forward a plan for the attainment of economic and monetary union. Following this report, the 'Snake' was created in 1972, the European Monetary Co-operation Fund was set up in 1973 and the first decision on economic convergence was taken in 1974.

However, the process of integration initiated at that time was hampered by member states' divergent responses to the economic shocks that occurred. The European Monetary System (EMS) was set in place in 1979 and has succeeded in creating a zone of growing monetary stability [16]. The discipline it imposed had contributed to the introduction, in countries with relatively high rates of inflation, of monetary policies geared to price stability, thereby laying the foundations for economic convergence between member states.

In early 1985, the Commission proposed a series of detailed measures for the removal of physical, technical and fiscal barriers, and for the creation of a unified economic area in which persons, goods, services and capital would be able to move around freely. It , as against this background of the European Council meeting in Hanover in June 1988, entrusted to a committee the task of studying and proposing concrete stages leading towards economic and monetary union.

3.11.2 Maastricht Treaty

The second half of eighties and early nineties had proved to be years of rapid developments, transforming overnight the very geo-political and economic structure of Europe. The psychological damage inflicted by the world wars - a complete wastage of more than three decades - was dramatically undone in a few years [17].

The pace and process of European integration had to be speeded up further in the face of such momentous changes across the globe as the withering away of the erstwhile USSR, the marketisation of Central and East European countries, the end of East-West hostility, and the collapse of the Berlin wall and subsequent unification of Germany.

In view of the changed scenario, the then twelve member states decided to strengthen their political and monetary bonds and negotiated a new treaty at the meeting of Heads of States held in the Dutch city of Maastricht on December 9 and 10, 1991. The negotiated agreements, called the Maastricht European Union Treaty (in short Maastricht Treaty), was signed by foreign and finance ministers of member states in February, 1992. In a sense, the Maastricht Treaty constitutes a grand finale of the inter-governmental conferences on Economic and Monetary Union and on Political Union held earlier in Rome in December, 1990.

The Treaty lays the foundation for three principal tasks:

(1) Continued internal development from a single market to economic and monetary union with the ultimate objective of creating an European Union.

(2) Evolving a strategy for the future enlargement of the European Union.

(3) Expanding external responsibilities of the European Union by helping define a new post-cold war world order and by being a role model

for the East European countries which are edging towards market economies and democratic set-up.

The Maastricht Treaty had set numerous goals in regard to various issues, selected ones are discussed as follows:

3.11.2.1 Economic and Monetary Union: The Maastricht Treaty provides a legal and political framework and a three stage time-table for the formation of the European Monetary Union (EMU), the ultimate goal being emergence of a single currency.

Stage 1: As proposed in the Delors' report, stage 1 of economic and monetary union began on July 1, 1990. The principal steps in stage-1 were:

- Removal of physical, technical and fiscal barriers within the Union in line with the programme for completing the internal market by the end of 1992;

- Increase in the resources, and improvement in the machinery of the structural funds in order to promote regional development and to correct regional imbalances, as part of the reform of the structural funds agreed in 1988;

- Strengthening of economic and fiscal policy co-ordination, this being the aim of the new convergence arrangements adopted in March, 1990 and based on multilateral surveillance.

In the monetary field, the principal steps in Stage-1 were:

i) Complete freedom of movement of capital, something already achieved in eight member states, with only minor exceptions remaining in the other four;

ii) Elimination of all obstacles to financial integration in the Union, i.e. freedom to provide the whole range of banking, financial and insurance services;

iii) participation of all Union currencies in the exchange rate mechanism of the European Monetary System;

iv) Strengthening of the co-ordination of decisions on monetary and exchange-rate policy.

Major economic events during Stage-1 were as follows.

Nominal Convergence : Achievements and Challenges: Stage-1 of EMU was characterised by major economic events. The implications of German unification not only determined economic developments in that country, but also had important repercussions on the Union economy as a whole during the period under consideration. While the initial effects were favourable for Europe, the adopted policy triggered restrictive effects later on. Spain and U.K. joined the Exchange Rate Mechanism (ERM) in June 1989 and October 1990, respectively. Both countries were facing special challenges. In Spain the catching up process required adequate responses in policies while in U.K. the policy assignment had to be altered as monetary policy was no longer available for short-term anti-cyclical stabilisation purposes. Portugal, subsequently, joined the ERM in April 1992. The Danish 'NO' in June 1992, the uncertainties surrounding the outcome of the French referendum, the political process of ratification in the U.K., and the challenging of the Treaty on European Union before the German supreme court delayed the ratification process.

The Exchange Rate Mechanism (ERM) of the European Monetary System (EMS) went through a period of marked instability from mid-1992, during which several realignments took place and the U.K. and Italy suspended their participation in the ERM system. In August 1993, the fluctuation margins were widened markedly.

These events caused a major correction in the financial markets' expectations on EMU. In consequence, the markets began to question the wisdom of their portfolio positions in high-yielding currencies; the so-called 'convergence plays' began to unwend as institutions sought to prevent themselves against newly-perceived devaluation risks.

The ensuing period of 18 months was characterised by repeated bouts of market pressure on ERM currencies as huge amounts of capital flowed between currencies, primarily into the DM. The severity of pressure resulted in a sequence of adjustments within the ERM, involving the withdrawal of two currencies from the system, five realignments involving four currencies and ultimately in early August 1993, the temporary widening of fluctuation margins to + 1.5 per cent.

The widening of ERM bands implies a major change of regime in monetary co-operation in the Union. A system of quasi-fixed exchange rates had been temporarily replaced by a system allowing, in principle, greater flexibility in exchange rate movements within wide bands. The weakening of exchange-rate discipline within the ERM represented a setback to the integration process within the Union as previously envisaged; but in the circumstances wider ERM bands were the most pragmatic response to the recurrent tensions on the foreign exchange markets.

Any effort to re-establish narrow bands without improved economic convergence among member states would almost certainly not be accepted by the financial markets and would incite renewed speculative attacks on the ERM grid. The experience of the recent crisis has demonstrated that a necessary condition for exchange rate stability is achieved by the pursuit of credible and consistent economic policies designed to foster economic convergence in conditions of economic growth, while focusing on the fundamentals of price stability and sound public finances.

Inflation: Reducing inflation rates or maintaining an already satisfactory inflation performance has been one of the central objectives of the convergence programmes. The progress achieved has so far been broadly in line with indicative targets set in the programmes, although in Germany headline inflation is coming down more slowly than projected.

Visible progress was achieved in inflation performance during stage 1, both as regards the level and the degree of convergence. The inflation rates in 1993 in seven member states were estimated to be within the limits to be aimed for according to the Treaty, which was of the order of 3-4 per cent. Of these member states, six (Belgium, Denmark, France, Ireland, Luxembourg and the Netherlands), have shown a remarkable regularity during the period, while the U.K. had entered the reference range for the first time in 1993. As regards the remaining member states, the somewhat poorer performance of Germany in the recent period had been mainly due to the special circumstances of unification; in Spain and Italy inflation had been decelerating and the 5 per cent plateau had been broken in 1993; in Portugal inflation was much closure to the reference range compared with the double digit inflation in the early nineties. Although progress had been achieved, inflation in Greece remained far above the Union's average.

Public Finance: Member states' public finances deteriorated significantly during stage-1 of EMU. It appears that fiscal policy has to play a major role in accommodating the recession either through the working of the automatic stabilisers or, in a few cases, as a result of a deliberately anti-cyclical budgetary stance. The deficit of the general movement represented, for the Union as a whole, 6.4 per cent of GDP in 1993, a figure clearly above that of the beginning of the decade. Decisive action is necessary to reduce budgetary imbalances in the Union, supported by an adequate policy-mix leading to steady and sustained economic growth; indeed, developments during Stage-1 have shown that the convergence of budgetary positions to the benchmark values of the Treaty while recession persists is a very difficult task.

Budgetary Situation: The deterioration of the budgetary situation had been generalised throughout the Union. In 1993, with the exception of Ireland and Luxembourg, no other member states was expected to comply strictly with the deficit benchmark of 3 per cent of GDP. The deterioration was most evident in Denmark, Germany, France and United Kingdom (where the public deficits in percent of GDP in 1993 were estimated to reach 4.4 per cent, 4.2 per cent, 5.9 per cent and 7.6 per cent respectively), given the low level of earlier deficits. Except for Germany, these countries took deliberate measures to mitigate the effects of the economic slowdown.

In Spain, the widening of the deficit in 1993 to 7.2 per cent of GDP more than offset the progress achieved in the previous year; a similar development occurred in Portugal. Some other member states aiming at fiscal consolidation either remained on a gradual upward trend or achieved a stabilisation in their government deficit e.g., Italy. In the Netherlands, the deficit was brought down after 1990 and was kept at relatively low level (4.0 per cent of GDP in 1993), while Ireland and Luxembourg stand as the member states with the lowest deficits.

Having occurred in a period of low, if not negative, real growth and of low or decelerating inflation, the widening of governments' deficits had led to a rise in the public debt to GDP ratios throughout most of the Union. This situation is particularly worrying for those member states where the public debt to GDP ratio is clearly above the 60 per cent benchmark; the public debt to GDP ratio is now over 100 per cent in three member states and has not yet been stabilised, which must first be achieved before the required steady decline.

Progress was achieved as far as convergence in long term interest rates within the Union is concerned. Long term interest rates have declined since 1990 and the dispersion among member states has narrowed; all but four member states already satisfy the interest-rate criterion of the Treaty. This trend largely reflects the favourable development of inflation and illustrates the high level of financial integration achieved in the Union.

Although not spelled out in Article 109 of the Treaty, real convergence cannot be ignored. Achievements in this domain were disappointing, given the sharp increase in the unemployment rate in the Union, from 8.3 per cent in 1990 to 10.6 per cent in 1993. However, supply conditions have improved in the Union through the implementation of structural reforms; in addition, the profitability of investment, which is important to cope with the challenge of unemployment, does not seem to have been damaged over much by the current cyclical downswing.

Stage-2: The second stage of Economic and Monetary Union commenced on January 1, 1994 and ran till June 1998, although provisions were included in the text to prolong stage-2 further, if necessary until 1999.

In this phase, member states made determined efforts to achieve performance convergence. A new body, the European Monetary Institute (EMI), was set up at the start of stage 2, which among other functions undertook surveillance of progress towards meeting performance criteria. In accordance with Article 109F (6) of the Treaty, "The EMI shall be consulted by the Council regarding any proposed Community act within its field of competence"[18].

The Institute replaced the committee of central bank governors and the European Monetary Co-operation Fund (EMCF) and consists of the national central bank governors and a President appointed by the Heads of Stages and Governments. Its principal task is to monitor developments in the European Monetary System (EMS) and in the matter of economic performance criteria and prepare the ground for the establishment of the European Central Bank in Stage-III.

Article 4 (2) of the statute of the EMI assigns to the EMI the task of specifying the regulatory, organisational and logistical framework necessary for the European System of Central Banks (ESCB) to perform its tasks in the third stage. It specifies some particular tasks in this respect, namely, to prepare the instruments and procedures for a single monetary policy, to promote the harmonisation of rules and practices for statistics, to prepare the rules for operations of national central banks in stage-III, to promote the efficiency of cross-border payments and to supervise the technical preparation of ECU bank notes.

Stage-3: The provision in the Treaty was that stage III would commence at the earliest from January 1, 1996 and at the latest from January 1, 1999. For stage-III to commence, it was necessary for the EU council of ministers to determine whether seven or more member states meet the economic performance criteria indicated below:

Inflation Differentials: A member state's consumer price inflation not to exceed more than 1.5 per cent points the inflation rates of the three best performing member states.

Exchange-Rate Stability: The exchange-rate to be held for two years within the narrow band of fluctuation of the Exchange Rates Mechanism of EMS without a devaluation.

Interest-Rate Differentials: Long-term interest rate not to be more than 2 percentage points above those in three member states with the lowest inflation.

Government Deficit: Consolidated deficit of the central, state and local governments and the social security funds not to surpass 3 percent of GDP.

Public Debt: Ratio of public debt to GDP not to exceed 60 per cent of GDP.

If seven or more states do meet the criteria, then the European Council may decide by a qualified majority to allow them to proceed to stage-III. If no decision is taken, the countries meeting the performance convergence criteria, irrespective of the number, will automatically progress to stage-III on January 1, 1999. A European Central Bank was set up at the beginning of stage-III (May 1998). It will be independent of national governments and will manage the monetary policies of the member states that have progressed to stage-III. It will have a Governing Council, consisting of an executive board and of the governors of the national central banks.

Each member state entering stage-III will be required to make their central banks independent of government's direction. National central banks will not be permitted to provide credit to the public sector or to purchase its debt directly.

There is a provision in the Treaty that on reaching stage-III, the States qualified to join the European Monetary Union, will set up European System of Central Banks (ESCB), which will consist of ECB and national central banks.

Under a protocol to the Treaty, the U.K. has reserved the right to opt out of stage-III, even if it meets the economic performance criteria. In another protocol, Denmark has been permitted to submit its participation in stage-III to a referendum.

The most important objective of the Monetary Union was to introduce a single currency six months after the establishing of the ECB.

3.11.3 Amsterdam Treaty of 1997

In the aftermath of the second world war, Jean Monnet had the idea of pooling European countries' economic interests. His aim was political, rather than economic. A lot has been done since then [19].

In 1957, the Treaty of Rome set up the European Economic Community. In 1987, the Single Act gave fresh impetus to the internal market, after which the Maastricht Treaty of 1991 paved the way for economic and monetary union. It also introduced the 'pillar' of European foreign policy and the desire to create an area of free movement in safety.

On June 17, 1997, the leaders of every member State of the European Union agreed on a new Treaty for Europe, the Treaty of Amsterdam.

The Treaty of Amsterdam has four main objectives:

to place employment and citizens' rights at the heart of the Union;

- to sweep away the last remaining obstacles to freedom of movement and to strengthen security;

- to give Europe a stronger voice in world affairs;

- to make the Union's institutional structure more efficient with a view to enlarging the Union, with new member states joining.

In other words, the Treaty of Amsterdam consolidates each of the three great 'pillars' which have been the foundation for the Union's work since the Maastricht Treaty of 1 November, 1993:

The European Communities (first pillar); the common foreign and security policy (second pillar); and co-operation in the fields of justice and home affairs (third pillar).

First Principle: Putting employment and citizens' rights at the heart of the Union.

The inclusion of this clause in the Treaty of Amsterdam is a new approach. Each member State will retain control over its own policy, but from now on will fit into a co-ordinated European strategy, bringing the social and economic spheres together.

In Amsterdam, the Governments agreed to :

(1) align their employment policies in a way consistent with the Community's economic policy;

(2) promote a skilled and adaptable work force, as well as labour markets which respond quickly to economic change.

The co-ordinated strategy for employment will be applied each year.

(a) The heads of State or Government will first examine the employment situation.

(b) The Council, acting by a qualified majority on a proposal from the Commission and after consulting the European Parliament, the Economic and Social Committee and the Committee of the Regions, will then draw up guidelines for the member states.

(c) At the end of the year, the Council will examine how these guidelines are being implemented and will, if it considers it appropriate, make recommendations to the member states.

(d) Lastly, incentives will be given for the financing of pilot projects for employment.

3.11.3.1 A Common Social Policy: As the U.K. joined the social protocol in 1997, which it had not in 1991, the Protocol has been incorporated into the Treaty's provisions on social policy, education training and youth.

3.11.3.2 New Rights for Citizens:

-Fundamental Rights: The Union is founded on the principle of liberty, democracy, respect for human rights and fundamental freedoms, and the rule of law. Henceforth any citizen has the possibility, on the terms set out in the Treaty, of bringing an action in the Court of Justice if he or she considers that an instrument issued by the institutions violates fundamental rights.

-Consumer rights and human health protection.

In order to promote the interest of consumers and to ensure a high level of consumer protection, the Community shall contribute to protecting the health, safety and economic interests of consumers.

-Right to Information: Any citizen of the Union and any natural or legal person residing or having its registered office in a member State shall have a right of access to documents originating from the European Parliament, the Council and the Commission subject to general principles and conditions governing this right.

-Freedom to Move Freely and Live in a Secure Environment

To guarantee that an 'area of freedom, security and justice' is established gradually in the Community, there will be a five-year period from the entry into force of the Treaty during which the Council will continue to take decisions by unanimous vote. At the end of the five years, Community decision-making procedures may be introduced.

The Amsterdam Treaty incorporated the Schengen arrangement into the Union's single institutional framework. Applying the system of 'closer co-operation', the 13 Schengen countries will continue their co-operation within the legal order established by the new Treaty.

In conclusion, the goal of establishing freedom of movement for individuals included in legal texts for the last 10 years, can now be achieved in practice. Citizens will not only be guaranteed that decisions will be taken democratically, but will also have access to effective legal recourse if their rights are not respected.

-Third Principle - Giving Europe a Message and a Voice in the World

From the outset the Community has defended commercial interests on behalf of all the member states. But international trade in the 1990s is very different from what it was in the 1960s, when it chiefly involved agricultural and industrial products. Invisible goods now account for a major proportion of the wealth which Europe's people produce. The Amsterdam Treaty aims to extend the competence of the Union to the key areas of intellectual property and services.

-Foreign and Security Policy: Setting Up Common Strategic Framework

The 15 Member States share important interests, and they will defend them better if they do so together. European leaders will decide by consensus on common strategies to guide the Union's action. The Council decides, normally by unanimity, an action to take.

The President of the Council will represent the Union and will be assisted in the task by a secretary-general, who will help to implement these political decisions. The Commission will be fully associated with this process.

-Anticipating Crisis and Creating Conditions for Quick Decision-Making

A new policy planning and early warning unit will monitor international developments, their possible implications for the Union and potential courses of action. The unit will consist of specialists from the member states, the Council and the Commission, as well as from the Western European Union (WEU).

The Amsterdam Treaty acknowledges both that most member states have obligations within NATO, and that others are not members of it. All of the states, however, believe that a common and security policy involves all aspects of the Union's security, including - increasingly - those relating to defence. It is a step towards a European identity in security and defence.

Fourth Principle: Effective Institutions for an Enlarged Europe: The new treaty emphasises to put efficient, legitimate institutions in place. The Amsterdam Treaty shall work in the following manner:

(a) Legislative Acts: The Parliament and Council will 'co-decide'.

The Treaty considerably increases Parliament's responsibilities by making the co-decision procedure more or less the general rule.

(b) More use of qualified majority voting in the Council of Ministers.

(c) There will be a stronger presidency for the European Commission.

(d) There will be closer ties with the national Parliaments.

(e) Groups of member states will be able to move faster and go further than others.

(f) The weighting of member states in the institutions will be modified when new states join in the future.

3.11.4 Conclusions

The internal market is now in its third stage. The already well established legal framework provides the basis for the elimination of non-tariff trade barriers. The strategic programme identifies new ways for managing this area without internal frontiers. As far as it is judged, by now, the single market is operating without major difficulties, apart from transitional problems for small and medium sized enterprises. It is still too early to assess the full economic impact of the internal market, as firms have not yet had sufficient time to adjust to the new legislation and the process of transposition is still going on.

The internal market programme is also not being constructed in an economic vacuum. The current recession and the world-wide economic situation has overshadowed the process of adaptation to the emerging single market framework. Nevertheless, there are indications to believe that restructuring and investment undertaken during the late 1980s, in anticipation of the internal market, have helped to mitigate to a certain extent some of effects of the downturn. In this context, the successful completion of the GATT-Uruguay round has improved the economic outlook.

The internal market legislation has injected new dynamism into key industries and services by providing open and, therefore, increased cross-border competition. The key competitive yardsticks are price and quality. The transformation of this competitive environment forces enterprises to adapt to the new conditions by increasing their efficiency. The process of the completion of the single market has already strengthened mutually profitable economic and commercial links between the member states. This has been reflected in a steady increase in the proportion of intra-EU trade as a component of industrial and services output. Europeanisation of company corporate and investment strategies to allow firms to take advantage of newly accessible commercial opportunities in other member states has been indicated by an increasing number of mergers and acquisitions as well as foreign direct investment in anticipation of the effects of the internal market.

The 1st January, 1993 was a deadline for the establishment of the legal framework for the single market removing the physical, fiscal and technical barriers; it has been largely respected. It marked a high point in the life of the internal market, but neither the end nor the beginning of an ongoing, dynamic and irreversible process. This legislation is coming on stream and opens up new possibilities for trade and investment. The challenge is now to realise the full potential of the internal market. Other Union policies also contribute to the proper functioning of the internal market by providing appropriate complementary measures concerning competition policy, consumer policy, special initiatives for SMEs and the establishment of trans-European networks. The single market framework provides environment within which to do business. But, it is also up to firms and consumers to take advantage of the new possibilities and to draw attention to cases where they have experienced problems in availing of single market freedoms.

To summarise, it can be said that Post-Maastricht message to Europe has been that the era of absolute sovereignty of nation states is almost over. Though, not very visible at present, the federalist approach has helped in constant balancing of national and common interests and in forging of a separate identity.

Notes

1. Willy de Clercq and Leo Verhoef ; 'Europe Back to the Top' - An Inspiring Vision of Europe's Present and Future; Printed in Belgium; 1990.

2. 'Opening up the Internal Market' ; European Documentation Series, pp. 11-15; Commission of the European Community ; Printed in Belgium.

3. Report of the Ambassador's Committee on *"The Single European Market 1992 and India"*; 1992.

4. *"Opening Up the Internal Market"*; European Documentation Series; June 1991; printed in Belgium.

5. A paper presented by Jurgen Wiemann at German Development Institute, Berlin; 1992.

6. Report of the ambassador's Committee on 'The Single European Market 1992 and India'

7. *"Completing the Internal Market - White Paper from the Commission to the European Council"*; Commission of the European Communities; Milan; 28-29 June, 1985.

8 Report of the Ambassador's Committee on *"The Single European market 1992 and India"*; 1993.

9. *"Reinforcing the Effectiveness of the Internal Market'*; A working document of the Commission on a strategic programme on the Internal Market; June 2, 1993; Brussels.

10. *"Opening up the Internal Market"*; European Documentation Series; June, 1991.

11. *"Completing the Internal Market"*; The elimination of frontier controls; Commission of the European Communities; December 31, 1990.

12. *"Reinforcing the Effectiveness of the Internal Market'*; A working document of the Commission on a strategic programme on the Internal Market; June, 1993.

13. *"Opening up the Internal Market"*; European Documentation Series; Commission of the European Communities; Luxembourg; 1993.

14. As from January 1995, EU consists of 15 member countries with the inclusion of Austria, Sweden and Finland.

15. *"European Union News"*; Newsletter of the delegation of the European Commission in India; Vol. 6, No. 2, May 1994.

16. *"Economic and Monetary Union"*; Commission of the European Communities; Luxembourg; 1991.

17. Report of Conference on *"Europe after Maastricht - A Backgrounder"*; jointly organised by PHD Chamber of Commerce and Industry; January 25, 1993.

18. *"Secondary Legislation for the Second Stage of Economic and Monetary Union*"; Commission of the European Communities; Luxembourg : September 22, 1993.

19. *"Citizens Guide - A New Treaty for Europe*"; Bulletin of European Union; Office for official publications of the European Communities; July, 1997.

Chapter 4

Indo-EU Trade Relations

4.1 Trends in India's Foreign Trade

International trade is an activity of strategic importance in the development process of a developing economy. India's foreign trade shares in the ups and downs of the economic growth and development of the country.

India had an active and mutually enriching trade with all the early civilisations. The history of India's trade and commerce goes back to the Phoenician times when not only did cotton and teak, spices, silks and precious stones change hands, but a whole series of ideas and thought systems were shared. Indian silks and fine muslins were highly prized and there is contemporary evidence of a flourishing trade between India and the distant European countries since pre-christian times.

Indian trade existed even before the christian era. During the Kushana period, India's trade and commerce with the Roman empire reached its zenith. Pliny described India as a source of precious stones. During the seventh and eighth centuries A.D., Indian trade had developed further, though by the eighth century, the Arabs had already proved themselves to be very strong competitors obtaining a foot-hold in Sind.

In the tenth century B.C., India had commercial relations with foreign countries in which the Arabs played the role of 'Intermediaries'. In the first two centuries of the christian era, there was a considerable increase in trade between India and Rome. The Gupta period, however, is regarded as the golden age in Indian history and Indian trade and culture during this period made a great impact on Central Asia and Malaysia. It can, therefore, be said that trade existed in our country from times immemorial [1].

Some of those who are reputed to have discovered certain countries, like Columbus, actually were in search of our country which came to be known as 'Golden Bird', largely through the trade which we had with other parts of the world. Archaeological discoveries, in India and other parts of the world, have proved the existence of flourishing trade in the Gupta and Mauryan periods, as stated above also. The trade, however, in those times was mainly 'visible trade'. The Europeans, particularly British, formed trading companies in their countries with a view to develop trade with India. East India Company was an example of this. It came to carry away precious goods - gold, silver, raw-materials and even finished goods to England and gave in turn services like Defence, Civil administration etc. Trade, then, became both 'visible' and 'invisible'.

The stupendous task of economic reconstruction and industrialisation beckoned the dawn of India's independence in 1947. The goals of achieving an all round economic self-sufficiency transforming the backward agrarian Indian economy into an industrial nation and ensuring the millions a better quality of life. This warranted colossal amount of resources quite apart from building the requisite infrastructure and marshalling foreign exchange to translate the set objectives into actual reality.

Tables 4.1 and 4.2 give a bird's eye-view of the foreign trade of India with the world in Indian currency and U.S. dollars.

In the first decade starting from 1950-51 to 1959-60, the trade deficit was on an increase; starting from Rs. 2 crore to Rs. 321 crore in 1959-60. The imports were increasing at a faster rate than the exports. The exports, as a part of the world's exports, however, were less than 2 per cent

In the second decade, starting from 1960-61 to 1969-70, trade deficit was still on an increase. However, there was a decline in the deficit from Rs. 551 crore to Rs. 169 crore . Exports, as percentage of world exports, however, fell from 1 per cent to 0.67 per cent .

In the seventies, however, there was a trade surplus for the first time in the year 1972-73; but, in the following year, again, the trade deficit was of the tune of Rs. 432 crore . It was on an increase for two consecutive years, i.e. 1974-75 and 1975-76. However, the year 1976-77 was a crucial year for Indian economy [2]. From a trade deficit of Rs. 1,299 in the preceding year i.e. 1975-76, trade surplus was experienced by Indian economy in 1976-77, a second time.

The deterioration in India's balance of payments during 1974-75 stemmed primarily from the increased trade deficit resulting from sharp increases in import prices particularly of POL, fertilisers and food grains.

The widening deficits in the balance of payments had to be bridged with great difficulty at a great cost. A series of internal measures, fiscal and administrative, were taken to limit the consumption of oil products and to increase internal production and, thus, reduce the dependence on import. The drive to increase exports was intensified resulting in an increase of 27 per cent in export earnings over the previous year (i.e. 1976-77 compared to previous year 1975-76).

However, end of 70s (i.e. 1979-80) again witnessed a sharp increase in imports to the tune of Rs. 9,143 crore (i.e. 34 per cent rise over the previous year) and exports shot up to the tune of Rs. 6,418 crore (i.e. 12 per cent rise) resulting in a trade deficit of Rs. 2,725 crore .

In the early part of the 1980s, deficit was within the range of Rs. 5,800 crore to Rs. 6,000 crore . In the latter part, trade deficit increased and was in the range of Rs. 6,500 crore to Rs. 8,800 crore .

In the Nineties, trade deficit fell from Rs. 10,640 crore in 1990-91 to Rs. 3,809 crore in 1991-92. It was possible mainly due to sharp increase in exports at the rate of 35.3 per cent over previous year. In 1993-94, again, India experienced an increase in exports at the rate of 30.4 per cent over previous year bringing the trade deficit to Rs. 3,259 crore as compared to Rs. 9,572 crore deficit in the year 1992-93, a fall of approximately 65 per cent .

As stated above, trade deficit in the year 1990-91 stood at Rs. 10,640 crore . This increase was mainly due to the Gulf crisis which took place in 1990.

In 1995-96, India experienced an increase in exports to the tune of 20.7 per cent over the previous year, imports also rising by 28 per cent, resulting in an increase in trade deficit by 110 per cent over the previous year. In 1996-97, however, exports rose by 5.3 per cent only over the previous year, and imports by 6.7 per cent, trade deficit rising by Rs. 782 crore over the previous year.

4.1.1 Balance of Payments Position: Impact of Gulf Crisis

The Gulf crisis which began with the invasion of Kuwait by Iraq on August 2, 1990 lasted for about seven months and ended on February 28, 1991. The crisis has had serious economic implications for both industrial and developing countries.

This Gulf crisis has been different in terms of its impact from the earlier two episodes of sharp spurts in petroleum prices. First, it did not have some of the compensating features of the earlier two oil shocks i.e. large inflow of remittances, surge in exports and tendency of non-fuel commodity prices to rise in sympathy with oil prices. Secondly, it imposed an additional cost of repatriating non-resident Indians from the affected countries of the region.

The Gulf crisis had a serious impact on India's POL import bill. First, alternative sources for imports of crude oil and petroleum products had to be identified to substitute for imports earlier obtained from Iraq and Kuwait. Second, since contracts for crude oil and products were market-related, higher prices entailed a sharp escalation in India's import bill of POL. The spurt in prices of crude oil and petroleum products brought about a massive surge in the POL bill raising India's total imports during the year 1990-91 [3].

The Gulf crisis constrained India's export performance during 1990-91 in more than one way. In 1989-90, West Asian countries accounted by 7.2 per cent of India's exports with Kuwait accounting for 0.7 per cent and Iraq about 0.5 per cent . The immediate impact of the Gulf crisis arising out of trade embargo on Iraq and occupied Kuwait and dislocation of trade to other countries in West Asia led to significant loss in exports of our country.

Table 4.3 gives a clear picture of balance of payments position of India from 1991-92 to 1996-97.

4.1.2 Commodity Composition and Direction of Trade

4.1.2.1 India's Exports: India's exports by major commodity groups are: manufactures which include Engineering goods, Chemicals and allied products, Cotton yarn, fabric etc., Jute manufactures, Leather and its manufactures, Ready-made garments and Gems and Jewellery. Together, they accounted for 75.7 per cent in 1997-98, as is evident from Tables 4.6 and 4.7 which depict composition of India's exports in percent share from 1960-61 to 1997-98.

Agriculture and allied products category includes Cashew Kernels, Coffee, Marine products, Raw cotton, Rice, Spices, Sugar, Tea and Mate, Tobacco, etc. Together, these accounted for 18.8 per cent of total exports in 1997-98.

Exports in 1996-97 were of the order of $ 33470 million (Table 4.5). A growth rate of 5.26 percent in exports during 1996-97 was experienced. In 1995-96, however, exports experienced a growth rate of 20.7 per cent.

India's exports by major commodity groups is reflected through Tables 4.4 and 4.5 from the year 1960-61 to 1996-97.

Tables 4.6 and 4.7 give composition of India's major export items from the period 1960-61 to 1997-98. As is clear from the table, in the year 1993-94, share of Gems and Jewellery within the Manufactured Goods was the largest (18.04 per cent), followed by Agriculture and allied products (18 per cent), Ready-made Garments (11.58 per cent), Machinery and electronic goods (11.4 per cent).

Tables 4.6 and 4.7 indicate that from a share of 44.2 per cent in 1960-61, Agriculture and its allied products have fallen to 18 per cent in 1993-94. However, export of manufactured goods has shown a rise from 45.33 per cent in 1960-61 to 75.5 per cent in 1993-94. Gems and Jewellery and Ready-made Garments have shown a sharp rise from 0.16 per cent each in 1960-61 to 18.04 per cent and 11.58 per cent respectively in 1993-94.

However, export of Leather and leather manufactures including Footwear have shown a fall from 19.47 per cent in 1960-61 to 6.09 per cent in 1993-94.

From Table 4.7, it is clear that share of gems and jewellery fell slightly to 17.1 per cent in 1994-95 and still further to 14.3 per cent in 1997-98. Agriculture and allied products, however, increased from 16 per cent in 1994-95 to 18.8 per cent in 1997-98. Readymade garments rose slightly in 1994-95 to 12.5 per cent but fell to 11.1 per cent in 1997-98. Leather and its manufactures fell still further from 4 per cent in 1994-95 to 2.8 per cent in 1997-98.

4.1.2.2 India's Imports: India's major imports are Petroleum oil and lubricants, Capital goods, Pearls and Precious stones, Fertilisers, Iron and Steel, Chemicals and Edible oils. Together, they accounted for more than 70 per cent in 1996-97, as is evident from Tables 4.10 and 4.11.

Table 4.8 gives a brief summary of imports of our country from 1960-61 to 1996-97; imports of our country in 1992-93 to 1996-97 in US $ can be seen from Table 4.9.

Tables 4.10 and 4.11 give percent share of major commodity groups of India's imports from the world from 1960-61 to 1997-98. A glance at Tables 4.10 and 4.11 reveal that share of India's imports of Cereal and its preparations has fallen remarkably from 16.13 per cent in 1960-61 to 2.40 per cent in 1993-94. However, share of Petroleum, oil and Lubricants registered a rise from 6.15 per cent in 1960-61 to 24.70 per cent in 1993-94. Similarly, imports of Precious, Semi-precious stones also registered a sharp rise from 0.09 per cent in 1960-61 to 11.30 per cent in 1993-94. Iron and steel, however, showed a decline. Imports of Capital goods was 31.72 per cent in 1960-61, which fell remarkably to 15 per cent in 1980-81 and rose again to 25.90 per cent in 1993-94. In 1997-98, share of petroleum, oil and lubricants rose to 25.5 per cent from 19.2 per cent in 1996-97. Imports of precious, semi-precious stones, however, fell from 11.3 per cent in 1993-94 to 6.9 per cent in 1997-98. Capital goods maintained a steady growth and were of the tune of 25 per cent in 1997-98, falling slightly from 27.7 per cent in 1996-97.

4.1.2.3 Direction of India's Trade: The direction of India's trade, as depicted in Tables 4.12 and 4.13, gives a picture of both the destination of exports and the origin of imports from 1980-81 to 1996-97. Table 4.14 shows direction of India's trade with selected East Asian countries.

Table 4.12 gives direction of India's exports to the world from 1980-81 to 1996-97. Table 4.13 gives direction of India's imports from the world for the period 1980-81 to 1996-97.

Tables 4.15 and 4.16 give percentage share of India's major trading partners for the period 1980-81 to 1996-97. Table 4.15 indicates that share of India's exports to EU was 21.6 per cent in 1980-81. In the early 90s, EU countries together accounted for 27.56 per cent of India's exports to the world. EU, as in 1992-93, was India's largest trading partner; USA was closely behind it accounting for 18.8 per cent of India's total exports to world in 1992-93. In 1994-95, EU's share was 26.7 per cent, fell a little to 25 per cent in 1996-97. USA was at second position with a share of 19.8 per cent in 1996-97.

Within EU, Germany has been India's largest trading partner accounting for 6.4 per cent of India's total exports in 1989-90 and rising continuously to 7.7 per cent in 1992-93, followed by U.K. (Table 4.15). Germany remained India's largest trading partner till 1994-95. Since then, UK has taken over with a share of 6.1 per cent in 1996-97 as against 5.6 per cent of Germany.

Table 4.16 gives percentage share of India's major trading partners (imports). EU accounted for 21 per cent share of India's total imports from the world in 1980-81 and was the maximum at 33.2 per cent in 1989-90. In 1992-93, EU accounted for almost 30 per cent of India's total imports from the world. EU accounted for 30 per cent of India's total imports from world in 1993-94 but fell to 25.6 per cent in 1996-97. Within EU, Germany is India's largest source of imports with UK closely behind it.

From the Tables 4.15 and 4.16, it is clear that EU has emerged as India's largest trading partner.

A quick glance at Table 4.17 shows that LDCs followed EU countries in 1993-94 and 1994-95 as far as India's exports to world is concerned. USA emerged as third largest trading partner accounting for 18 per cent and 19 per cent in 1993-94 and 1994-95 followed by OPEC and Japan. LDCs share, however, was 25.89 per cent in India's total exports to world and 17.20 per cent in India's imports from the world.

From Table 4.17, it is evident that while India's share of exports to OPEC and LDCs showed a rise, India's share of exports to OECD (except Japan) and Eastern Europe showed a decline in 1993-94.

India's share of imports from OPEC and LDCs showed a rise in 1993-94 (Table 4.17), whereas Eastern Europe showed fall in 1993-94. U.K., Germany, U.S.A. and Japan showed a rise, whereas other EU countries showed a fall in 1993-94. In 1996-97, India's share of exports to OPEC and LDCs was 9.54 per cent and 25.89 per cent respectively. India's share of imports from these countries was 24.75 per cent and 17.20 per cent respectively in 1996-97.

4.2 India's Trade with EU

4.2.1 History of Indo-EU Trade

International trade relations constitute the single most important plank of the EU's external relations. After having established a common external customs tariff, as a corollary to its internal customs union, the European Union embarked on the road of a common trade policy. The EU had taken its place on the world stage as a trading partner in its own right and constituted, as a matter of fact, one of the largest trading blocks in the world [4].

4.2.1.1 First Phase: The 'Six' and India: Indo-EU economic relationship is now more than three and a half decades old. India's relationship with the Union has always been marked by mutual co-operation and trust. India took early steps to ensure that mutual trust and co-operation that it had built up with each one of the 'six' [5] in the past is not only continued but is indeed strengthened further. In pursuance of this objective, in 1962, it took opportunity of establishing formal diplomatic relations with the European Union and posted an Ambassador at Brussels. The intervening years have witnessed a remarkable development in relations between them to the point, where the EU, known as EC earlier, has emerged as India's principal trading partner and India as one of the main beneficiaries of the instruments devised by the Union to help developing countries raise the living standards of their people.

During the first phase of this relationship, which lasted some ten years, India was primarily concerned with securing better access to the Union's market for its exports.

For historic reasons, its commercial and financial ties were with the U.K., but a greatly expanded import programme, aimed at accelerating the pace of economic development, had resulted in trade deficits with the EU. It was in order to correct this imbalance that India sought tariff and other concessions from the Union. Its initial request was for the implementation of the tariff reductions, which the 'Six' had agreed to, in the course of the abortive 1961/63 negotiations for Britain's entry [6].

The result was a Union decision to suspend its tariffs on tea in bulk, certain spices and East India Kips on an autonomous basis. Again, at India's request, the EU opened zero-duty tariff quotas for handloom fabrics and handicrafts. Following the negotiations of self-restraint agreements covering jute and coir products, the EU partially suspended its tariffs on these products.

A third such agreement, covering cotton textiles, was negotiated at about the same time. Although a bilateral agreement like the others, it was concluded under an international agreement, the Long-Term Arrangement (LTA) on international trade in cotton textiles, which had been adopted by the contracting parties to the GATT in 1962.

Another international decision, in UNCTAD, was the basis of the Union's decision to introduce its own Generalised System of Preferences (GSP) in 1971. Both India and EU had played an important part in the UNCTAD agreement and it was only fitting that Indian exporters should be among the main beneficiaries of the Union's scheme.

4.2.1.2 Second Phase: Enlarged Union and India: The second phase of EU-India relations began in 1973 with the Union's enlargement, following the entry of the U.K., Ireland and Denmark. During the negotiations for enlargement, the Union had accepted a Joint Declaration of Intent (JDI) on the development of trade relations with Ceylon, India, Malaysia, Pakistan and Singapore under which the enlarged EU declared itself ready "to examine with these problems as may arise in the field of trade with a view to seeking appropriate solutions". This Joint Declaration of Intent was annexed to the Act of Accession, which demonstrates the importance the Union attached to it.

The enlarged Union redeemed another much older pledge, when it concluded a 5-year Commercial Co-operation Agreement (CCA) with India in December, 1973. (At the same time of the 1961/63 negotiations for Britain's entry, the two sides had agreed to conclude a comprehensive trade agreement with India following enlargement). The CCA, which reflected an advance on the traditional bilateral trade agreement, was to set the pattern for the agreements between the EEC and the other South Asian countries. Under the CCA with India, the two sides undertook to "consolidate, deepen and diversify their commercial and economic relations to the full extent of their growing capacity to meet each other's requirements on the basis of comparative advantages and mutual benefit".

4.2.1.3 Third Phase: New Co-operation Agreement: This may be said to have begun with the signature of the new 5-year Commercial and Economic Co-operation Agreement on June 23, 1981. A non-preferential agreement like the first, it too was based on the principles of comparative advantage and mutual benefit. But it represented a considerable advance on the 1973 agreement. The provisions for commercial co-operation had been strengthened in order to expand and diversify their trade; the two sides agreed to promote trade and industrial delegations foster the organisation of fairs and exhibitions, encourage their commercial organisations to cooperate with each other and generally help their economic operators identify sectors and products in which each side enjoys comparative advantage and support market development programme based on such identification.

In 1982, the EU launched an important programme aimed at encouraging EU firms to embark on industrial collaboration with Indian partners. They were given details of the opportunities offered by India in a series of seminars in four European cities. These seminars were followed by conference in New Delhi. European Commission financed major studies on the transfer of technology to India and organised a seminar in Berlin in 1984 to discuss their conclusions. As a part of the new programme of industrial co-operation, launched in 1987, the EU had continued with its efforts to bring together India and European economic operators with the focus being on sectoral basis. In 1987, a delegation of Indian machine tool manufacturers visited the European Machine Tool exhibition in Milan for discussions with their European counterparts. These revealed a complementarity of interests and resulted in an agreement to consider joint action programmes.

In 1988, the scope for collaboration in the manufacture of medical and surgical equipment was investigated with Union backing for a joint study and support from European companies which took part in the "Health India" exhibition in New Delhi in September 1988 [7].

Since 1987, India and the European Commission are collaborating on a different programme of industrial co-operation. It was agreed, under the new industrial co-operation programme, that Indian companies would be helped both to produce more efficiently and to produce to internationally agreed technical standards followed in the EU and other international markets.

The industrial co-operation programme, which led to the signing of first memorandum of co-operation in June 1987, gave a new dimension to Indo-EU relations. Areas identified for promotion of industrial co-operation include establishment of data banks, upgradation of industrial standards, co-operation in sectors like energy, human resource development, steel, electronics, telecommunications and bio-technology. The objective of such a co-operation was to make Indian market more attractive for European technology and products and inject competitiveness in India's exports to EU and world markets. EU had also drawn up a comprehensive plan in the area of quality control, standards and certification. It has set up a venture capital fund - European Community Investment Partners (ECIP) scheme for providing assistance in establishing joint ventures in India.

A major development was the establishment of Indo-EU Business Forum (Indo-EC known earlier) in 1992 to promote joint ventures and investments and to provide a platform for interaction between European and Indian businessmen.

4.2.1.4 Co-operation Agreement on Partnership and Development (December 1993): A co-operation agreement between India and European Union was signed on December 20, 1993. The agreement aims at building a closer and enhanced relationship between India and the European Union and lays special emphasis on promoting trade and joint ventures with the unified European market. It duly takes into account India's commitment to economic reforms and recognises that the economic environment that would emerge as a result of reforms would create opportunities for joint venture investment in variety of industries [8].

Under the agreement, economic co-operation is structured to encourage the private sector with the expectation of resulting multiplier effects. It will involve three broad fields:

- improving the economic environment in India by facilitating access to European know-how and technology;

- facilitating contacts between economic operators and other measures designed to promote commercial exchanges and investment; and

- reinforcing mutual understanding of their respective economic, social and cultural environment as a basis for effective co-operation.

In the broad fields described above, the aims shall be in particular to :

- improve the economic environment and business climate;

- co-operation in the protection of the environment and natural resources;

- co-operation in the field of energy and energy efficiency;

- co-operation in the field of telecommunications, information technology, and related matters;

- co-operation in all aspects of industrial standards and intellectual property;

- encourage technology transfer in other sectors of mutual benefit;

- exchange information on monetary matters and the macro-economic environment;

- reinforce and diversify economic links between them;

- encourage the two-way flow of EU-Indian trade and investments;

- activate industrial co-operation including agro-industry;

- promote co-operation in order to develop agriculture, fisheries, mining, transport and communication, health, banking and insurance, tourism and other services;

- encourage close co-operation between the private sectors of both regions;

- promote support of undertaking by means of trade promotion and market development;

- promote scientific and technological development;

- promote training and specific training programmes; and

- cooperate in the fields of information and culture.

The new agreement is qualitatively of an entirely different character from the earlier ones, as it vastly expands the scope of co-operation. There are thirty articles in the agreement and detailed outline is given in respect of each of the above mentioned seventeen action areas.

- exchange of information and ideas;

- preparation of studies;

- provision of technical assistance;

- training programmes;

- establishment of kinds between research and training centres, specialised agencies and business organisation;

- promotion of investment and joint ventures;

- institutional development of public and private agencies and administrations;

- access to each other's existing data bases and creation of new ones;

- exchange of experts.

Some of the important provisions of the agreement are as follows:

Trade: In the matter of trade, within the ambit of the MFN framework, India and the Union have agreed to improve market access to the highest possible degree which will enable them to strengthen their relations in a dynamic and complementary way. In this context they are committed to granting each other the highest degree of liberalisation of imports and exports.

Under the Agreement, both India and the Union will give consideration to exempting, from duties and taxes, goods imported temporarily into their territories for subsequent re-export or goods that re-enter their territories after processing in the other country. This will enable them to get involved in inward processing arrangements for third country markets. The agreement also underlines the need for a bilateral consultative mechanism for settling disputes without prejudice to their obligations under GATT.

Standards: Maintenance of new standards, in the wake of the creation of the single market, is one of the most important challenges that India has to face in increasing its exports. The need is to keep pace with the changes through constant technological upgradation of India's industry. The new agreement establishes co-operation in the area of standards.

Development Co-operation: In the area of development co-operation, the Union has indicated its preparedness to strengthen the existing co-operation and enhance its efficiency. Programmes will, in particular, be directed to rural development and public health. The most important Union funded development assistance programme so far in India has been the "Operation Flood" - India's co-operative dairy development programme. This programme is widely regarded as one of the Union's most important and successful aided programmes in the world. A significant development in the new agreement has been the Union's decision to give sectoral assistance to India for the national programme of primary education.

Apart from its economic content, the new agreement has a political component too. The EU-India joint statement on political dialogue issued after the signing of the main agreement, reaffirms commitment of the two parties to a political dialogue based on shared values and aspirations. The dialogue will aim to :

- underline the parties' common attachment to democracy and respect for human rights and their common commitment to safeguarding peace and establishing a just and stable international order in accordance with the UN charter;

- reinforce the parties' common interest in closer co-operation to promote prosperity, the commitment to economic reforms and liberalisation of the economy, free trade and the enhancement of economic stability, social progress and the development of cultural ties;

- enable each party to consider the position and interests of the other party in their respective decision-making processes;

- bring about mutual understanding, increase co-operation and work towards defining areas of agreement on international issues, particularly those of concern like non-proliferation and disarmament, combating terrorism, drug trafficking and money laundering, and other matters relating to peace and international stability.

- the political dialogue between the parties will take place through contacts, exchanges and consultations, particularly in the following forms:

(a) meetings at ministerial level between India on the one hand and the EU Troika on the other, with the purpose of promoting the relationship;

(b) providing mutual information on foreign policy decisions, taking full advantage of diplomatic channels, including contacts in the bilateral as well as the multilateral field, such as the UN and elsewhere;

(c) development of contacts at parliamentary levels; and

(d) any other mean which would contribute to consolidating and developing the political dialogue between the parties.

4.2.1.5 Textile and Clothing Agreement (December 1994): Binding of Tariffs on Textiles and Clothing Items: It has been agreed that India will bind its tariffs on textiles and clothing selected under chapters 51, 52, 53, 55, 56, 58, 59, 61, and 63 according to an agreed time table. The scheme is as follows [9].

Tariff Bindings as Agreed to in the Agreement Reached on December 30-31, 1994.

Item	Tariff Bindings by India					Market Openings	
	1.1.95	1.1.98	1.1.2000	1.1.2002	1.1.2005	SIL	FREE
Applicable to Products under Chapters 51 to 59 and 63 (Yarn, Thread, Fabrics & Blanket)	65%	40%	35%	35%	35%	1.1.91	1.1.2002
Applicable to Products Under Chapters 61-62 (Garments)	70%	50%	40%	40%	40%	1.1.95	1.1.2000

It can be seen that in the case of products under chapters 51-59 and 63, tariffs as on 1.1.95 were reduced by 25 percentage points by 1.1.98 and thereafter there would be a further reduction by 5 percentage points over the next two years, that is by 2000. So far as products in chapters 61 and 62 (basically garments) are concerned, the cut by 1998 was by 20 percentage points and thereafter a further cut by 10 percentage points by 2000.

Removal of Quantitative Restrictions (QRs): On all products under chapters 51-59 and 63, India will remove all QRs and will permit free imports in 2002. In so far as the products under chapters 61-62 are concerned, imports in India will be completely free in 2000.

- **Dual Pricing Policy:** It has been agreed that Government of India will not apply dual pricing policy for export of raw cotton from India.

- **Under Restraint:** For all Indian exports under restraint in terms of MFA, the phasing out time table as incorporated in the GATT agreement on textiles and clothing will be applicable.

- **Request for Exceptional Flexibilities to be Considered Favourably by the EU:** EU will give favourable consideration to request from India for exceptional flexibilities for any or all categories under restraint upto the following for each quota year:

1995	7000 tonnes
1996	7000 tonnes
1997	7000 tonnes
1998	8000 tonnes
1999	8000 tonnes
2000	8000 tonnes
2001	8000 tonnes
2002	8000 tonnes
2003	8000 tonnes
2004	8000 tonnes

India will invoke such exceptional flexibilities in the order of carry-over, inter-category transfer and carry-forward to the extent of the possibilities existing on the basis of the utilisation of quotas. Moreover, in each quota year, the total amount of flexibilities shall not exceed 2500 tonnes for any particular textile category or 3000 tonnes for any particular clothing category.

- **Removal of all restrictions on Indian Exports of Handloom Products and Cottage Industry Products:** European Union agreed to remove, w.e.f. 1.1.95, all restrictions on India's exports of handloom products and cottage industry products. From the point of view of India, this is definitely a very substantial concession.

4.2.1.6 GSP Scheme of EU: It was on July 1, 1971, that EEC had come out with its first GSP Scheme, under which generalised tariff preferences were given for imports of finished and semi-finished industrial products from developing countries. Thereafter, it was revised after every 10 years. The revision which was to be held on 1.1.91 was postponed and was finally taken up in 1994. EU has now notified the new GSP Scheme which has entered into force w.e.f. 1.1.95.

The new GSP will be applicable to industrial products, including textiles and will be valid for four years, viz till the end of 1998. For agricultural products, a new scheme was introduced in 1996 and was valid for three years viz. till the end of 1998.

Salient features of the new GSP Scheme are as follows:

- **Use of Principle of Tariff Modulation in Place of Quotas and Ceilings:** In the new Scheme, there are no quotas or ceilings. They have been replaced by tariff modulation, reflecting the sensitivity of different sectors (products or groups of products). The admissible products have been classified under four lists, the criterion for classification being the level of sensitivity of each product/product-group. Each list will be subjected to different rates of preferential duty, the most sensitive ones enjoying lower degree of concessional element in duty than the others. The four lists are as follows:

Classification of Products for Tariff Modulation Purposes

Nature of Products	Preferential Duty (Expressed as Percentage)	Extent of Concession Enjoyed (Expressed as Percentage of MFN Duty)
Most sensitive products (essentially Textiles and Ferro-alloys)	85 per cent of MFN duty	15 per cent of MFN duty
Sensitive Products (ranging from basic chemicals to electronics and automobiles)	70 per cent of MFN duty	30 per cent of MFN duty
Semi-sensitive products	35 per cent of MFN duty	65 per cent of MFN duty
Non-sensitive	Fully exempt from duty	100 per cent of MFN duty

- **Countries Enjoying Zero Rate of Duty for All Four Categories:** Following categories of countries will enjoy duty free access and the four-fold classification for tariff modulation will not be applicable to them.

(a) Least developed countries as per UN classification.

(b) Five Andean group countries (Columbia, Venezuela, Ecuador, Peru and Bolivia).

(c) Central American Common market (CACM) countries (Costa Rica, El Salvador, Guatemala, Honduras and Nicaragua) provided they continue their efforts to combat drug menace.

- **Review of Sensitivity Classification:** No review of either preferential duties or of sensitivity classification.

- **Graduation Mechanism:** The new scheme seeks to spread the benefit of GSP to those countries which have not gained enough through it so far. This objective is sought to be achieved through the graduation mechanism. The graduation mechanism is both country and product specific. Its criteria of application is related to (i) the level of development of the beneficiary countries and (ii) their respective specialisation.

The system incorporates sector/country graduation on the basis of specialisation index and development index.

Specialisation Index is based on the ratio of a beneficiary country's share of total EU imports in general to its share of total EU imports in a given sector. The larger the sectoral proportion compared with the general proportion, the greater the specialisation.

Development Index represents each country's overall level of industrial development compared with that of the EU. An index of zero means the beneficiary's level of industrial development is equal to that of the EU.

Application of Development Index

-	Countries with per capita GNP of over US $ 6000 in 1991 (Hongkong, Singapore, S. Korea, S. Africa, Oman, Brunei, Qatar, UAE, Kuwait, Bahrain, Libya & Nauru)	- w.e.f. 1st April 1995 got only 50 per cent of GSP benefits; will be excluded from GSP w.e.f. 1.1.96.
	Countries with per capita GNP	- Upto 31 December 1996 all GSP

of less than US $ 6000 in 1991	concession applicable.
	- Thereafter 50 per cent reduction of benefits in sectors where they have achieved a high degree of specialisation.
	- GSP to be withdrawn completely w.e.f. 1.1.98.

- **Solidarity mechanism:** The sector/country graduation system is supplemented by a 'solidarity mechanism' which applies to beneficiary countries whose exports of products covered by GSP, in a given sector, exceed 25 per cent of all beneficiaries' exports of those products in that sector. For the concerned countries and sector, thus identified, preferential access will end from 1st January 1996.

- **Withdrawal of GSP concession:** The EU has decided that preferential access for individual beneficiary countries will be curtailed with immediate effect, if it is proved that operation of the graduation mechanism has resulted in providing certain beneficiary countries much greater access for specific products than available to them under the existing GSP Scheme.

- **Most advanced of the beneficiary countries:** The most advanced of the beneficiary countries will be excluded from EU's GSP scheme w.e.f. 1st January 1998 on the basis of objective and clearly defined criteria, on which the Commission has been invited to present proposals to the Council to 1st January 1997.

- **Withdrawal (total or partial) of GSP concession:** The withdrawal (total or partial) of preferences under GSP Scheme is possible in the following circumstances:

(a) fraud or failure to provide administrative co-operation as required for the verification of certificates etc;

(b) unfair trading practices adopted by a beneficiary country, including discrimination against the Union;

(c) practice of any form of forced labour;

(d) export of goods made by prison labour;

(e) inadequate controls on export or transit of drugs or money laundering;

(f) failure to comply with obligations, under the Uruguay Round, to meet agreed market access objectives;

(g) the temporary withdrawal shall last for one year and shall be renewed unless it can be shown that the facts which led to adoption of the measure no longer remain.

- **Special incentive scheme:** The EU decided that starting from 1st January 1998, 'Special Incentive Scheme' in the form of additional preferences may be granted to those beneficiary countries that make a written request and provide evidence that they have adopted and actually applied the provisions of ILO conventions concerning freedom of associations, protection of the right to organise and to bargain collectively and minimum age for admission to employment. Similar provisions are foreseen for environment-related standards, i.e., special incentives would be available to beneficiary countries which undertake effective environmental protection policies consistent with the objectives set out in international conventions on the environment.

- **Safeguard clause:** The new scheme also has a safeguard clause, analogous to the provisions of GATT, to cope with significant unexpected imports of a product which causes or threatens to cause serious difficulties to a Union producer of the like or directly competing product. In such a case, common customs tariff duties may be reintroduced on that product at any time at the request of a member state or on the Commission's own initiative.

- **Anti-dumping and Anti-subsidy:** Under the new GSP Scheme, preferences will not be granted in respect of products subjected to anti-dumping or anti-subsidy measures, unless it can be shown that the said duties were based on a price reflecting the preferential tariff arrangements granted to the country concerned.

- **Date of coming into force:** The new scheme has become operational with effect from 1st January 1995. Transitional arrangements have been provided for any goods for which contracts have been concluded already in 1994 and shipped (have left the country of origin) before 1st January 1995 and were released in the Union market before 15th March 1995.

Indo-EU relations, for the reasons stated above, exhibit a special character. The rapid developments taking place in Europe and the structural adjustment and stabilisation moves initiated in the Indian economy by the government, open up host of opportunities for both to strengthen their relationship.

4.2.1.7 EU's Joint Collaborations and Foreign Investments in India: The EU countries are playing a leading role as investors and collaborators. Joint ventures with EU in India have been in widely diversified fields. These include chemicals, textile, ceramics, activated carbon, plastic moulded goods, diamond and jewellery, multiwall paper sacks, leather goods, Tuna fishing, dredging activity, frozen marine products, cosmetics and toilet items, woollen knitwear, lubricants, construction and consultancy services and various engineering products.

Indian joint ventures in the EU countries are largely in the service sectors such as restaurants, erection services, financial consultancy, marketing of pumps, electronic products, garments, automobile and industrial rubber products, book publishing and assembly of diesel engines.

Table 4.18 gives country-wise details of Indo-EU joint collaboration for which approvals were given during 1991, 1992 and 1993. Table 4.19 gives approval of country-wise foreign investment in India from 1991 to 1995. Table 4.20 gives sector-wise breakup of FDI from August 1991 to February 1996. Table 4.21 gives a picture of states attracting approved FDI from 1993-95.

4.2.2 Indo-EU Bilateral Trade

Foreign trade makes an important contribution to economic growth in both the European Union and India and bilateral trade has been the bedrock of the Indo-EU relationship. Over the years, the European Union has emerged as India's largest trading partner, with a share of 25 per cent of its global exports in 1997-98 and 24 per cent of its imports coming from EU. Over the past decade, EU has become a major destination for India's products and a source of supplies for the critical imports including important raw materials and investment goods.

4.2.2.1 India's Widening Trade Deficit With EU: Tables 4.22 and 4.23 highlight Indo-EU bilateral trade. In the 1970s, India's trade balance with EU rose from a deficit of Rs. 67.39 crore in 1973-74 to Rs. 472.61 crore in 1978-79, registering a growth of eight-times over the period. The year 1976-77, however, saw a trade surplus of Rs. 298.2 crore. This was possible as exports in that year had grown by 4.9 per cent over the previous year whereas imports registered a fall by 13 per cent over the previous year. In the span of a decade starting from 1980-81 to 1989-90, trade deficit rose from Rs. 504.70 crore in 1980-81 meteorically to Rs. 5024.36 crore in 1989-90, rising ten times of the initial figure over the decade. The reason for the rising trade deficit can be found in the pattern of India's exports and imports. Between 1980-81 to 1989-90, the share of EU countries in India's exports had increased from 22 per cent to 26 per cent, whereas, on the other hand India's imports had risen much more dramatically from 16 per cent to 34 per cent in 1989-90. In absolute values, India's exports to and imports from EU increased by five times over the initial figure in each case - in exports from Rs. 1496.3 crore in 1980-81 to Rs. 7088.6 crore in 1989-90, while in imports from Rs. 2001.0 crore in 1980-81 to Rs. 12112.9 crore in 1989-90.

In early nineties, i.e. from 1990-91 to 1993-94, trade deficit of India with EU countries fell down remarkably. From a deficit of Rs. 5024.43 crore in 1990, it fell down to Rs. 2068.2 crore in 1991-92. However, deficit rose again to Rs. 3972.52 crore in the following year. Deficit fell down remarkably in 1994-95, when it was only Rs. 663.43 crore. The reason being that exports increased by 21.63 per cent over the previous year whereas imports rose only by 2 per cent. However, in 1997-98 trade deficit was Rs. 4400.35 crore, falling slightly as against Rs. 5617.93 crore in 1996-97.

The reason for this fall in deficit can be seen from a glance at Tables 4.24 and 4.25. The share of imports fell from 34 per cent in 1990 to 29 per cent in 1992, the share of exports, however, did not register a large increase. From a share of 26 per cent in 1990, it rose to only 27 per cent in 1992. The reason in the fall of trade deficit was due to a substantial fall in imports from EU countries. In 1993-94, India's share of exports and imports to EU countries was 26 per cent and 30 per cent respectively.

India's share of exports to EU was 24.89 per cent and 25.18 pre cent in 1996-97 and 1997-98 respectively.

4.2.2.2 EU's Share in India's Trade: For India, EU is a major trading partner. It is a leading market for India's exports, as can be seen from Table 4.24.

In the 1970s, from 25 per cent in 1973-74 its share rose to 27 per cent in 1979-80. In the decade starting from 1980-81, its share rose from 22 per cent to 26 per cent in 1989-90. From 1981-82 to 1985-86, there was a fall in the share of exports, but, it again increased in 1986-87 continuously till 1989-90 from 23 per cent to 26 per cent approximately. The early nineties, i.e., 1990-91 to 1993-94, also saw a continuous rise in the share of exports to EU. From a share of 27 per cent in 1990-91, it registered a rise to 28 per cent in 1992-93. 1993-94, however, experienced a fall by 2 per cent in exports. In 1994-95, India's exports to EU represented 26.71 per cent of total exports to the world. Its share fell down a little in 1997-98, representing 25.18 per cent of total exports to the world.

India's exports to European Union during the period 1980-81 to 1989-90 rose five times over the initial figure and India's global exports rose four times over the initial figure for the same time period.

EU is also an important source of imports for India. India's imports from EU have expanded at a much faster rate than India's global imports. India's imports from EU countries was almost five times over the initial figure, whereas, India's global imports was only two and a half times of the initial figure from 1980-81 to 1989-90.

From the table 4.25, share of EU in India's imports can be seen over a period from 1973-74 to 1997-98. Imports from EU have steadily increased over this period. In the 70s, its share rose from 24 per cent in 1973-74 to 31 per cent in 1978-79. Starting from a share of 25 per cent in 1979-80, its share rose substantially to 34 per cent in 1989-90. In the early 90s, i.e., from 1990-91 to 1993-94, share of imports remained within a limit of 29 per cent -30 per cent . Share of EU in India's imports, over a period of 20 years, i.e., from 1973-74 to 1993-94, rose from 24 per cent to 30 per cent In 90s, imports from EU constituted nearly 1/3rd of our total imports. However, imports registered a fall of 4 per cent in 1993-94 which had a substantial effect on our balance of trade. The deficit from Rs. 50,244 million in 1989-90 fell to Rs. 37,488 million in 1993-94. Imports from EU to India, however, declined in 1994-95, representing only 24.83 per cent. They further declined to 24 per cent in 1997-98.

4.2.2.3 India's Share in EU's Trade: India's share in EU's trade is very small.. In the late 1970s, India's share in EU's total exports had been within the range of 0.38 per cent to 0.52 per cent and share in EU's total imports had been in the range of 0.42 per cent to 0.46 per cent .

In 1980, India's share in EU's total exports was 0.48 per cent ; in mid-1980s, i.e. in 1985, it grew to 0.71 per cent and dropped slightly to 0.68 per cent in 1989. In the early 1990's, however, it fell down and was the least i.e. 0.41 per cent in 1991 and increased a little to 0.52 per cent in 1992. India's share has been less than 1 per cent over these years.

India's share in EU's total imports has also been very small. In 1980, India's share was 0.33 per cent and was 0.39 per cent in 1989 with a little increase to 0.41 per cent in between in 1982. In early 1990s, however, it was 0.39 per cent on an average (for the three years from 1990-1992). As in 1997-98, India's share in EU's trade continues to be still less than 1 per cent.

4.2.2.4 India's Exports to EU: Composition of India's Exports to EU: India's exports to EU can be classified into following broad categories:

- Agricultural and Marine products;
- Leather and its products including Footwear.
- Chemicals and allied products.
- Textiles and Garments.
- Jute and Coir products.
- Gems and Jewellery.
- Engineering and Electronic goods.

Nearly 70 per cent of India's exports to EU comprise of commodities which include leather, tea, diamonds, cotton fabrics, tobacco, precious and semi-precious stones and coffee.

The residual exports of about 30 per cent comprising engineering goods, chemicals and software form a dynamic area which still has a wider scope for exploitation. Table 4.26 gives a break-up of the total exports to each member country of EU by India. Table 4.27 gives a percentage share of each member country of EU in India's exports to EU. A look at the table reveals that from 1973-74 to 1997-98, major partners have been U.K., Germany, Belgium, Italy, the Netherlands and France. In the 1970s, i.e. from 1973-74 to 1979-80, U.K. dominated the European Union by having a share of 29 per cent (maximum share of 46.60 per cent in 1975-76).

In the 1980s, however, its share started declining from 26.39 per cent in 1980-81, it fell down to 22.53 per cent in 1989-90. At the same time, share of Germany rose to 25 per cent in 1989-90. Share of other major trading partners, i.e. Italy, the Netherlands, and France maintained an almost constant level over the years. Belgium, however, showed a rising trend till 1989-90 (17 per cent), its share falling slightly to 13 per cent in 1992-93.

From 1995-96 onwards, share of U.K. in India's total exports to EU started rising and that of Germany started declining. As in 1997-98, U.K. is the leading trade partner followed closely by Germany. A notable feature from 1993-94 onwards is that Belgium has become an important trade partner, its rank being third.

Greece, Luxembourg, Portugal, Denmark, Ireland and Spain are small partners. Share of Luxembourg till 1992-93 had almost been negligible. Share of Portugal, Greece, Ireland was even less than 1 per cent of India's total exports to EU. In 1997-98, these countries together accounted for 9.95 per cent of total exports to EU, showing a remarkable increase from 1992-93. Share of Spain has risen from 1.98 per cent in 1983-84 to 5.03 per cent in 1997-98.

4.2.2.5 Product-wise Analysis of India's Exports to EU:

Ready-made Garments: Exports of Ready-made garments to EU from India had been showing a rising trend for the past several years, i.e. from 1973-74 to 1997-98. From 1985-86, especially, the exports had grown more rapidly from Rs. 360.40 crore in 1985-86 to Rs. 2719.8 crore in 1992-93 (Table 4.28). In the early 1990s, i.e. from 1990-91 to 1992-93, Ready-made garments represented 19 per cent of total exports to EU. In 1994-95, ready-made garments represented 15.61 per cent which fell down to 13 per cent in 1997-98. Within EU, largest importer of Ready-made garments from India is France, with exports of this item worth Rs. 324.49 crore in

1992-93 representing 42 per cent of total exports of India in that year to that country, followed by Germany (Rs. 907.12 crore representing 22 per cent share), U.K. (Rs. 741.48 crore sharing 21 per cent), Italy (Rs. 286.22 crore sharing 16 per cent) and Netherlands (Rs. 242.31 crore having a share of 20 per cent in 1992-93 (Tables 4.29-4.35).

In 1997-98, however, imports of readymade garments by France from India fell down, the share coming down to 31.62 per cent as against 42 per cent in 1992-93. Share of Germany's imports of this item also fell to 17 per cent; U.K.'s share was 11.39 per cent; Netherlands share was 15 per cent in 1997-98.

India's main exports in this group comprised of T-shirts, blouses, jerseys, pullovers, skirts and shirts.

Though there is a strong garment industry in the Union, it should be possible for India to exploit the enlarged Union market more effectively mainly because the European industry is expected to orient itself to high-fashion items and because personalised items such as garments' design, colour, shape, appearance etc. matter a great deal [10].

India's exports of textiles and clothing are also governed by the GSP scheme. EU's new GSP scheme for 1995-2004 had been finalised and had become effective from January 1, 1995. It is in India's interest to maintain and improve GSP access as over two-fifths of our total exports enter EU under preferential tariffs [11].

Other factors that are likely to influence India's exports of garments to EU are :

- Competition from East Europe and from low labour cost countries such as Portugal, Greece and Ireland within EU.

- New packing standards.

- Technological developments,leading to less labour-intensive and/or high-skilled labour oriented production and

- Advantage of low level of inventory and shorter delivery period within EU.

Leather, Leather Manufactures and Footwear: Leather and its manufactures including footwear is another important item of exports to the EU. Table 4.28 reveals that its share was approximately 10.51 per cent in 1997-98 (it was almost 18 per cent in 1990-91). This commodity group had been representing a large share of total exports to EU since 1973-74 (share of 11 per cent in that year) and its exports had grown continuously since then, but falling down to 10.51 per cent in 1997-98.

Tables 4.29 to 4.35 reveal that market in Italy for leather manufactures appears quite strong (representing 14 per cent share of total exports to the country in 1997-98), followed by Germany (13 per cent in 1997-98), France (7.7 per cent in 1997-98) and U.K. (6.85 per cent in 1997-98).

This is a sector where there are substantial domestic supplies with Italy, Spain, Portugal, Germany, U.K. and France having strong supply base. ACP countries, which have the benefit of STABEX support under the Lome Conventions, are also emerging as significant suppliers in particular of bovine leather. Besides, exports of a number of items in this category are subjected to GSP ceilings in the Union.

On the other hand, due to a number of factors such as the demand in EU countries over-stepping domestic supplies, the problem of environmental pollution posed by the domestic industry, the shortages of hides and skins within EU, the relative cost advantages enjoyed by countries like India in this labour intensive sector and the fact that leather manufactures are personalised items, supplies from third countries to the EU are not expected to be affected to any great extent in the future.

There is, however, a possibility that countries like Spain, Portugal and Italy might try to expand their share of finished leather goods in the EU market. This could make the competition for India in the leather goods more severe, but it could also throw up opportunities for supply of finished leather goods to feed the expanding leather industry in the Union. The nature of Union's new GSP regime (1995-2004) will also influence further prospects of India's exports of leather and leather goods in Europe.

Gems and Jewellery: Another important category of exports to EU by India is represented by pearls, precious and semi-precious stones with diamonds (worked) being the main export item. Its share from 6 per cent in 1973-74 rose continuously to 18 per cent in 1978-79 (Table 4.28); it fell substantially to 9 per cent in the following year (i.e. 1979-80) and again showed a rising trend from 1980-81 at 11 per cent to 19 per cent in 1988-89. However, its share had declined to 9 per cent and 8 per cent in 1984-85 and 1985-86 respectively. Till 1990, it was the second largest item of exports. However, in the early nineties, i.e., from 1990-91 to 1992-93, it represented third important item of exports; its share had been within the range of 11-14 per cent ; in 1992-93, its share was 11 per cent. In 1993-94, share of gems and jewellery rose to 12.51 per cent as against 11 per cent in 1992-93, falling slightly to 10.52 per cent in 1996-97. Its share, as in 1997-98, is 11.33 per cent (Table 4.28)

In the case of diamonds, Belgium stands out among all the EU countries with a share of 65 per cent of total exports of India of diamonds in 1997-98.

Agro-Based Goods: This category of products includes Coffee, Tea and mate, Rice, Sugar, Tobacco and its substitutes, Spices and Cashew-kernels. Share of this group was very high from 1973-74 to 1986-87, representing 13 per cent in 1986-87; it, however, declined from 1987-88 and in 1993-94 it was averaged at 6.27 per cent , representing fourth important category of export item from India to EU (Table 4.28). From 6.35 per cent in 1994-95, it has risen again to 9.80 per cent in 1997-98.

In this group, Coffee, Tea and Spices dominate other products. Export of tea is mainly to U.K., whereas, its share of coffee is small; Coffee is exported mainly to Italy and Germany.

In the case of Spices, pepper is an important item of exports. The important partners for this group are France, Netherlands and U.K.

The other items have a low share in this category. However, exports of Cashew-kernels are showing a rising trend; major markets for this product are U.K., the Netherlands and Germany.

For coffee, tea and spices, the Union is entirely dependent on third countries. Competition to India comes mainly from Kenya and some other ACP countries which have stepped up their exports of all the three items in the recent years. They have also availed of the Union's substantial financial support for development of production and stabilisation of export earnings in these products. Moreover, they enjoy tariff benefit in the EU market for coffee. Non-ACP competitor countries are the South American countries for coffee, Sri Lanka and Indonesia for tea and Malaysia, Indonesia and Brazil for pepper. Though European unification has increased demand for these products, India will now have to face challenge from these countries, some of which are associated with the Union under the Lome Conventions and stricter and uniform application of health and sanitary standards.

Chemical Materials and Products: The EU is also an important export destination for chemical material and its products. Around 25 per cent of total global exports of this group from India was sent to EU (in the early 90s). The Table 4.28 shows, in value terms as well as in percentage, the export of this product group to the countries of European Union. From a low percentage of 1 per cent in 1973-74, its share had risen to 5.96 per cent in 1993-94 and 7.2 per cent in 1997-98.

About Rs. 2289.68 crore worth of chemical materials were exported to EU in 1997-98. Within EU, Netherlands had a share of 16.25 per cent in 1997-98 followed by Spain (13.84 per cent), Germany (10.9 per cent), Italy (7.78 per cent), U.K. (6.58 per cent) and France (6.07 per cent).[tables 4.29-4.35].

Cotton and Manufactures: Cotton represented a low figure of 0.38 per cent in 1973-74, its share rising to 1.97 per cent in 1983-84. In 1997-98, its share fell down again to 0.38 per cent.

Italy is the largest importer of this product. Rs. 4923.57 crore worth of cotton was imported by Italy in 1997-98 accounting for 1.20 per cent share of total imports from India. U.K. is the second largest importer of this product accounting for Rs. 3099.94 crore worth of cotton in 1997-98, followed by Germany, Netherlands and France.

Export of items in this group is regulated under the Bilateral Textile Agreement and specific quotas for cotton yarn, fabrics, bed linen and table/toilet linen. The growth in the exports by India of items under this group indicates the capacity of the Indian industry to meet the demands of consumers in the European union, the increasing competitiveness of Indian products partly due to the decline in the value of rupee and the flexibility in the implementation of the bilateral agreement.

Though the Union's textile industry is one of the largest in the world accounting for substantial exports, the decline in its relative share in global production and employment coupled with the rise in textile consumption within the EU and the concentration of the domestic industry of high value-added items indicate bright prospects for Indian items.

In this sector also, the industry should gear itself up to face the challenges of European unification that have been posed by the Union level quotas bringing textiles under GATT regulations or modifications in GSP scheme of the Union. All the other factors that have been enumerated as likely influences on India's exports of garments apply equally to the exports of this group of items also.

Engineering Goods: EU has also emerged as an important market for Indian engineering goods. EU's share in India's export of engineering goods has grown spectacularly in 1992-93 to above 15 per cent [12]. It represented a share of 5.41 per cent of total exports to EU in 1997-98 by India. Major markets in the EU for Indian engineering goods are Germany, U.K., France, Italy, Netherlands and Belgium.

This category includes machinery, transport equipment, metal manufactures, electronic goods etc. The Union, however, offers good prospect for a number of engineering items (due to increased industrial activity).

India's strategy to raise the level of engineering exports to the Union should take into account the following developments within the EU: (a) harmonisation of standards (b) use of improved technology (c) increased volumes of production and automation (d) improved buying power of European firms (e) introduction of product liability clauses (f) economies of scale and improved productivity and (g) vacation of industrial areas due to environmental reasons and rising labour costs.

Carpets and Other Floor Coverings: Exports of carpets by India to EU showed a rising trend from 1990-91 to 1995-96, when the share was 6.78 per cent of total exports to EU (Table 4.28). However, its share started declining and in 1996-97 and 1997-98, the share came down to 3.21 per cent and 2.65 per cent respectively. Germany alone contributed 7.23 per cent share in 1997-98, followed by Netherlands and U.K.

Marine Products: The Union's imports of Fish, Crustaceans and Molluscs from third countries as well as from India is small. Its share in India's total exports to EU was less than 1 per cent till 1978-79. This share increased a little coming to 2 per cent in 1982-83 and 1983-84. In 1985-86, its share rose to 4 per cent . However, it declined again and in 1992-93, its share in the exports to the EU was 3 per cent. Its share further declined to 1.21 per cent in 1997-98 from 3.47 per cent in 1993-94.

Major partners are U.K., Italy and France. India's major export item in this group is frozen shrimps. The competition for India comes mainly from China, Indonesia, Thailand, Bangladesh, Cuba and Tunisia besides ACP countries. The fisheries sector in the latter has benefited substantially under the Lome Conventions through financial support for development and exploitation of fishery resources for higher processing and for stabilisation of export earnings. Besides, the EU countries can, by agreement, operate their fishing vessels in ACP waters. The ACP countries also enjoy tariff advantages over India.

The development to be considered by the Indian industry in this sector should include (1) increased competition from some of the Union countries themselves consequent to the rights that they may secure under the Lome Convention, (2) increased competition from third countries including ACP countries, (3) the uniform and stricter implementation of health regulations and packaging and labelling laws throughout the Union, (4) the major sea-food firms in the Union joining hands through mergers and acquisition for large scale operations,(5) the limitations faced by India due to concentration of its supplies in one product group namely, shrimps and (6) the inelastic supply base of the country [13].

Together, the above stated commodities constituted 66 per cent and 65 per cent of total exports from India to the EU in 1995-96 and 1997-98 respectively.

4.2.2.6 Past Performance of India's Major Export Items to EU: In order to assess the past performance and to work out the rate of growth of individual commodity group of India's Exports to European Union, a period of twenty years starting from 1973-74 to 1992-93 has been taken. The reason of starting from 1973-74 being that U.K., an important trading partner of India, entered the Union on January 1, 1973.

1. Gems and Jewellery = 5.87 + 0.19(T), n = 20
   (1973-74 to 1992-93)

   T-Ratio = 12.49 9.5 (The first and second values pertain to the Constant and Coefficient of time respectively).

   R^2 = 0.86

2. Ready-made garments = 5.91 + 0.21(T), n = 20
   (1973-74 to 1992-93)

   T-Ratio = 19.06 21

   R^2 = 0.86

3. Carpets and other floor coverings: = 5.26 + 0.17 (T), n = 20
   (1973-74 to 1992-93)

   T-Ratio = 17.53 17

   R^2 = 0.88

4. Cotton = 7.61 + 0.25 (T), n = 6
   (1987-88 to 1992-93)

   T-Ratio = 31.71 4.17

   R^2 = 0.83

5. Chemical Material and its Products
   (1973-74 to 1992-93) = 4.01 + 0.24 (T), n = 20

   T-Ratio = 11.14 24

   R^2 = 0.95

6. Fish and its Preparations
   (1973-74 to 1992-93) = 3.14 + 0.26 (T), n = 20

   T-Ratio = 8.72 26

R^2 = 0.95

7. Engineering Goods
(1973-74 to 1992-93) = 5.33 + 0.15 (T), n = 20

T-Ratio = 11.59 7.5

R^2 = 0.80

8. Leather, etc.
(1973-74 to 1992-93) = 6.39 + 0.16 (T), n = 20

T-Ratio = 20.61 16.00

R^2 = 0.91

9. Agro-based Goods
(1973-74 to 1992-93) = 7.17 + 0.08 (T), n = 20

T-Ratio = 28 8

R^2 = 0.79

From the above analysis, the commodities can be ranked according to their rates of growth. From the regression results, coefficients have been taken as rates of growth for comparison purposes (though, the actual rates of growth would be slightly more).

Cotton had the highest growth rate of 38 per cent and can be ranked number one. Export of this commodity was subject to a number of ceilings and restrictions.

Regression was run for cotton from the period 1987-88 to 1992-93 and following results were obtained. Since the export of cotton became significant from 1987-88, coefficient was obtained for a period of six years.

Cotton = 7.61 + 0.25 X T, n = 6
(1987-88 to 1992-93) (0.24) (0.06)

$R^2 = 0.83$

For cotton, average rate of growth was 38 per cent from 1973-74 to 1992-93, R^2 being 0.67, whereas it is 25 per cent for the period of six years, i.e., from 1987-88 to 1992-93 when export of cotton had gained momentum and R^2 was 0.83.

Fish and its preparations had second highest growth rate of 26 per cent. Third important category of exports was chemical material and products which had a trend growth rate of 24 per cent. Fourth important group of export items was Ready-made Garments whose rate of growth was 21 per cent.

Fifth category of export commodities was Gems and Jewellery (growth rate was 19 per cent). An important aspect to be noted in case of Gems & Jewellery is that India exports very huge quantity of this item to European Union, especially to Belgium. Similarly, India imports the same item very heavily from Belgium; the net earnings in respect of this commodity are negative.

From Table 4.36, it is clear that there has been a continuous negative trade balance from 1978-79 onwards till 1997-98. Trade surplus was obtained only in three years in the 70s. The rough diamonds are obtained in huge quantities from EU and export of Gems and Jewellery to EU countries is in much less quantity as there are many other markets for it in the world.

Sixth category of exports item, according to growth rate, is carpets and other floor coverings having 17 per cent trend rate of growth.

Seventh category is leather and its manufactures including footwear with a growth rate of 16 per cent. Eighth category of export item is engineering goods, with 15 per cent rate of growth and the last or ninth category is of Agro-based goods with 8 per cent growth rate.

Commodities exported by India to EU-12: According to their rates of growth (Period 1973-74 to 1992-93)

Commodities	Rank	Rate of Growth
Fish and its preparations	1	26 per cent
Cotton	2	25 per cent
Chemical material and products	3	24 per cent
Ready-made Garments	4	21 per cent
Gems & Jewellery	5	19 per cent

Carpets and other floor coverings	6	17 per cent
Leather, its manufactures etc.	7	16 per cent
Engineering Goods	8	15 per cent
Agro-based Goods	9	8 per cent

A projection can also be made about the exports of each item to EU in the year 1999-2000, if all other things remain constant (Value in Crore Rupees).

Commodities	1992-93	1999-2000
Fish, molluscs and its preparations	481.1	2584.8
Cotton	846.8	8245.4
Chemical material and its products	1069.6	3595.4
Ready-made Garments	2719.8	10693.8
Gems and Jewellery	1693.3	5987.4
Carpet and floor coverings etc.	825.5	1895.8
Leather, its manufactures including footwear	2087.2	4480.2
Engineering Goods	780.2	1184.9
Agro-based Goods	1042.5	1127.1

The projected values have been worked out in the following manner: (Time being 27 years from 1973-74 to 1999-2000):

1. Fish, molluscs and their preparations:

   $Y = 3.14 + 0.26t$

   $Y = A.\log(10.16)$

   Value in year 2000 = Rs. 2584.8 crore

2. Cotton:

   $Y = 1.06 + 0.38t$

   $Y = A.\log(11.32)$

Value in year 2000 = Rs. 8245.4 crore

3. Chemical material and its products:

$$Y = 4.01 + 0.24t$$

$$Y = A.\log(10.49)$$

Value in year 2000 = Rs. 3595.4 crore

4. Ready-made Garments:

$$Y = 5.91 + 0.21t$$

$$Y = A.\log(11.57)$$

Value in year 2000 = Rs. 10693.8 crore

5. Gems and Jewellery:

$$Y = 5.87 + 0.19t$$

$$Y = A.\log(11.00)$$

Value in year 2000 = Rs. 5987.4 crore

6. Carpets and other Floor Coverings:

$$Y = 5.26 + 0.17t$$

$$Y = A.\log(9.85)$$

Value in year 2000 = Rs. 1895.8 crore

7. Leather, its manufactures including footwear:

$$Y = 6.39 + 0.16t$$

$$Y = A.\log(10.71)$$

Value in year 2000 = Rs. 4480.2 crore

8. Engineering Goods:

$$Y = 5.33 + 0.15t$$

$$Y = A.\log(9.38)$$

Value in year 2000 = Rs. 1184.9 crore

9. Agro-based goods:

$$Y = 7.17 + 0.08t$$

$$Y = A.\log(9.33)$$

Value in year 2000 = Rs. 1127.1 crore

4.2.3 Trend Growth Rates of India's Exports to EU

An attempt has been made to work out the trend growth rate, both in terms of exports in rupees and in US Dollars, to find out the growth of Indian exports to European Union (Table 4.37).

Following results were obtained for both Indian currency and US Dollars when regressions were run in Log Natural form to obtain the trend growth rate from 1974-1993:

For Indian currency :

$$Y = 8.49 + 0.15\,t, \quad n = 20$$

$$(0.30) \quad (0.01) \quad R^2 = 0.91$$

For US $:

$$Y = 7.00 + 0.09\,t \quad n = 20$$

$$(0.20) \quad (0.01) \quad R^2 = 0.87$$

The two growth rates obtained were 15 per cent for exports in Indian currency and 9 per cent for exports in US Dollars. This trend indicates that difference of 6 per cent is due to devaluation of Indian currency.

A Projection can also be made about the magnitude of Indian exports to EU, both in Indian currency and in US Dollars, in the Year 1999-2000.

For Indian currency :

$Y = 8.49 + 0.15\,t$

(time being 27 years from 1974-2000)

$Y = A.Log\,(12.54)$

Value in year 2000 = Rs. 27928.8 crore

For US Dollars:

$Y = 7.00 + 0.09\,t$

(time being 27 years from 1974-2000)

$Y = A.Log\,(9.43)$

Value in the year 2000 = $ 12,456.53 million.

4.2.4 Impact of European Unification on India's Exports

European unification implies increase in Gross Domestic Product (GDP) of the European Union, increase in Population, increase in imports of the EU from world etc. To see the impact of this on India's exports to EU, multiple regressions were run and following results were obtained:

India's Exports to EU (X) = f(EU's imports, GDP, Population)

Here the Dependent Variable was India's Exports to EU.

Independent variables were EU's GDP, EU's Imports and EU's Population.

Unit of currency was Million US $.

Time period was 20 years from 1973-74 to 1992-93.

Regressor	Coefficient	St. Error	T-Ratio
Constant	-131.9934	55.3433	-2.3850
EU's Imports	0.1284	0.0736	1.7456
EU's GDP	0.0159	0.3789	0.0419
EU's Population	23.9326	10.1239	2.3640

$R^2 = 0.9049$

As there were a lot of fluctuations in the imports, a two stage least square method was adopted using the fitted values of imports regressed against GDP. Because of high correlation amongst these three variables, no statistically significant result could be obtained. Hence, the Ln values of India's exports were regressed against each individual variable separately.

Following results were obtained.

LnExp dependent variable.

C	Lnlmp	Lnlmpf	LnGDP	LnPoP	R^2	F·Value	
-4.8729	-	0.9504	-	-	0.8391	93.8826	
(-3.69)		(9.68)					
-0.1770	-	-	1.0185	-	0.8426	96.34	
(-0.2145)			(9.81)				
-150.46	-	-	-	27.45	0.8868	140.95	
(-27.45)				(11.87)			
-148.76	-	-	0.0122	27.14	0.88	66.56	
(-2.57)			(0.0304)	(12.57)			
					TIME		
6.99	-	-	-	-	(0.0866)	0.86	
(73.68)					(10.92)		
-1.17	0.1600	-	0.8748	-	-	0.87	57.73
(-1.27)	(1.96)		(7.22)			(1.16)	

A number of salient features emerge from these results:

1. The impact of EU's income on India's exports is significant.

2. The impact of EU's imports from world is also significant on India's exports to EU.

3. The impact of increase in EU's Population on India's exports is also significant.

Through index number techniques (as shown in Table 4.38), it was found that GDP of EU has grown by 4 times, imports of EU from rest of the world grew by 3 times while India's exports to EU grew by almost 6 times over a period of 20 years. Population did not register a significant growth.

Regressions were run to see the impact of European unification on India's exports of major commodity groups to EU, the results of which are shown below:

1. Gems and Jewellery:

Here the Dependent variable was India's Exports of Gems and Jewellery to EU.

Unit of currency was Million US $.

Independent variables were:

EU's GDP, EU's Imports of the commodity from the world except India and EU's Population.

Time period was 20 years from 1973-74 to 1992-93.

On Multiple Regression:

Regressor	Coefficient	Std. Error	T-Ratio
Constant	-20134.1	140.73	143.06
EU's Imports	1.526	0.476	3.185
EU's GDP	9.470	2.086	4.539
EU's Population	194.14	83.173	2.334

$R^2 = 0.9318$

2. Leather, its manufactures including footwear:

Here the Dependent variable was India's Exports of Leather, its manufactures including footwear to EU.

Unit of currency was Million US $.

Independent variables were:

EU's GDP, EU's Imports of the commodity from the world except India, EU's Population.

On Multiple Regression:

Regression	Coefficient	Std. Error	T-Ratio
Constant	-5161.05	56.03	-102 82
EU's Imports	0.3341	0.2218	1.5063
EU's GDP	4.2819	0.9816	4.3621
EU's Population	54.6612	36.3918	1.5020

$R^2 = 0.9516$

3. Agro-based Goods:

Here the Dependent variable was India's Exports of Agro-based Goods to EU.

Unit of currency was Million US $.

On Individual Regression:

When Independent variable was EU's Imports of Agro-based Goods from world except India.

Regressor	Coefficient	Std. Error	T-Ratio
Constant	141.06	42.69	3.30
EU's Imports	0.18	0.15	1.20

$R^2 = 0.08$

When Independent variable was EU's GDP

Regressor	Coefficient	Std. Error	T-Ratio
Constant	144.35	39.99	3.61
EU's GDP	0.14	0.06	2.33

$R^2 = 0.19$

When Independent variable was EU's Population

Regressor	Coefficient	Std. Error	T-Ratio
Constant	-1066.72	36.74	-29.03
EU's Population	12.13	4.22	2.87

$R^2 = 0.32$

Following results, however, were obtained when multiple Regressions were run:

India's Exports to EU (X) = f (EU's Imports, EU's GDP, EU's Population)

Regressor	Coefficient	Std. Error	T-Ratio
Constant	-5890.10	32.84	-179.36
EU's Imports	0.185	0.161	1.15
EU's GDP	-0.106	0.578	-0.18
EU's Population	60.24	21.45	2.81

4. Cotton:

Here the Dependent variable was India's Exports of Cotton to EU.

Unit of currency was Million US $.

On Individual Regression:

When independent variable was EU's Imports of cotton from the world except India.

Regressor	Coefficient	Std. Error	T-Ratio

Constant	-1.68	2.62	-0.64
EU's Imports	0.57	3.84	0.15

$R^2 = 0.51$

When independent variable was EU's GDP.

Regressor	Coefficient	Std. Error	T-Ratio
Constant	-26.88	1.84	-14.61
EU's GDP	3.71	0.85	4.36

$R^2 = 0.51$

When independent variable was EU's Population

Regressor	Coefficient	Std. Error	T-Ratio
Constant	-574.53	1.85	-310.56
EU's Population	100.05	23.21	4.31

$R^2 = 0.51$

When Multiple Regressions were run, following results were obtained:

Regressor	Coefficient	Std. Error	T-Ratio
Constant	-614.21	1.51	-406.76
EU's Imports	9.21	3.77	2.44
EU's GDP	-25.54	8.79	-2.91
EU's Population	126.44	80.85	1.56

$R^2 = 0.92$

As can be seen from Multiple Regression results for cotton, the signs were not the expected ones, hence, individual regressions were run for cotton to get the desired signs.

5. Fish and its preparations:

Here the Dependent variable was India's Exports of Fish and its preparations to EU-12.

Unit of currency was Million US $.

Independent variables were EU's Imports of Fish etc. from the world except India, EU's GDP and EU's Population. Following results were obtained on Multiple Regression:

Regressor	Coefficient	Std. Error	T-Ratio
Constant	-35809.7	215.33	-166.30
EU's Imports	1.59	0.88	1.81
EU's GDP	0.95	4.88	0.19
EU's Population	355.32	135.37	2.62

$R^2 = 0.91$

6. Carpets and other floor coverings:

Here the dependent variable was India's Exports of Carpets etc. to EU-12.

Unit of currency was Million US $.

Following results were obtained on Individual regression:

When independent variable was EU's Imports of carpets etc. from world except India.

Regressor	Coefficient	Std. Error	T-Ratio
Constant	-212.67	196.58	-1.08
EU's Imports	3.69	0.48	7.69

$R^2 = 0.77$

When independent variable was EU's GDP

Regressor	Coefficient	Std.Error	T-Ratio
Constant	-204.86	133.40	-1.54
EU's GDP	2.86	0.23	1.24

$R^2 = 0.89$

When independent variable was EU's Population

Regressor	Coefficient	Std.Error	T-Ratio
Constant	-19124.2	110.53	-173.02
EU's Population	191.27	12.67	15.09

$R^2 = 0.93$

Following results were, however, obtained when multiple regressions were run:

Regressor	Coefficient	Std.Error	T-Ratio
Constant	-27261.6	94.14	-289.59
EU's Imports	-0.27	0.63	-0.43
EU's GDP	4.56	1.86	2.45
EU's Population	270.72	67.88	3.99

$R^2 = 0.96$

Since the signs were not the expected ones when multiple regression results were obtained for exports of carpets, individual regressions were also run for the same commodity.

From the Multiple as well as Individual Regression results on India's Exports to EU, it can be concluded that -

1) Impact of increase in EU-12's imports from world except India on exports of Gems and Jewellery, Cotton, Fish, Agro-based goods, Leather, Carpets and Ready-made Garments is very significant.

2) Increase in Gross Domestic Product of EU has a positive impact on India's all the major export commodity groups to EU-12.

3) Impact of increase in EU'ş Population on India's major export commodity groups is also significant.

4.2.5 India's Imports from EU

India imports almost 1/3rd of its total imports from European Union. Table 4.25 suggests that imports of India from the EU, from 1973-74 to 1985-86, were in the range of 24 per cent to 28 per cent of the total imports from the world. From 1986-87 to 1989-90, it grew to the extent of

34 per cent . However, share of India's imports from EU fell in the early 1990s; in 1993-94, its share was 30 per cent. It however, started declining from 1994-95 and as in 1997-98, its share was 24 per cent.

Table 4.39 gives a country-wise break-up of total imports from leading trading partners of EU and percentage share of these member countries respectively.

India's imports from EU cover a wide range of items like

- Iron and Steel
- Gems and Jewellery, particularly rough diamonds.
- Capital goods, particularly machinery and transport equipment.
- Organic chemicals.
- Inorganic chemicals.
- Chemical material and products.
- Non-ferrous metals.
- Professional and Scientific instruments etc.

Together, they accounted for 74.55 per cent of total imports in 1997-98. Table 4.40 suggests that import of capital goods was 46.35 per cent of total imports in 1973-74 and was 33 per cent in 1983-84 but started declining from 1987-88 and fell to 25 per cent in 1997-98. Share of Gems and Jewellery, however, rose from 8 per cent (approx.) in 1973-74 to 31 per cent in 1997-98. Share of chemical material and products fell from 13 per cent in 1973-74 to 5.5 per cent in 1997-98.

Share of professional and scientific instruments has almost been the same; sharing 2.4 per cent in 1997-98 of total imports from the EU.

Within EU, in 1997-98, major import sources were U.K. (21 per cent), Germany (19 per cent), Belgium (11 per cent) followed by Italy (8 per cent) and France (7.5 per cent) (Table 4.39). Share of U.K. fell from 34 per cent in 1973-74 to 21 per cent in 1997-98. Belgium has emerged as the most important source for imports as its share has risen from 9 per cent in 1973-74 to 12 per cent in 1997-98.

Thus, imports from EU are highly concentrated in countries like Germany, U.K., France, Italy and Belgium. In the case of Belgium, a high proportion (86 per cent) consisted of Gems and Jewellery item in 1997-98.

Greece, Luxembourg, Ireland, Denmark, Portugal, Spain, and the then GDR had an almost negligible share in India's total imports from EU, as is obvious from Table 4.35.

4.2.6 India's Trade with EU Member Countries

Tables 4.29 to 4.35 and 4.41 to 4.47 show India's exports and imports from leading EU member countries over the period 1973-74 to 1997-98. A look at the tables reveal that Germany, U.K., France, Italy and Netherlands are important partners in trade with India.

4.2.6.1 Germany: Tables 4.31 and 4.43 reveal that Germany is not only the largest market for Indian exports but also the most important source of imports for India among all the EU member countries, sharing 22 per cent of total exports and 20 per cent of total imports in 1997-98.

India's major exports to Germany include Ready-made garments (17 per cent), Leather and its manufactures (13 per cent), Carpets and other floor coverings (7 per cent) in 1997-98 (Table 4.31). Exports to Germany increased from Rs. 108.34 crore in 1973-74 to Rs. 473 crore in 1983-84 and shot up spectacularly to Rs. 1773 crore in 1989-90 before the German unification.

After the unification in 1990, exports increased from Rs. 2548 crore in 1990-91 to Rs. 6892 crore in 1997-98 registering a growth of 170 per cent

A glance at Table 4.43 shows that major imports from Germany include capital goods, especially electrical and non-electrical machinery (43 per cent), Iron and Steel (7 per cent), Organic chemicals and Chemical material and products (12 per cent each approximately) in 1997-98.

In 1997-98 imports from Germany amounted to Rs. 9294 crore. India's imports from Germany stood at Rs. 29,469 million or DM 2,947 billion in 1990, registering an increase of 16.6 per cent over the previous year. During the period from 1980-81 to 1989-90, India's imports from the then West Germany increased by 325 per cent . The exports during this period increased by 361 per cent . They grew faster than the imports. The decade of 80s witnessed a several fold increase in trade between the two nations. In 1988, the trade volume crossed Rs. 5,000 crore or DM 5 billion mark for the first time in the history of Indo-German trade relations. Since

Germany was our leading trade partner within EU, India's trade deficit with it was also the highest. In 1987-88, India's trade deficit declined by almost 10 per cent . In the early 90s, i.e., 1990-91 to 1992-93, India had witnessed a constant fall in the balance of trade with Germany. In 1992-93, trade deficit with Germany declined by 4.5 per cent over the previous year. The exports in 1992-93 grew faster than imports over the previous year, exports registered an increase of 31.5 per cent , whereas imports grew at a rate of 24.8 per cent only.

Germany has also emerged as India's leading source for foreign technology and foreign direct investment. In 1989, Germany topped the list of foreign investors for the first time with over Rs. 120 crore (DM 120 million) of sanctioned investment. In fact, German investment proposals accounted for 38 per cent of all foreign investments sanctioned by the government in that year. In the early 90s, i.e., 1991-92, Germany had maximum number of foreign collaborations approved and had second position in the country-wise foreign investments in India; Germany accounted for 35 per cent of the total foreign investments approved in India from 1991 to 1994.

Despite increases in volume and value in the bilateral trade, from the Indian point of view, the share of Indo-German trade in Germany's aggregate trade has been very small, being merely about 0.5 per cent of the total German trade volume in the last years of the 1980s. German imports from India constitute only a minuscule of its total imports (around 0.3 per cent) and German supplies, in terms of its world-wide exports, also form a very negligible portion (about 0.5 per cent). Germany's main trading partners have remained unchanged, namely, France, the Netherlands, U.K. Italy, Belgium, Luxembourg inside Europe, and U.S.A. This trade profile has largely been the result of the global and regional framework within which Germany evolved itself in the post-war years.

Germany had witnessed an eco-politico resurgence as the country entered into the 1990s. The unification of the Germany and the integration of the European market in 1992 are having profound effects on its economy.

For Germany the Single European Market by the end of 1992, could not have been better timed. The market took shape at a time when Germany had emerged as a big technological power, following all pervasive modernisation and technological upgradation and some of the other EU member nations were lagging behind in meeting the tough competition given by the German firms.

Moreover, German unification has brought tremendous opportunities for India. Unification has led to steep rise in German imports as the German industry alone cannot possibly supply all the goods needed for the reconstruction of the economy. India should avail of these opportunities in the present as well as future. India should also be cautious from East Asia, a region which has been maintaining its exports at a commendable rate despite various restrictions. The four NIC - S. Korea, Taiwan, Hongkong and Singapore - account for nearly 40 per cent of German exports to the south, South East and Far East Asia combined excluding Japan. The share of these four economies in the German market is about 53 per cent of the total imports from this region. India's position among the East Asian nations, in the early 90s, was fifth or sixth with regard to trade with Germany. China, Taiwan, S. Korea and Hongkong scored over India in exporting to Germany in aggregate, as also selected commodities of India's interest such as garments, leather products and engineering goods.

India having a developing country with relatively less sophisticated technology, small volumes of production and low labour productivity in the modern sector industries afflicted by high input costs of basic industrial materials (steel, plastics, copper, furnace oil etc.) as compared to international prices, the structure of its exports is dominated by traditional products of low value, although a modest degree of commodity diversification can be noticed in its trade composition in recent years (early 90s).

Garments and other finished products have become one major category now in Indian exports to Germany. Garments alone constituted 17 per cent of total exports to Germany in 1997-98.

Leather and its manufactures and Gems and Jewellery have shown consistent improvement from mid-70s to early 90s. Together they accounted for 25 per cent of total exports to Germany in 1992-93 (Table 4.31). Carpets and other floor coverings also constitute a good share. Their share had dropped in the mid-80s, but it rose again in 1997-98 accounting for almost 7 per cent of total exports to Germany.

Exports of engineering goods, on the other hand, have shown a very marginal improvement. From a share of 3.7 per cent in 1980-81, their share had risen slightly to 4.2 per cent in 1992-93 and 6 per cent in 1997-98. However, this product should be given more importance as there is enormous scope which India can tap.

The prospects of Indian exports, however, cannot be viewed independently of the EU framework and, to some extent, global concerns like quota restraints and MFA regimes. It is argued that there have been two sets of factors affecting the performance of Indian textiles in EU markets. The first is domestic, like lack of modernisation of textile machinery, pull of domestic market, high cost of production due to use of outdated machinery and other factors like escalations of cotton prices, heavy internal taxation and low productivity of labour etc.

Among the external factors, severe competition from Hongkong, Pakistan, S. Korea and China (mainly on account of low prices) hit India's exports adversely. Exchange rate variations and quota spread or concentration were the other major setbacks. Also exporters and industrialists are reluctant to invest in technological upgradation which leads to inferior quality of products. They are not adaptable to demand, design and fashion, and more important, have a short-term outlook leading to problems like non-adherence to quality and delivery schedules. Consequent to hike in wages among the traditional suppliers and structural adjustments in the industrial patterns, a number of new competitors such as Thailand, Philippines and Brazil have emerged. The East Europeans and the Chinese are also putting up stiff competition for woven fabrics in the German market.

Indo-German trade has to be seen in a broader perspective viewed on a holistic frame. The new targets of the trade relationship cannot be achieved merely in terms of quantitative parameters. A new qualitative element will have to be introduced with a time frame as reference point [14]. Since the Indian economy, like many other developing economies which pursued the import substitution strategy, could not build a strong scaffolding for a national economy to realign its global relations on the internal strength, this qualitative change will have to be obtained through external factors - by greater participation in the global division of labour attracting foreign capital and technology. Indo-German trade relations in this context would develop if,

- Indian industrialists, by seizing initiatives become competitive enough in terms of quality production, concentrate on the export of sophisticated finished products with proper adherence to quality, time and delivery schedules, joint production through proper identification of sectors and opportunities where mutually productive operations could be established with the help of joint ventures.

- Exporters adopt professional and aggressive marketing strategies keeping the suitability of channels of distribution and proper marketing analysis in mind; study market structure, identify consumer needs, tastes, preferences and develop new products in conformity with the consumption trends; analyse distribution sector and adopt joint marketing with the local German importer/distributor.

United Germany offers tremendous opportunities for India. India should strengthen its economic relations and make Germany its major economic partner if it has to take advantage of unification of Germany.

4.2.6.2 U.K.: As a market for Indian products, U.K. was a close second to Germany till 1994-95. From 1995-96 onwards, it is the number one trading partner with India. India's major exports to U.K. included Ready-made garments (11 per cent), Leather (7 per cent), gems and Jewellery (6 per cent), Engineering goods (6 per cent) in 1997-98 (Table 4.35).

Exports in 1985-86 to U.K. amounted to Rs. 521.4 crore (26 per cent of total exports to EU) as compared to exports to Germany which amounted to Rs. 5091.4 crore with 25 per cent share.

From 1986-87 onwards till 1992-93, Germany had been our major export destination with U.K. following it. In 1993-94, exports to U.K. amounted to Rs. 4319.79 crore with a share of 23.8 per cent of total exports to EU as compared to Rs. 4803.19 crore exports to Germany with a share of 26 per cent . U.K. is also a leading source of imports for India. Major imports from U.K. include Gems and Jewellery, Electrical and non-electrical machinery, Transport equipments, Capital goods, iron and Steel and Chemical material and products (Table 4.47).

From 1973 till 1983-84, U.K. was our number one source for imports. In 1983-84, total imports from U.K. amounted to Rs. 1152.7 crore as compared to Rs. 1122.9 crore from Germany (Table 4.47).

Share of U.K., however, started declining from 1984-85 till 1993-94. In 1993-94, total imports from U.K. amounted to Rs. 4319.79 crore, with a share of 20 per cent as compared to Rs. 4803 crore, with a share of 22 per cent from Germany.

In the field of foreign investments, however, U.K. is number one at present. For the period 1991-94, investment of U.K. in India was 9.7 per cent of total investment as compared to 3.1 per cent from Germany (Table 4.19).

U.K. has been taken as a sample country in Table 4.48 to find its share in India's total exports to the world. It is evident that U.K.'s share of tea and mate in India's total exports of it to world is the highest (13 per cent in 1997-98). India's exports of tobacco etc. to world in 1997-98 was Rs. 1058.51 crore and U.K.'s share was Rs. 138.12 crore representing a share of 13 per cent.

Exports of leather, its manufactures including footwear to world by India was Rs. 4294 crore and to U.K. was Rs. 519.59 crore representing a share of 12 per cent in 1997-98. Exports of readymade garments to world amounted to Rs. 11720 crore and to U.K. alone were Rs. 863 crore, representing 7.36 per cent. U.K.'s share in the export of cashew kernels was 6.6 per cent, rice 5 per cent, cotton 4 per cent, spices 6 per cent, carpets 4 per cent, gems and jewellery 2.3 per cent, engineering goods 6 per cent, products of chemicals 5 per cent in 1997-98.

India's export of remaining items to U.K., i.e. Fish, Sugar, and Coffee is very low. Together, they accounted for 2.96 per cent in 1997-98.

4.2.6.3 Belgium: Among the EU members, Belgium is fast emerging as an important export destination for India. India imports Pearls and Precious stones especially rough diamonds from Belgium in huge quantity among other things such as Iron and Steel, Capital goods and Chemical material and products.

Pearls and precious stones imported from Belgium amounted to Rs. 485.5 crore in 1983-84 with a share of 75 per cent of total imports from Belgium; their imports rose to Rs. 775.75 crore in 1997-98 (Table 4.41) with a share of 85.5 per cent Main exports to Belgium were cut and polished diamonds and pearls (Rs. 2757.14 crore) with a share of 65 per cent in 1997-98 (Table 4.29).

Since diamond industry is an import intensive industry and depends entirely on imported rough diamonds, India's trade with Belgium has increased over the past decade (from 1982-83 to 1992-93). Imports from it grew by 665 per cent over a period from 1973-74 to 1981-82 and then grew by 738 per cent over a period of 1982-83 to 1992-93. Exports, however, grew by 565 per cent over a period from 1973-74 to 1981-82 and witnessed a rise of 824 per cent over a period from 1982-83 to 1992-93. Total trade between the two countries grew spectacularly over a period of decade mentioned above due to a sharp rise in the trade of diamonds.

4.2.6.4 France: France is an important source of imports for India within EU. Major imports from France include Electrical and non-electrical machinery. Capital goods, in 1997-98, alone constituted 34 per cent of total exports of France to India. Besides capital goods, other major imports are Iron and Steel (4.5 per cent), Chemical material and products (8.8 per cent), Organic chemicals (6 per cent), Professional and scientific instruments (2.4 per cent) (Table 4.42).

France is also a major market in the EU for India's exports, especially for Ready-made garments (31 per cent), Leather and its articles and footwear (8 per cent), Products of chemical (6 per cent) and Engineering goods (5.6 per cent) in 1997-98. Exports to France stood at Rs. 4857.0 crore in 1973-74 and grew to Rs. 14803.6 crore in 1981-82, rising by 204 per cent and then from Rs. 14582.6 crore in 1982-83 exports rose to Rs. 136170.4 crore in 1992-93 rising by 834 per cent over the period (Table 4.30). In 1997-98, exports to France stood at a figure of Rs. 275056 crore.

4.2.6.5. Italy: Italy is fast emerging as an important market for Indian exports, especially for Textiles and Garments and Leather and its manufactures. Ready-made garments constituted 9 per cent of total exports by India to Italy in 1997-98. Leather and its manufactures, Engineering goods, and Chemical materials had a share of 14 per cent , 6 per cent and 7.8 per cent respectively in 1997-98. India's exports to Italy had risen from Rs. 69.32 crore in 1973-74 to Rs. 157.5 crore in 1981-82 and from Rs. 139.7 crore in 1982-83 to Rs. 4081.98 crore in 1997-98 rising almost thirty times over the period (Table 4.32).

4.2.6.6 The Netherlands: India's exports to Netherlands has been steadily growing over the years. In the seventies, from Rs. 73.26 crore in 1973-74 it grew to Rs. 221.30 crore in 1979-80, rising three times over the period. In the eighties, after falling from Rs. 221.30 crore in 1979-80 to Rs. 152.04 crore in 1980-81, it increased to Rs. 528.75 crore in 1989-90, rising more than five times over the period. From the Table 4.33, it is obvious that India's exports to Netherlands has been increasing continuously from 1986-87. In 1997-98, the total exports to the country were valued at Rs. 2903.67 crore.

Major exports to Netherlands in 1997-98 included Apparel (14 per cent), Cashew-kernels (11 per cent), Products of chemical, especially pharmaceuticals (16 per cent), Leather and its manufactures (4 per cent), and engineering goods (5.45 per cent).

Main commodities imported from Netherlands in 1997-98 were capital goods (25 per cent), chemical materials (13.59 per cent), organic chemicals (11.28 per cent), iron and steel (5 per cent), and non-ferrous metals (4 per cent) (Table 4.45).

4.6.6.7 Other Members of European Union: India's trade with the remaining EU member countries, namely Denmark, Ireland, Greece, Luxembourg, Portugal and Spain is not very significant as is obvious from tables showing exports to and imports from these countries.

Together, these countries accounted for 10 per cent share in total exports of EU to India in 1997-98. Spain and Portugal, however, offer markets which have great potential. Their potential has not been fully exploited which is evident from the export figures. Even imports from these member nations are minimal and imports from Luxembourg and Portugal are almost negligible.

Therefore, there is need for greater co-operation between India and other EU member states in the field of trade.

4.2.6.8 Effect of New Member Countries on India's Trade: On January 1, 1995, three new member countries: Austria, Sweden and Finland joined the European Union. An attempt has been made to analyse what effect would these member countries have on India's exports to and imports from EU. Data have been collected to analyse the effect of newly joined member nations on India's trade with EU.

Year	India's Imports from EU-15 (Rs. crore)	India's Imports from World (Rs. crore)	Per cent share of EU-15
1991-92	14713.96	47850.83	30.75
1992-93	20057.59	62923.42	31.88
1993-94	22808.09	73101.01	31.20
1994-95	23797.16	89970.70	26.45
1995-96	34468.06	121646.59	28.33
1996-97	37717.77	138919.88	27.15
1997-98	38081.91	151553.52	25.12

Before the entry of new member countries, the share of India's imports from EU was 30 per cent in 1993-94 and 24.83 per cent in 1994-95. A look at the above table indicates that share of India's imports from EU-15 has not increased substantially. The share would have risen from 30 per cent in 1993-94 to 31.20 per cent in the same year if Sweden, Finland and Austria were also the member countries of EU. Similarly, the share would have increased from 25 per cent to 26.45 per cent in 1994-95. In other words, it can be stated that as far as imports from the new member countries are concerned, they are not very significant partners.

EU's share in India's exports with 15 member countries from April 1991 to March 1992 till April 1997 to March 1998 is as follows

Year	India's Exports to EU-15 (Rs. crore)	India's Exports to World (Rs. crore)	Per cent share of EU-15
1991-92	12404.66	44042.21	28.17
1992-93	15768.32	53351.84	29.55
1993-94	18876.93	69748.85	27.06
1994-95	22975.48	82673.40	27.79
1995-96	29040.43	106464.86	27.27
1996-97	30640.63	118817.32	25.79
1997-98	32907.86	126285.76	26.06

A look at the above table suggests that if the new member nations had joined earlier, then the share of India's exports to EU in India's total exports to world would have been 28.17 per cent in 1991-92 and 29.55 per cent in 1992-93 as compared to 27 per cent and 28.3 per cent in 1991-92 and 1992-93 respectively with 12 members only. In 1993-94 and 1994-95, share of India's exports to EU would have been 27 per cent and 28 per cent as compared to 26 per cent and 27 per cent if the new members had joined in. Thus, as far as exports are concerned, the new member countr. do not contribute significantly.

Indo-EU Bilateral Trade
(Rs. crore)

Year	Exports	Imports	Trade Balance
1991-92	12404.66	14713.97	-2309.31
1992-93	15768.32	20057.59	-4289.27
1993-94	18876.93	22808.09	-3931.16
1994-95	22975.48	23797.16	-821.68
1995-96	29040.43	34468.06	-5427.63
1996-97	30640.63	37717.77	-7077.14
1997-98	32907.86	38081.91	-5174.08

The trade deficit in 1991-92 was Rs. 2068 crore, when EU comprised of 12 member nations; if the new member countries were a part of EU in 1992 and 1993, trade deficit would have been Rs. 2309.3 crore in 1991-92 and Rs. 4289.3 crore in 1992-93. In other words, deficit would have increased by 11.65 per cent in 1991-92 and by 7.97 per cent in 1992-93. The reason for a rise in deficit can be attributed to a steeper rise in imports than exports.

Imports after the entry of new members would have risen by 5.3 per cent as against exports which would have increased by 4.2 per cent only in 1991-92. Similarly, imports in 1992-93 would have increased by 4.88 per cent with the entry of new members, whereas exports would have risen by 4 per cent only leading, thereby, to an increase in trade deficit by 7.9 per cent .

On the basis of above analysis, it can be predicted that unless India's exports to Sweden, Finland and Austria increase substantially in coming years, these member countries will remain marginal partners only. Trade deficit can be bridged to a considerable extent in future only if exports are increased and imports reduced substantially.

Hence, our conclusions will not be seriously affected even with the inclusion of these new member countries to the European Union.

4.2.7 India's Strategic Response to European Unification

EU-92 has created demand conditions which, in turn, have created keener competition in almost all segments of exportable products from India in the EU market. To meet this challenge, countries need to formulate their strategic response appropriately. Speed of action on the supply side and 'breath-taking flexibility' in responding to new managerial challenges for augmenting international competitiveness are equally necessary for actually staying ahead of competitors.

The EU-92 had generated 'Europhobia' in the EU countries. India had to think and act EU-wide treating the entire EU as a thrust market in its global export marketing network. India's strategic response to the EU-92 challenge had to be a determined action programme of substantially improving the degree of international competitiveness of its products and services. India's strategic managerial challenge and opportunities for exports thrown by EU-92, was formulated at two distinct levels; the first level related to the established products and the second level related to new products and relatively unexplored new market within the EU [15].

4.2.7.1 Strategy for Established Products: The basic objective of India's strategic response for its established export production in the EU was to preserve and maintain the market share in the increasing competitive market. India had to pay much greater attention in two basic areas, namely, 'Product Management', and 'Marketing Management'.

First and foremost attention had to be paid to up-gradation of quality of products and their adaptation to strictly meet the new harmonised standards and specifications set by EU.

Productivity should be increased in these areas by scale expansion and better management to bring costs and prices to international standards. India had to move away from supplying low value added items (like raw cotton, hides and skins) to higher value added products (like better quality cotton and mixed textiles and leather products). Innovative designs in textiles and leather products by tie-ups with fashion design organisations in the EU countries have helped in improving 'Product Management'.

The 'Marketing Management' dimension required adoption of aggressive marketing techniques like intensive promotion of better quality products. Market penetration strategies helped in increasing the market share. A competitive commercial intelligence system and a constant feedback mechanism from customers was developed. Joint marketing ventures, including equity participation in distribution channels and warehouses further strengthened India's efforts at market penetration. Strategic alliances were formed wlth potential competitors from the less developed EU members like Spain, Portugal and Ireland and with the ACP partners. These took the form of joint ventures in the labour-intensive manufactured products vulnerable to protectionist moves. by EU. These products included apparel, footwear and leather products.

4.2.7.2 Strategy for New Products/Services: The strategy for diversifications into new products had to be highly selective. Indian entrepreneurs had to identify few new products in which India could hold dynamic comparative advantage. These included products like auto components, hand tools, electronic components and processed fruits and foods. The engineering products could best be developed by tie-ups with original equipment manufacturers in the EU using their specification and exploiting economies of scale.

New joint ventures were set up and existing ones expanded in India with the help of investors from the EU who also provided and are still providing the latest research and development technology and making buy back arrangements.

The marketing strategy for processed fruits and foods had to rely on concluding mutually beneficial long-term supply contracts between Indian firms and the European distribution channels including chains of supermarkets [16].

Market-entry strategies were adopted initially for new products. They included price discounts supply of unbranded products etc. India also set up joint marketing ventures in the EU which helped to market these new products under India's own brand names.

India's most important resource which certainly retained dynamic comparative advantage was its skilled manpower. Since the demand for services of technical, scientific and managerial professions had risen after European unification, India could export several types of services to EU markets such as engineering services, financial services, audit and accounting services, architectural services, medical services, and most importantly software services.

The formulation of an integrated strategic response from India to EU-92 required going beyond the narrow questions of increasing India's exports. Strengthening economic relations between EU and India in the wake of EU-92 required a comprehensive policy in promoting two-way trade and two-way joint ventures.

India has been successful in setting up export-import technology upgradation oriented joint ventures with EU. India has also been able to woo European Foreign Direct Investment (FDI) into India.

For future, Indian entrepreneurs who can mobilise foreign funds from European banks and other sources under EU's preferential locational policy should venture to set up joint ventures with the European partners and Indian skilled manpower. The resourceful entrepreneurs who can mobilise investible resources from international sources should also venture into takeovers of sick but potentially viable production and marketing units in the EU.

To promote India's exports to the EU, the steps already undertaken by the Government of India need to be pursued in future also. A further aggressive diplomatic drive towards securing greater co-operation of the EU secretariat and the member nations of the EU to provide more assistance to India to meet the challenges thrown up by EU-92 is required.

4.2.8 Measures to Enhance India's Trade With EU

There are a set of broad strategies that Indian business and policy-makers, in general, could follow in preparing to build enduring industrial and trade links with the European Union. The attempt is to derive, from the implication of European integration, certain generic policy recommendations. The strategies are divided into firm-specific, industry-specific and country-specific actions, although there would be some degree of overlapping between the three categories.

4.2.8.1 Firm-specific Actions: The driving force behind any initiative to enhance commercial and trading links with a unified European Union is the enterprise. Indeed, in Europe it is the prompt reaction and reorientation of strategies by European corporations and their response to the Single market measures that have enhanced the viability of the programme. Their active participation in the progress has lent credence to official measures which otherwise would have simply remained on paper. Similarly, the task of making substantial inroads into European markets is largely the task of individual firms [17].

An outline of a set of actions that could be applied, in general, at the firm level is given below:

(a) Establishing an Organic presence in the European Union:

It is evident that an organic and continuous presence in the EU market is vital in promoting Indian exports to the region. The strategy should, therefore, hold good at all the three levels - firm, industry and country. Establishing or strengthening presence in Europe should be assigned top priority in preparing for an integrated Europe.

The setting up of an outlet in Europe in some form or the other, such as a marketing office, branch, subsidiary etc. will give an enormous advantage to Indian companies in terms of access to timely information on market trends and potential customers. Proximity to the market and the consequent ability to respond quickly to changing market demand would also substantially improve Indian competitive strength, given the tenuous communication links between India and Europe. Gaining a foothold in the European Union market will confer a number of advantages:

- Ability to plug into a European Economic Interest Grouping (EEIG): The EU regulation providing for the creation of an EEIG encourages co-operation between business across national frontiers in the Union by enabling them to form an informal alliance called an EEIG, for common, non-profit making support activities. Any European business can be a member of an EEIG and this includes European subsidiaries of third country companies. Thus, setting up a subsidiary, albeit small, will enable Indian companies to become a part of the new European corporate culture.

- Ability to take advantage of the European company Statute: The proposal for the European Company Statute provides for a new framework of law that would enable the creation of "European" companies. Once this statute comes into force, a "European company", which can be formed either through mergers or creation of joint undertakings, will be governed by one set of EU law rather than by different national company laws. Such a European public limited company can be formed by two or more Union-based businesses from at least two member states, and these could include European subsidiaries of third country companies.

(b) Giving priority to Quality Assurance and Standards: By far the most important step for Indian firms to take is on standards. The issue of standards has been a point of contention between the EU and the developing countries. On the one hand, the biggest type of the Single Market programme is based on the harmonisation of standards and technical regulations across the EU, paving the way for the emergence of "European" standards and single testing and certification procedures leading to substantial cost reductions. Developing countries, on the other hand, have been expressing fears over standards being used or a non-tariff barrier against exports to the EU.

The EU-India standards and quality programme is a major component of bilateral co-operation. From modest beginnings in 1987, as essentially an information exchange action, the standards programme has over the years grown both in content and coverage. It includes the modernisation of Indian testing laboratories, the setting up of a National Accreditation Scheme to international norms, and the introduction of education in quality in engineering colleges.

Under the scheme of Harmonisation of Standards, a number of Indian standards have been harmonised with European standards. In March 1995, under Quality Training, sixty Indian officers belonging to various government and private agencies have been trained to become qualified assessors by Batalas, U.K. A further batch of five Indian officers were trained as lead assessors.

(c) Strengthening Marketing Capability: Individual companies have to adopt a professional approach to marketing. There is a need to establish and strengthen marketing tie-ups, in particular with European partners. Indian companies should seriously explore the possibilities of utilising the services of professional bodies, which provide a range of support services for Indian exporters in improving their trade with the EU. Services offered include market surveys and information and identification of potential business partners and buyers.

(d) Establishing links with European SMEs: Entering into tie-ups with small and medium enterprises (SMEs) in the European Union is a relatively easier way of tackling the competitive rigours of the Union market. SMEs are receiving special attention in the progress towards completion of the EU market unification. The European Commission has put in a place a number of special schemes which seek to help them to position themselves more competitively in the run-up to an integrated Europe.

Tie-ups with European SMEs would, therefore, lead to easier market access for Indian companies and will facilitate exploitation of new opportunities emerging in the internal market. Co-operation with European SMEs, which have exploited the "learning economies" of the internal market, and which have good R&D skill and marketing resources, would be particularly beneficial in seeking a penetration of European markets. The SMEs are extremely dynamic in terms of flexibility to technological change and innovation. They also maintain special relationships with customers and suppliers and exercise control over a diverse range of products. Links with European SMEs will also enable Indian companies to be involved in the European Union's research and technology programmes, thereby providing access to much-needed technology and technical expertise.

EU-India Partenariat '99, the biggest ever EU-India business event, will be held in March 1999 in New Delhi. This is a multi-sectoral business meeting, focusing on the small and medium sector. A joint initiative of the Government of India and the European Commission, it will bring together around 700 European and Indian small and medium-sized enterprises (SMEs) - an equal number from each side - providing them an opportunity through an intensive series of pre-programmed one-on-one meetings to discuss business partnerships, joint ventures, collaborations and strategic alliances. [18]

The European Commission organises Euro-Partenariat in Europe every six months. These are aimed mainly at bringing together European SMEs. Building upon the success of these events, the EC has recently launched this initiative in Asia.

In November 1997, the first EU-ASEAN Partenariat was successfully held in Singapore. India has been selected as the next Asian destination.

Co-organisers of the EU-India partenariat are the three apex Indian industry associations (CII, ASSOCHAM and FICCI) and the Council of the EU Chambers of Commerce in India. They constitute the secretariat to identify and select the Indian companies for participation in the Partenariat.

The Partenariat will focus on six key factors : Chemicals and plastics processing, electronics and information technology (hardware), environmental technology, food processing and packaging, software and other services. Each of these sectors has been further subdivided to simplify identification and selection procedures.

Since the announcement of the meet in May 1998, the first phase of the preparatory work - selection of the Indian companies for participation in the Partenariat - has been successfully completed. The Indian co-organisers have selected 350 Indian companies for the meet.

From the side of the EU, representatives of the 15 member states, designated National Counsellors, visited India in September to apprise themselves of the economic situation in the country. This will help them to make a presentation to the EU companies on the Indian business scenario. For the benefit of these National Counsellors, a presentation on the Indian economy was made by Mr. T. R. Prasad, Secretary, Ministry of Industry, Government of India. Mr. Prasad pointed out that, since the economic reform process began in India in 1991, a total of 5,600 investment and technology transfer agreements have been approved between India and Europe. To further build upon this, he urged the European National Counsellors to present the advantages of doing business in India on their return to Europe to attract the best participation in the EU-India Partenariat.

The Ambassador and Head of the Delegation of the European Commission in India, Mr. Michael Barrie McGeever, also emphasised the same point. "The recent liberalisation and consequent increase in income levels has given rise to a huge middle class of over 150 million people", he said, and due to this investment in India is very attractive owing to its tremendous market potential. It was also pointed out that India has abundant natural resources, skilled and inexpensive scientific and technical manpower, vibrant capital market and a large private sector as well as a large domestic market.

The Partenariat is designed to be a major step in promoting EU-India economic cooperation, which has taken rapid strides in the last decade. The EU is India's largest trading partner, accounting for about one-third of both India's exports and imports. The EU is also the largest source of foreign direct investment (in terms of actual flows) in India as well as the largest donor of grant aid to India. Over the last couple of years, it has launched several regional and India-specific programmes, such as the EU-India Economic Cross Cultural Programme, Asia Investment and Asia Urbs, which have given a new dimension to EU-India relations.

(e) Maximising use of official schemes: A number of important schemes are already in place to promote trade and co-operation between the European Union and India within the ambit of the EU-India Industrial Co-operation Programme. These include the Bureau Rapproachment Enterprises (BRE) facility, the EC Investment Partners (ECIP), etc. These existing institutional arrangements should be exploited to the maximum by individual companies for securing joint ventures and co-operation agreements with European companies.

The European Union has extended its BRE service to small and medium enterprises in India that seek to find suitable joint venture partners in Europe. The ECIP facility seeks to provide investment finance to potential joint venture schemes by Indian companies with Europeans. This facility provides seed money for undertaking various actions leading up to the setting up of a joint venture. The four major activities for which finance is provided are (a) identification of potential projects and partners, (b) preparations for the creation of a specific joint venture, (c) financing of capital requirements and (d) human resource development, training and management expertise.

This facility, which was hitherto routed through a select number of European banks, is now also channelled through three financial institutions in India, namely, IDBI, ICICI and EXIM Bank. For small and dynamic enterprises, this facility would constitute a very viable option of gaining a foothold in the EU market by joining hands with a European partner. The latest Indo-EU Business forum also provides a platform for continuous interaction and co-operation between India and European businessmen.

4.2.8.2 Industry-Specific Actions: Business lobbies often wield so much power that, if properly directed, they could fuel beneficial synergetic effects on trade. A weakness observed in the Indian corporate sector is that there is insufficient co-operation among companies for undertaking joint export efforts. Greater co-ordination among Indian firms, therefore, needs to be nurtured. In particular, it is felt that concerted and co-ordinated actions from Indian industry are needed to make a dent in the European market.

A set of strategies are presented in this part, that could be adopted at an industry level, for instance by Industry Associations and Exporters' Associations.

(a) Promoting Indian presence in the EU: Indian industry, as a whole, should strive to make its presence felt in the EU and project India's image in it. Since the cost of launching promotional schemes in Europe are fairly heavy, it is all the more necessary to make joint efforts. First, the offices of Industry Associations already present in the Union should be rapidly upgraded so that they actively pass on timely information to companies in India. These association offices should also develop databases of all useful information on the EU directives, standards, policies etc. Participation in all important European-level trade fairs is essential. In addition, Indian industry should aim at having well-equipped showrooms in the major cities of Europe that would display the range of Indian technical as well as product-specific expertise.

(b) Promoting Co-operation on Standards: Indian industry should play a catalytic role in spreading, across the country, the concept of Total Quality Management (TQM). Quality assurance will give the crucial edge to competitiveness, and individual firms should be persuaded to realise the benefits of producing to standards. Industry should assist the government in enforcing quality assurance requirements. More specifically, an industry-level effort to establish quality-control systems and assistance to a large number of companies to qualify for ISO 9000 would be a valuable contribution. In specific industrial sectors where India has a potential comparative advantage in exporting to Europe, time-bound programmes to introduce and implement quality control systems covering all the firms should be given urgent priority. Manufacturers' Associations should play an active role in this exercise.

(c) Encouraging technology absorption: The advantage of low labour costs has considerably diminished in recent years due to increased automation and advent of new technologies. Thus, it is imperative for Indian industry to compete on the basis of state-of-the-art technology and capability in design engineering and flexible manufacturing systems. This is particularly crucial for engineering items. The translation of technological advances into productive efficiency in this sector has made such rapid strides that is no longer possible to compete without a fair degree of technical expertise. While earlier, competitive advantage was derived from economies of scale in mass production, it has now become necessary to produce differentiated products without sacrificing price competitiveness.

(d) Undertaking aggressive marketing: An integrated Europe will demand much more strenuous marketing efforts than before on the part of India. European unification will alter the modes of trading and distribution across the Union. The retail sector is particularly set for far-reaching changes and it is important for Indian exporters to establish links with super-market and hyper-market chains with a Europe-wide network. For market information, Indian businessmen should procure access to the relevant databases in the Union. Here, chambers of commerce can play a useful role. Companies also need to co-ordinate their marketing efforts. The formation of supplier cartels or consortia may go a long way in achieving bargaining strength. For a large single market, it may be better to offer "package solutions" rather than only isolated, single products.

A group of Indian auto component companies from the Northern region have come together to form a trading company to tackle a more competitive and unified EU. This trading company is modelled on the lines of a Japanese trading company and is expected to bring large benefits to the member companies. Such steps should be encouraged for other sectors also.

Participation in all the relevant European-level trade fairs would not only provide market exposure but also often act as the beginning of a stream of orders. In order to get over official export restrictions, Indian businessmen should consider identifying and liaisoning with organisations in Europe, for example, the Foreign Trade Association, which lobby for the interests of European importers and that often coincide with the interests of developing country exporters.

4.2.8.3 Country-specific Actions: Country-specific strategies typically fall within the realm of official policy. Certain critical areas of policy support are pinpointed here that could qualitatively improve trading relationships with the EU. Given the importance of the European market for India, the reform policies should specially target the European Union for enhanced effectiveness.

(a) Promoting greater Indian presence in the EU: Promotion of Indian presence in the EU constitutes a top priority for official policy as well. This calls for reorientation of economic policy in India to encourage actively direct Indian presence in the EU. Indian investments in Europe have been extremely negligible because of foreign exchange constraints. The emphasis, so far, has been to promote foreign direct investment into India. There is now need for an environment that is supportive of investing resources within European Union borders in order to break into markets.

The new economic policy has made important headway in allowing companies to partly use their foreign exchange earnings. However, specific plans to promote investment into the EU, for specific industrial sectors demonstrating comparative advantage and a track record of exports to Europe, should be drawn up.

It has now become fairly imperative to enhance the "visibility" of Indian enterprises and their capabilities in Europe and to project the country's image as a producer of not just handicrafts and textiles but also as manufacturer of sophisticated engineering and electronic products. To this end, the government should reinforce the role of export promotion councils and Indian diplomatic missions in giving sufficient publicity to the country's comparative strengths. Warehousing facilities in Europe provided by the government should be enhanced and better utilised.

The Indian Ambassadors' committee report had recommended upgradation of commercial and economic sections of Indian Embassies in EU member states. This would be a cost-effective way of monitoring developments in the region as well playing an active role through participation in ongoing EU discussions relating to external policies. Countervailing lobbies should be mobilised in Europe to offset any imposition of Voluntary Export Restraints (VERs) or other Non-Tariff Barriers (NTBs) in place of existing quantitative restrictions. Indian missions should also target to have on a priority basis, access to all important databases to undertake analyses on the field before passing information regarding important developments to the Indian government and the Indian business community.

(b) Providing marketing support: Marketing has been the backbone of Indian exporters. A coherent approach to marketing is essential, given that it would determine, to a large extent, India's export success in the EU. An integrated and spruced-up European market will call for a new approach to marketing. Trading and export houses should be revamped so that they could wield greater bargaining power.

The new policies with respect to trading houses and export houses should be further strengthened and redirected, particularly towards the EU. The role of trading houses is even more important in representing the interests of small and medium enterprises which do not have the financial viability to do it alone but have competitive products to offer in the European market.

(c) Sponsoring a standards "Offensive" : The emergence of European standards is probably the single most important repercussion of the 1992 market integration for third countries. The EU and India are currently implementing an important programme of co-operation in the area of standards. The EU is helping in training its experts on various aspects of quality assurance and the working of European standards.

The Confederation of Indian Industry (CII) was designated by the Government of India as the nodal agency for quality training under the EU-India programme. Two separate sets of training, one for certified quality engineers and the other for instructors were conducted by a German organisation.

Regarding the modernisation of laboratories, three key areas were pinpointed - automative sector, domestic electrical appliances and processed food. The assistance concerns transfer of technical know-how to establish modern installations and personnel training, with a view to giving them a knowledge of testing procedures and enabling them to operate and maintain installations according to internationally accepted norms so that testing is done indigenously.

The issue of standards needs to be tackled first on the domestic front. For an effective implementation of standards, it is essential that domestic quality assurance requirements are themselves tightened. Quality control requirements in India are very inadequate and are most often not enforced.

If Indian companies are to gear up to European standards, it is absolutely vital to tighten domestic quality assurance requirements. Therefore, mandatory quality assurance systems and homologation facilities should be set up for the domestic market as a first step. Companies should be made to produce to standards irrespective of whether it is for the domestic market or the export market.

The EU has also advised the Indian government on a National Accreditation Scheme for testing and certifying products in India. And, at the request of the Indian government, the EU has provided assistance in the preparation of National Accreditation Scheme (NAS) for India. Under this programme, a five-member European Expert Group (EEG) recommended a comprehensive NAS, the essential elements of which are:

The National Quality Council (NQC) would be the apex body for operating the scheme in India. It should be an autonomous body under which five separate boards will function:

(a) A national accreditation board for the certification of product and quality management systems.

(b) A national accreditation board for the certification of laboratories.

(c) A board for the registration of quality related personnel.

(d) A national enquiry service of standards and conformity assessment.

(e) A national awareness campaign.

The EU would be assisting India in training its experts. Foreseen for a duration of five years, this programme is intended to mobilise 50 percent of finances required from industry and 50 percent from government sources. This European Expert Group has made a number of recommendations such as harmonisation of the standardisation activities of different Indian agencies, adoption of European standards as Indian standards, an effective information service on standards and technical regulations, product certification for export markets, etc. Needless to say, acting upon these recommendations urgently is of prime importance. A coherent national policy needs to be evolved for quality certification and for developing indigenous institutions for certification. This would, then, pave the way for an early negotiation with the European Union of mutual recognition of test certificates, whereby products certified in India would be accepted in the EU.

(f) Promoting SMEs for Exports and Joint Ventures: Small and medium enterprises (SMEs) in the European Union are the focus of many special schemes that aim at helping them in preparing for an integrated Europe. The action programme for SMEs attempts, on the one hand, to make special provisions for taxation, company law and social policy and on the other hand, to promote their development through special schemes. Apart from providing information on the Single Market to SMEs through a network of Euro-Indo centres, special schemes to provide business advisory services and assistance to form joint ventures such as BE-Net and Europartenariat, promotion of R&D co-operation among SMEs and finance to tackle a large single market, are also in operation. We have already recommended that tie-ups between the SME sector in India and Europe would lead to large potential benefits. The SME sector in India is very broad and contains a mixture of firms. U.K.'s trade minister, Mr. Anthony Nelson, on his visit to India in mid-September 1995, also advocated the joint venture route for foreign companies wishing to invest in India. Mr. Nelson advocated stronger ties between small and medium industries particularly in Banking, Insurance and Services sector of both the countries [19].

The Government of India should also play an active role in identifying the dynamic segments of the SME sector to encourage partnership with European firms. The BRE service is an extension of part of the BC-Net service to Indian firms. Europartenariat is an important initiative for promoting the development of SMEs from specific regions. Thus,

Europartenariat is playing a big role in assisting companies from former East Germany to find Western partner firms that can help them in their restructuring and privatisation. India should explore possibilities of benefiting from such schemes so that Indian firms can actively participate in the economic development of the new German lander.

The sets of strategies presented above are fairly general in nature and can be applied to different types of businesses. They are by no means exhaustive. More work is needed at the micro level to identify specific actions for taking on the challenge of the European market. Strategies at all three levels should go hand in hand and should be undertaken without delay. Ideally, the initiative to tackle the integrated European market should begin at the firm level which then would build up to form actions at the industry level. Therefore, these actions should mobilise official thinking to bring about changes in policy.

4.2.9 Summary

India has had formal relations with the Union since as far back as 1962. Despite the fact that India and six other countries of the Commonwealth were denied special preferences even when they lost Commonwealth preferences under the Treaty of Accession, an enduring relationship has been developed between India and the Union over the years under the aegis of the Commercial Co-operation Agreement (CCA), first signed in 1973 and later renamed Commercial and Economic Co-operation in 1981.

Trade is central to the economic relations between India and the Union. The Union alone accounts for 24 per cent of India's imports and 25 per cent of total exports from India in 1997-98. Two disquieting features have, however, persisted. India has not been able to make a dent into the Union; India's share in the Union's imports and exports remains still less than 1 per cent . Secondly, India had run a large trade deficit with the Union from 1978-79 to 1989-90. From 1990-91 to 1991-92, for two years, deficit registered a fall by 26 per cent and 80 per cent respectively, which was a remarkable achievement for India. But again, in 1992-93, trade deficit rose by 92 per cent . 1993-94, however, experienced a fall in the deficit by 5.6 per cent. In 1997-98, trade deficit fell from Rs. 5617.93 crore to Rs. 4400 crore.

An important reason for this has been the increasing difficulty in gaining market access due to the protectionist policies of the Union in areas like clothing where India has comparative advantage. On the other hand, import liberalisation in India has provided a rapidly growing market for European Industry.

Apart from the structural imbalance in trade, the composition of India's exports to the Union is not well diversified. Three groups of items, i.e., leather and leather goods, textiles and textiles articles and pearls and precious stones taken together account for two-thirds of India's total exports to the Union.

The implication of the single market has been the faster growth of intra-EU trade. However, it may be noted that there are a large number of items, like marine products, tea, coffee, spices, articles of leather, fabrics and clothing and pearls and precious stones in which intra-Union trade is much lower than 50 percent. In these products, even relatively faster growth in intra-Union trade has left considerable scope for expanding India's exports. In future, India will not face a demand constraint as its share in imports from non-EU countries is still quite low in most of these products.

Similarly, India must particularly concentrate on the markets like Denmark, Germany, Italy, U.K. and Spain, where intra-Union imports are relatively of lesser magnitude. In certain products like apparel and clothing made-ups, knitted and crocheted goods, carpets, tobacco, animal feeds, metallic ores and pearls and precious and semi-precious stones, India has better price competitiveness with non-Union suppliers. Whereas, in other major products like marine, edible fruits and nuts, oilmeals and leather goods, India's competitiveness is very much behind the non-Union suppliers. It would, therefore, be all the more important to improve the productivity and competitiveness of these major products.

As stated earlier also, India would be able to export the following items to EU in the year 2000, keeping all other factors constant, to the tune of:

Ready-made garments	Rs. 10693.76 crore
Cotton	Rs. 8245.43 crore
Gems and Jewellery	Rs. 5987.41 crore
Leather, its manufactures etc.	Rs. 4480.16 crore
Chemical material and products	Rs. 3595.41 crore

Fish, molluscs etc.	Rs.	2584.83 crore
Carpets and Floor Coverings	Rs.	1895.83 crore
Engineering Goods	Rs.	1184.90 crore
Agro-based Goods	Rs.	1127.11 crore

Besides, the projections made above in respect of India's major export items to the EU, an attempt was also made earlier to see the impact of unification on India's overall exports to EU.

Through index number techniques, it was found that GDP of EU has increased by four times, imports of EU from the world grew by three times while India's exports to EU grew by almost six times over a period of twenty years. Population did not register a significant growth. Regressions were run to see the impact of imports, GDP and population of EU on India's exports.

India's chances of improving competitiveness with countries like Spain and Portugal are quite good, particularly in view of pressure on wages in these countries in the wake of the fixation of minimum working age under the social charter.

Restructuring of industry through mergers and pressure of competition will also have a major impact on the configuration of supplies to the EU. It is likely to increase sources of production and servicing facilities from outside. Apart from developing the capacity to meet large scale orders, business contacts with firms in Europe would have to be strengthened to develop market channels.

Development of large monopolies and cartels in the Union would reduce India's bargaining leverage. It is, however, possible to develop long term production and trade relations with the major European companies. The services sector, due to integration, will expand more rapidly in future. Indian banks must enter the area of investment banking so as to utilise the increasing opportunities. Another area where India can gain a foothold is foreign travel which is likely to increase faster in the years to come.

The completion of the internal market and a larger role in policy-making of the Union institutions would (i) reduce the national variations from common policy; (ii) help to improve predictability by (a) strengthening its contacts at the Union level and (b) developing a much more efficient information network.

It is necessary to restructure India's commercial and economic representation in Europe such that Union-wide institutions get more importance. The importance of a more efficient information network can hardly be over-emphasised as the impetus provided by Europe 1992 has (i) ushered in significant changes in technology and relocation of investment and (ii) increased the importance of consumer services.

The significant improvement in productivity in the Union and reduction in labour cost have lowered the prices of some items of machinery and equipment imported by India. At the same time, the same trend in other industries, where the Union countries compete with India in third markets, could adversely affect India's exports in future. Textiles is a clear case where increased use of structural funds, that formed part of the 1992 package, have imparted dynamism to the European industry.

Indian exporters must carefully follow the process of harmonisation of standards in the EU. Strict quality control in ago-based consumer products and safety standards in industrial machinery and engineering goods are major determinants of export performance in the EU market as a result of unification. National standards have been replaced by Union-wide standards in a number of sectors. This EU requirement of conformance, testing, certification and quality control involves additional costs putting pressure on India's competitiveness. Fortunately, EU-India co-operation in this area has made initial headway and consultations between the Bureau of Indian Standards (BIS), the European Committee for Standards (CES) and the European Committee for Electro-technical Standards have led to identification of area of co-operation.

Some Asian countries like Malaysia, Thailand and Indonesia are stated to have made tremendous inroads into the EU market. Indian strategy, therefore, should be carefully worked out. It must revolve around

a) proper choice of products;
b) professional marketing approach with an efficient information network and
c) development of catalytic institutions.

Three sectors, i.e. agriculture, engineering including electronics and textiles including clothing need particular attention.

Notes

1. Aggarwal P.N, *"The History of Indian Business"*, pp. 13, 1985.

2. *"Economic Survey"*; Government of India; various issues from 1974 to 1993.

3. *"Economic Survey"*; Ministry of Finance; Government of India publication; 1991.

4. Conference on *"Europe after Maastricht - A Backgrounder"*; PHD Chamber of Commerce and Industry; January 25, 1993.

5. Six nation Community comprised of Belgium, France, the then FRG, Italy, Luxembourg and the Netherlands.

6. *"Europe Information - External Relations"*; Commission of the European Communities; June, 1981.

7. Workshop on "EEC 1992: Opportunities and Challenges - A Backgrounder'; PHD Chamber of Commerce and Industry; May 2, 1989.

8. Workshop on 'EEC 1992: Opportunities and Challenges - A Backgrounder'; PHD Chamber of Commerce and Industry, March, 1995.

9. Workshop on 'EEC 1992: Opportunities and Challenges - A Backgrounder'; PHD Chamber of Commerce and Industry, March, 1995.

10. *"India, Germany and the European Community"*; Edited by K.B. Lall, H.S. Chopra, Thomas Meyer; Radiant Publishers, 1993.

11. *"Indo-EC Business Pulse"*; The Newsletter of the Council of EEC Chambers of Commerce in India; Volume 1, No. 6; October, 1994.

12. *RBI: Report on Currency and Finance*: Government of India publication; 1993.

13. The Associated Chambers of Commerce and Industry of India: *"Restructuring Indian Industry to meet the Challenges of EC 1992"*; Summary report of proceedings and background paper; 1992.

14. *"India, Germany and the European Community"* Edited by K. B. Lall, H. S. Chopra, Thomas Meyer; Radiant Publishers; 1993.

15. *"India, Germany and the European Community"* Edited by K. B. Lall, H. S. Chopra, Thomas Meyer; Radiant Publishers; 1992.

16. *"India, Germany and the European Community"* Edited by K. B. Lall, H. S. Chopra, Thomas Meyer; Radiant Publishers; 1993.

17. Shanti Jagannathan; *"EC and India in the 1990s - Towards Corporate Synergy"*; Indian Council for Research on International Economic Relations; Indus Publishing Company, New Delhi, 1993.

18. 'European Union - Newsletter of the Delegation of the European Commission in India'; Volume 9, Number 1, September-November 1998.

19. The Economic Times, Friday, September 15, 1995; New Delhi.

Chapter 5

Impact of European Unification on India's Trade : An a Priori Analysis

The European Union (EU), provides the most successful example of regional economic integration in the world today. The EU took a leap forward by its decision to establish a single internal market by the end of 1992; the move, known as 'EU-92', promises to be an event of far reading significance in the economic history of not only the EU but also for the entire world. The 'Unified Europe' will, naturally, also influence the fortunes of the developing countries (the third world) including India.

The 'Unified Europe' was a strategic response of the EU to various developments in its changing internal and external economic, technological and political environment. These developments over the last three decades had considerably undermined the international competitiveness of the member countries and also eroded the EU's economic and technological power base to retain its role for leadership in bio-tech industries in the world [1].

To take up the internal developments first, the moves towards the creation and strengthening of EU did not quite proceed in the way legislated by the founding fathers and subsequent Heads of the Union. The three Treaties constituting the core of the EU, referred to earlier, "have the same objective, namely, to achieve economic expansion and higher standard of living, through the united efforts of the States and people of Europe, and to work towards the Union. The conjoint function of the three European Communities provides the principal instrument for a supra-national action."

The EU has constantly been evolving to achieve political union. While the difficulties of working towards an economic and ultimately political union were sufficiently recognised by the policy-makers of the EU, in actual practice, the process of smoothening out the nationalistic approach for formulating EU-wide policies for the above objective had entailed growing number of difficulties and delays in the envisaged time schedule. The expansion of the membership from the original 'six' in 1957 to nine in 1973 and to ten in 1981 and further to twelve in 1986 and in 1995 to Fifteen further added to the complexities of forging unity on economic and political fronts.

Experience so far shows that it has been difficult to achieve progress even towards economic union. The EU had decided, in 1957, to form a Single European Common Market (ECM) among the member countries. By 1968, all tariffs on imports from the member countries had been dismantled and a Common External Tariff (CET) was imposed on imports from the extra-EU countries. An year earlier in 1967, in the move towards harmonisation of economic levies, an identical system of taxes on goods and services, namely, Value Added Tax (VAT) had been introduced in all member countries.

However, the markets of the member states were still working as separate units and the economies of scale, which an integrated market could bring about, were not in sight. Free circulation of goods or services within the Union was being hampered in view of the various border controls, differing technical standards and nationally oriented public procurement policies.

The GDP, which grew at a rate of 5.1 per cent between 1958 and 1973, dropped to 2.2 per cent between 1973 and 1980 during the oil crisis and further down to 1.8 per cent after 1980. The initial dynamism with which the Union had started, appeared to have been exhausted and Europe was slowly receding from the forefront among the industrialised countries giving way to Japan and USA in terms of economic advancement, employment and new technologies [2].

The increasing globalisation of international business and innovations in technology, accompanied by a further integration of international financial markets, resulted in providing primacy to the degree of international competitiveness as a force for determining patterns of world trade and payments. The hub of economic activity in the world shifted further away from the EU and the North America to the countries of the Asia-Pacific region including Japan and the Newly Industrialised Countries (NIC) of the region like South Korea, Singapore, Taiwan and Hongkong.

The EU countries faced "eurosclerosis" recording lower growth, higher unemployment and greater technological obsolescence compared to other OECD countries and the NICs. It was clear that if Europe was to get back into race, something radical had to be done.

It was recognised that only a truly single EU-wide internal market could provide the necessary strategic response to reverse the process of "Eurosclerosis", and to restore a degree of economic and technological leadership to the EU in the world by improving the international competitiveness of its products and services.

The Dublin summit of December, 1984, took stock of the situation. The Brussels summit of March, 1985 asked the Commission to draw up a detailed programme with a specific time-table to achieve a Single Market by 1992. A White Paper was produced in June, 1985. The Single European Act (SEA), which was agreed to by the then twelve and came into force in July 1987 gave a political impetus and a more specific legal mandate for its completion.

Internal dimensions of Project 1992 had been analysed in a study - published at the beginning of 1988 by Paulo Ceccihini - 'The European Challenge - 1992' under the auspices of the European Commission. It had been estimated that four major consequences could arise from the combined impact of the elimination of barriers and the subsequent boost to competition; these are:

(1) Significant reduction in costs, resulting from improved exploitation by companies of economies of scale in production and business organisations;

(2) Improved efficiency within companies, widespread industrial organisation and rationalisation, and a setting of prices closer to costs of production under the pressure of more competitive markets;

(3) Adjustment between industries on the basis of a fuller play of comparative advantage in an integrated market;

(4) Increased innovation, new business processes and products generated by the dynamics of the internal market.

In more specific terms, the study quantified that the Internal Market programme will result in a one time addition of 200 billion ECUs in the Union's GDP and an all round reduction in prices to the tune of 6 per cent. Although there may be some job losses over the short-term, but if the Union adopted the necessary macro-economic policies and other associated measures, the gains could be as much as 7 per cent and the employment opportunities may increase by 5 per cent without inflationary risks or deterioration of public finances.

The above mentioned changes throw up a challenge as well as other opportunities for India and if export expansion has to be promoted, the impact of recent developments in Europe should not be underestimated.

In early 1990s, one quarter of India's exports went to the EU and another 16 per cent to Eastern Europe. Thus, about 40 per cent of India's foreign trade was done with Europe with the Western share increasing and that of the East declining. This tendency will become even more visible as a result of the actual economic crisis in Eastern Europe. Therefore, the Single Market of the EU will have some impact on India and its impact would increase during the 1990s and later.

While discussing the implications of the Single European Market for India, it must be remembered that the impact of European integration will vary from one sector to another. However, in most of these sectors, there are a number of common elements of impact. The implications for India and the necessary steps to be taken could be summarised as follows:

(1) Over 70 per cent of India's exports to the EU comprise consumer goods, such as cotton textiles and garments, handicrafts, carpets, leather and leather products, gems and jewellery, marine products, tea, coffee, cashews, spices and other food items. The market for these items is expected to expand with the predicted higher economic growth of the Union finding reflection in higher rate of consumption. This will apply, in particular, to items in which domestic production in the Union does not

exist or is inadequate. As is obvious from the above Table 5.1 also, consumer goods account for more than 70 per cent of India's exports to EU.

(2) In textiles, India would stand to benefit if the restraint levels for the restricted categories are Union-wide and are not apportioned into member states level quotas. This should enable us to optimise the quota utilisation and thereby increase our export earnings. It needs to be pointed out, however, that the textile sector has always been governed by special provisions and much would depend on the manner in which arrangements are finally worked out.

(3) Restructuring of industry, the formation of larger trading companies through mergers and acquisitions etc. in the Single Market would result in bigger supply orders. This would call for parallel restructuring and export orientation of concerned industrial sectors in India so as to generate export surpluses of larger magnitude on a competitive, continuing and dependable basis. We need to set machinery for close monitoring of trends of production and competition in the Union [3].

(4) In the internal market any Union company, including European subsidiaries of foreign firms, will be able to freely tender for government contracts in any other member states. This can open larger possibilities for Indian exports through Indian subsidiaries or even through local companies bidding for such tenders, provided they have a strong Indian presence or have traditionally been importing from India. Sectors such as public health, water supply, sanitation and communications, could be the relevant areas in this regard where potential opportunities could arise.

(5) Enhanced global competition and the imperative of increasing cost efficiency could lead to a search for production/servicing facilities even outside the Union, particularly in labour-intensive sectors. On a selective basis, India's opportunities could be explored in the fields of textiles and clothing, automobile components, gems and jewellery, machine tools and hand tools, electronic goods and components, software development, processed food products etc.

(6) Progressive harmonisation of technical standards is likely to bring about marked expansion, especially in engineering, electrical and electronic goods and other industrial products. To take advantage of this

development, Indian industry will need to adapt and realign its production patterns which have so far been linked to limited traditional markets like the U.K. Evaluation of progress in harmonisation must be closely monitored. India needs to ensure that its standards are in tune with the standards of the Union.

(7) The harmonisation in relation to environmental, health, safety and labelling requirements would also considerably increase opportunities for Union-wide exports, particularly in agro-based processed items. Non-compliance with strict health and safety regulations has in the past led to a severe decline in India's exports of agricultural products like de-oiled cakes. Considerable effort in planning and co-ordination is called for to respond to uniform standards in these fields in the case of sea-food, processed food items, spices, cashew, fresh fruits, vegetable and flowers, tea and coffee.

(8) There would be areas where India's exports may come in direct competition with Union products. The general lowering of prices (6 per cent) that is expected as a result of more efficient means of production, distribution and marketing, could have a negative effect on some of India's exports where demand may be price-elastic. Examples in this sector would be certain categories in textiles, engineering products, chemicals and pharmaceuticals, leather goods and electronic components. India would also have to contend with competition from a restructured and expanded industrial and manufacturing base in member states like Spain, Portugal, Greece, and neighbouring countries with preferential links and arrangements like Turkey and the EFTA countries.

(9) To benefit from the anticipated market expansion on the one hand and to meet the enhanced competition on the other, India needs to develop an export strategy based on upgradation of technology, product adaptation to changing market requirements and special efforts to achieve cost reduction through higher capacity utilisation. Special attention would also need to be paid to factors such as quality conformance, strict adherence to delivery schedules, good packaging and reduction of the lead time between order and delivery.

(10) India is suffering from the inherent disadvantages due to the small size and limited financial resources of Indian companies; even companies of big business houses like the Tatas and Birlas, say, in the field of leather,

sea food, etc. have individually only limited marketing operations. By and large, products like tea, tobacco, coffee are being exported in bulk only to be blended, packaged and marketed with huge value additions by European companies. Indian companies need to improve packaging. In certain selected areas it would be advantageous for Indian companies to enter into joint ventures and tie-ups for blending, packaging and distribution with European firms which have Union-wide and world-wide distribution network.

(11) In regard to the above mentioned factors, a closer co-ordination is needed between the Ministry of Commerce and the Ministry of Industry so that policies made by the former can be implemented effectively.

(12) Such a co-ordination would also facilitate timely dissemination of information to concerned Export Promotion Councils. The efficient functioning of the Export Promotion Councils, in particular, will benefit from a thorough review.

(13). The Single European Market would also have some impact on India's imports where the European Union has the single largest share. They may, on the one hand, become more competitive vis-à-vis other suppliers, namely the USA, Japan and the EFTA countries. On the other hand, the development of large monopolies and cartels in the Union could reduce our bargaining leverage. Further disadvantages could result from the evolving competition laws in the Union which could eliminate the state or other subsidies which are now available from individual member states to some of the exporters.

(14) Electronics, telecommunications and information, engineering are emerging as promising fields for Indian exports to the integrated Union market. It was estimated that the market demand in the EU for electronic hardware may be of the order of US $ 200 billion and for computer software and services US $ 70 million in the mid-90s. India's share in this market was negligible in the early 90s. As the Indian computer software and electronic industry develops, it should pay special attention to expanding Union demand through the establishment of marketing network, anticipating technology trends and establishment of software centre in India with dedicated links in India and Europe.

(15) There is need for a single trade centre in one of the EU's leading commercial centres, co-ordinating export promotion activities of various trading bodies and Export Promotion Councils. Frankfurt or London would be most suitable places. Isolated and often ill-co-ordinated functioning of foreign branch offices of various Export Promotion Councils, TDA, CEI and other bodies has led to a lot of wasteful effort in the past.

(16) It is necessary and important that legitimate concerns of our trade and industry will need to be systematically examined and, where appropriate, communicated to the EU authorities. For this purpose, a division under a joint secretary should be created in the Ministry of Commerce. It should include director or deputy secretary level officers from the Ministries of External Affairs and Industry.

(17) In the Single Market business firms would inevitably require a Pan-European service from their banks. Indian banks operating in the Union would be at a disadvantage unless they can offer similar services either by opening branches or setting up co-operative facilities with prominent European banks, perhaps preferably those that have branches in India.

Many foreign banks have converted their branches in the Union into subsidiaries, in order to avoid the application of the reciprocity clause. Indian banks operating in the Union must keep track of this development and examine, in consultation with the Reserve Bank of India, the question of conversion of their branches into subsidiaries. Banks registered as subsidiaries of Indian banks would have full flexibility to adjust to the widened market opportunities, whereas banks registered as branches of Indian banks would (despite the assurances of the Commission that developing countries interests would be protected) probably face severe constraints both in expanding the number of their outlets geographically and in the range of services they can provide.

Since the Indian banks are functioning with a relatively small capital base and offer only a limited range of services, the rationale for having a large number of Indian banks present in Europe becomes weaker. The Reserve Bank of India needs to give thought in enhancing the financial strength of banks operating in the Union by sufficiently increasing their capital base as well as by converting their branches into subsidiaries. If this is not done, the danger is that other Union-wide banking institutions may, in competition, make inroads even into the limited market in which Indian banks have been operating.

Since the Unification, permission to establish branches/subsidiaries in the EU has to be cleared not only by the regulators in the home countries but also by the European Commission. This aspect needs to be taken into account by the Government of India in terms of its own policy to grant access to European banks in India.

(18) Tourism has emerged as the world's third largest industry after the oil and motor-vehicles. In early 90s, it was estimated that economic growth in the EU of 2.5 to 3 per cent results in about 6.5 per cent increase in expenditure on travel. Thus, the relative share of this sector in the EU economy is expected to continue to increase both in terms of incoming as well as outgoing traffic.

Single Market has spurred foreign travel even from the relatively not so developed countries of the EU like Spain, Portugal and Greece, which did not have well-established outward travel trade. India needs to pay attention to this aspect and initiate a Union-wide effort to promote tourism to India. India should seek to project itself as a desired destination of the European traveller well before this trend towards greater travel manifests itself.

(19) The establishment of important freight hubs at selected European airports together with the removal of barriers and frontier checks on intra-European cargo are presenting a variety of new options to the expansion of freight services from India and the number of destinations that these services can reach. It is necessary to monitor the developments in this sector, identify European freight hubs which would best meet our export cargo requirements and establish air cargo routes to and from these hubs as well as ground infrastructure therein, including warehousing facilities.

(20) As an associated measure to the internal market programme, an ambitious programme of co-operation in the field of science and technology among the Union member states has already been implemented. The technological base in Europe has become increasingly sophisticated and advanced as a consequence of the R & D initiatives launched by the Union in the form of various projects such as ESPRIT (European Strategic Programme for Research and Development in Information and Technology), RACE (Research and Development in Advanced

Communication Technology for Europe) and BRITE (Advanced Technology for Traditional Industries). The Union has been quite forthcoming in offering co-operative projects in this sphere to third countries including India. This offer should be put to optimal use and the Department of Science and Technology should examine the Union's programme and pursue proposals of interest and relevance to India [4].

(21) The Union has embarked upon a common environmental policy since 1973. The focus has gradually changed from remedial action to preventive measures against pollution and the priority areas have been water, air, noise and chemicals.

The policy is likely to gain in importance and influence decisions in other areas. The developments in this regard should be reported extensively by the Missions and monitored by the Department of Environment in order to identify sectors in which Indo-EU collaboration and co-operation could be worked out, particularly in areas such as waste management, bio-technology and noise pollution.

Keeping in mind the above mentioned reactions of United Europe on India's exports, Indian Industry needs to be prepared accordingly.

An analysis of the Indian industry's attitudes and preparedness towards significant changes taking place in Europe, in the wake of the formation of a Single European Market, is given below. Indian companies can be effective in the European Union if they adopt the following measures:

- Consortium or horizontal alliances to bid for large projects under the EU's common procurement schemes or even large purchasing orders placed by mega companies in EU in order to minimise resource constraints faced by individual Indian companies.

- Co-operation with government agencies so that the government and industry work as partners to manage a joint challenge.

- Professional management which places emphasis on research, forecasting, advance planning, market analysis, restructuring of production processes whenever necessary, technological upgradation, warehousing, packaging, product liability, public relations, brand establishment etc.

- System for removing supply side problems which affect delivery schedules.

- Cost-effectiveness, with particular reference to foreign currency earning and expenditure, for quality control.

The above mentioned five-point criteria were used in the analysis of the Indian industry's firm-level preparedness for EU 1992.

5.1 Mergers and Acquisitions

With the creation of an integrated market, the European Industry has witnessed more and more mergers and acquisitions. Multinationals in the US, Japan and non-EU countries have also acquired EU companies.

Logically, mergers and acquisitions should lead to large orders or cancellation of orders. In practice, the result from the Indian perspective is less dramatic but more complicated.

- It is believed that in Indian private sector companies effect of mergers and acquisitions has been marginal. Indian companies have a negligent market share and there is enough scope to increase it irrespective of mergers.

Secondly, mergers have mostly affected the high-technology areas whereas Indian companies are in low-technology areas.

- Indian companies are in general agreement that mergers are relevant in practice to the extent that the personnel dealing with them are affected. If the personnel in the merged companies are promoted, or not transferred to other divisions, they may place larger orders but if they are transferred to other divisions in the new company, Indian companies have to build contracts with the new personnel.

- A few companies believe that mergers will improve prices. One company reported increase in unit value realisation by 15 percent in the 1990 calendar year on account of the apprehension of its agents that the contract might be transferred to another Europe-wide merged agency.

- In engineering goods and software, mergers can create a R &D market provided Indian companies can supply quality research products at low prices (possible in software) e.g. Nixdorf take-over by Siemens has made cash available to the former for R & D which was not earlier possible. Indian companies can get business in the new R & D markets.

- According to some executives, demand for Indian products will go down on account of mergers as technology gap will increase and financial restructuring will take place.

- At the operational level, types of products and types of European companies affected by mergers are important. With regard to bulk commodities, if Indian companies are dealing with nation-level companies and such companies are taken over by continent-level companies, Indian exporters will be benefited. This is because continent-wide orders will be placed and national brand names will be replaced by multinational brand names. But in the case of consumer products, take-over may not make such difference as nation-level companies will be allowed to operate as separate units of the merged entity because of the local brand name advantage.

Some companies have responded that mergers can affect agency business where principals are European. If there were two agencies of two separate companies, now there would be only one agency. One multiple-product company has reported additions to its agency business in some product lines while losses in some others because of the mergers of its principals.

5.2 Consortium Approach

There is a general impression that unification of the EU market will result in large orders for Indian products which individual companies will not be able to satisfy. It will, therefore, be essential for companies to engage in a horizontal alliance to be able to supply large quantities and negotiate profitable terms with the European giants. Many trade associations, government and the research community have, therefore, shown interest in the consortium approach; but this approach did not find favour at the operational level. All the companies covered by the present survey expressed strong opposition to the consortium approach in practice, though some of them appreciated it at the hypothetical level. A few reasons are offered for the corporate opposition to horizontal alliances. The prominent of them are as below:

- Generally, Indian business companies like to have the sole control of a project. It is not part of the Indian business culture to share power. Where a company has inadequate supply position, it prefers to expand ancillary units under its own umbrella instead of entering into arrangement with another large company.

- Most export benefits go to traders. Therefore, manufacturers like to have their own trading operations instead of forming alliances with trading companies. It is important to recognise that most Indian companies export for various benefits they receive from the government. In a consortium, there would be problem about the entitlement to the export incentives and benefits from its sale in the open market.

- Companies believe that in the specific Unified Europe context, expansion of supply capability through a consortium is not relevant. Each Indian company in the EU has such a negligible share in the market that it will be satisfied with two-fold or three-fold increase in exports to the region which can be achieved without any horizontal alliance. Large companies procure goods from the ancillary sector where the problem is to deliver quantity goods on schedule. The problem is not about size of the supply capability.

- Indian companies think in terms of small-size contracts. There are very few companies with a single export order of more than Rs. 5 or 10 crore for a single product in the EU market. There is not even one private sector company exporting one product of more than Rs. 50 crore to the EU on an annual basis. A majority of the Indian companies presently active in the EU have not shown desire for establishing their brand names in the unified EU. When the vision is so limited there is no question of concepts such as consortium which apply to units with wider vision. There are some exceptions to the general antipathy towards the consortium approach, which are:

1. Confederation of Indian Industry (CII) has set up an office in London which is shared by about 10 companies. It is, in fact, a business centre with common secretarial and market research support.

2. Four leading exporters in software once jointly planned to bid for a large contract in the EU but did not succeed due to differences in terms of sharing costs and benefits.

5.3 Marketing Strategy

- Executive of the Indian companies believe that the problem is not of market demand but it is of supply and hence marketing strategy has little importance in their plans.

- They are not in favour of undertaking any deliberate effort to expand their market geographically from their present positions of strength to other parts of EU. They are satisfied with current business and at the most they would like to penetrate further in the same markets.

- Exporters of the traditional product categories such as textiles, garments and leather believe that any special marketing strategy or change in their present practices is simply not required.

- Many exporters in engineering and software sectors are in the process of opening or strengthening their own offices in EU to keep themselves abreast of legal and marketing developments.

- Very few companies in India have a clear marketing strategy in the first phase, they plan to have tie-ups for marketing assembling and packaging in EU. In the second phase, they may buy EU brand names. In the third phase, they will try to establish their own brand names and give up the present sourcing job.

In brief, Indian companies do not place much emphasis on scientific analysis of strategies of companies from the competing countries, creating an impression that they are not serious about marketing in EU.

5.4 Warehousing

Warehousing has become an important factor in marketing process in EU. Buyers in Western Europe do not keep a long inventory and are used to getting supplies of their requirement at a day's notice. India's distant location from Europe is a disadvantage in this respect. Not only does shipping take a long time but also non-availability of shipping space on a short notice from Indian ports to ports in Europe and customs formalities are regular problem areas which make it difficult for Indian firms to keep their delivery schedules with their buyers in EU. Companies from South Korea, Taiwan, Hong Kong, Brazil etc. have made use of the warehousing facilities available in Rotterdam, Hamburg etc. Many Indian exporters also report that their importers try to persuade them to stock goods in warehouses in EU.

With this background, the government has secured warehousing space in Rotterdam which accounts for 66 percent of goods originating from India to EU. Engineering Export Promotion Council (EEPC) has been appointed as a nodal agency to manage it. The costing is done in such a manner that the government shares some cost of warehousing. But industry sources suggest that exporters are not satisfied with the degree of financial assistance and would like more of it, particularly on account of pre-shipment credit. As a result, only about a dozen companies take benefit of the warehouse.

In some cases the nature of product is such that it does not require warehousing. Where companies believe that warehousing at different stations will be required and cost of such an exercise would be prohibitive, they would depend on their buyers or agents to arrange warehousing.

5.5 Packaging

Indian companies have not yet been affected by EU's regulations on packaging though it may assume importance after 1995. Some companies have reported benefits from the European unification. Earlier, different labels were required for different markets within EU, now only one label and one type of packaging will be adequate. As Indian companies only export to one or two countries in EU and do not want to expand markets horizontally, the question of common or different packaging is not very relevant.

5.6 Product Liability

So far, product liability was an important factor in the United States. With the integration of EU and harmonisation of standards and insurance procedures, product liability has assumed importance in the EU. It is compulsory for end-use products, but it is also required for such intermediate products which affect the life of the final product. The General Insurance Corporation sets insurance premium rates for Indian exporters [5].

EXIM Bank of India had a programme to support exporters financially to the extent of 20 to 50 percent of the premium cost under its market entry programme. Eight companies in the early 90s took benefit of the EXIM Bank's scheme. Such a low number of beneficiaries was due to the fact that the scheme was a new one and also to the fact that very few companies, at least in the organised sector, were in product liability mould because few companies only were exporting products which were directly put to end-use in the EU market.

5.7 Distribution

The tendency in India is not to treat distribution in EU as exporter's problem. It is left to importers and agents. But, the role of the agent has changed due to unification of EU and the consequent new rules and market practices. Earlier, an agent was merely expected to generate or promote sales. Henceforth, in addition to sales promotion, an agent is expected to obtain product liability insurances, certificates of standards from testing laboratories and crucial information on changes in tariff and other business aspects. The agent will, therefore, not merely have to sell but also advice the Indian exporter what to sell and advice the buyers about what they are buying. Companies are, therefore, thinking in terms of increasing their direct presence in the EU.

There are also reports of Indian companies planning to buy EU companies, though details are not available as companies do not want to reveal this information. In this case, Indian companies will be responsible for distribution in EU. Companies in India believe that it is necessary to have offices in the UK, Germany and Belgium unlike East Asian/Japanese companies which have tried to buy companies or establish offices in 'soft' countries like Spain, Portugal, etc. There are reports of Indian companies also planning to buy offices or companies in 'soft' countries but they are only a few.

Many companies plan to continue with the present system of different distributors for different countries because they are in consumer products for which patterns vary from one country to another.

5.8 Joint Ventures

Indian companies are not inclined in favour of entering into joint ventures (JVs) in EU for the following reasons:

- It is possible to have more control through wholly owned subsidiaries rather than JVs and, where companies cannot afford subsidiaries, they would deal with buyers themselves or through agents.

- The experience of many companies is that in a JV an European company virtually gets monopoly control over an Indian company's operations which may be used to the disadvantage of the latter. Also, it is part of the Indian business culture to have sole control over a project.

But there are certain provisions:

- Some companies prefer JVs in India with European companies with buy-back arrangements.

- Some companies recommended JVs in Eastern Europe to facilitate entry into the EU since they believed that in future Eastern Europe will be amalgamated with the EU.

- A few companies favoured JVs in Turkey or Cyprus to ease entry into EU.

- A few companies also favoured JVs in Mauritius (i) to take advantage of LOME Convention trade preferences and (ii) to have access to South Africa as trade with it was expected to be allowed soon.

In reality, only a few companies had actively planned JVs in Mauritius. Some of those who had JVs in Mauritius have closed them down because of practical difficulties in managing the operation such as transport and communication problems were more than potential Lome Convention benefits.

5.9 Diversification

As a result of the Single European market taken in conjunction with certain other trends, the following type of diversification in India's product-mix has been considered.

- General trading companies are entering into granite exports specifically for the EU market.

- In the gems and jewellery sector, companies are shifting from diamond to jewellery exports.

- In software, companies favour a shift from bodyshopping to programme exports but the latter .depends on sound telecommunication facilities.

- In engineering, CII as well as operating companies believe that in future Indian companies must concentrate on the lower bracket in the technology ladder and in the long run attempt to move to a higher level. If India addresses the higher level of the technology ladder immediately, it will not have much scope in EU where mergers and acquisitions have led to an upgradation of the continent's technological edge. An ideal product-mix for India would be:

- intermediate technology areas (castings and forgings, handtools, machine tools)

- automotive components (on OE basis)

- software.

5.10 Standards

Different technical standards in different EU member states had proved to be big obstacles for Indian goods in the past. Manufacturers had to pursue different product lines for the different member states thereby denying themselves benefits of economies of scale and R & D effort on a streamlined basis. These barriers were reflected in differences between member states on account of mandatory technical regulations, standards and type testing and certification.

The EU 1992 process had assigned prime importance to technical harmonisation and standards. There was a three-tier approach towards standardisation.

(i) Minimum harmonisation of member states regulations.

(ii) Creation of harmonised European standards by European Standardisation bodies.

(iii) Mutual recognition of national standards in the interim period.

The issue of standards has been a point of contention between the EU and the developing countries. On the one hand, the biggest type of the Single Market programme is based on the harmonisation of standards and the technical regulations across the EU, paving the way for the emergence of "European" standards and single testing and certification procedures leading to substantial cost reductions. Developing countries, on the other hand, have been expressing fears over standards being used as a non-tariff barrier against exports to the EU.

The EU-India standards and quality programme is a major component of bilateral co-operation. From modest beginnings in 1987, as essentially an information exchange action, the standards programme has over the years grown both in content and coverage. It includes the modernisation of Indian testing laboratories, the setting up of a National Accreditation Scheme to international norms, and the introduction of education in quality in engineering colleges.

The introduction of ISO-9000 standards has been an important step for India, which is meant to assess manufacturing processes and not merely the specifications of the final product.

As per ISO-9000 norms, quality systems as installed and strictly adhered to by a company from the stage of acquiring a contract, to design, production testing and commissioning are examined and approved by an internationally recognised agency.

Under the scheme of Harmonisation of Standards, 142 Indian standards had been harmonised with EN Standards in 1995. Some companies such as Kirloskar Cummins, Sundaram Fasteners, Ralliwolf, WS Industries and Bharat Forge have already obtained ISO-9000 certificates. In July 1995, Eastern Medikit Ltd., which is India's first I.V. Cannula producing company, obtained ISO-9001 certificate from the National Accreditation of Certification Bodies [6].

In March 1995, under Quality Training, sixty Indian officers belonging to various government and private agencies had been trained to become qualified assessors by Batalas, U.K. A further batch of five Indian officers were trained as lead assessors.

The emergence of European standards is probably the single most important repercussion of the 1992 market integration for third countries. Common EU standards is a major issue for Indian firms exporting goods. As pointed out earlier also, EU-India standards and quality programme is a major component of bilateral co-operation. As in 1995, it included the modernisation of Indian testing laboratories, the setting up of a National Accreditation Scheme to international norms and the introduction of education in quality in engineering colleges.

Regarding the modernisation of laboratories, three key areas were pinpointed - automotive sector, domestic electrical appliances and processed food. The assistance concerns transfer of technical know-how to establish modern installations and personnel training with a view to giving them a knowledge of testing procedures and enabling them to operate and maintain installations according to internationally accepted norms so that testing is done indigenously.

The issue of standards needs to be tackled first on the domestic front. If Indian companies are to gear up to European standards, it is absolutely vital to tighten domestic quality assurance requirements. Therefore, mandatory quality assurance systems and homologation facilities should be set up for the domestic market as a first step.

The EU has also advised the Indian government on a National Accreditation Scheme for testing and certifying products in India. Under this programme, a five member European expert group recommended a comprehensive NAS, the essential elements of which are :

The National Quality Council (NQC) would be the apex body for operating the scheme in India. It should be an autonomous body, under which five separate bodies will function:

(a) A National Accreditation Board for the certification of product and quality management systems.

(b) A National Accreditation Board for the certification of laboratories.

(c) A Board for the registration of quality related personnel.

(d) A National Enquiry Service of standards and conformity assessment.

(e) A national awareness campaign [7].

The EU would be assisting India in training its experts. Foreseen for a duration of five years, this programme is intended to mobilise 50 percent of finances required from industry and 50 percent from government sources. The European Expert Group (EEG) has made a number of recommendations such as harmonisation of the standardisation activities of different Indian agencies, adoption of European standards as Indian standards, an effective information service on standards and technical regulations, product certification for export markets etc.

Needless to say, acting upon these recommendations urgently is of prime importance. A coherent national policy needs to be evolved for quality certification and for developing indigenous institutions for certification. This would, then, pave the way for an early negotiation with the European Union of mutual recognition of test certificates, whereby products certified in India would be accepted in the EU.

5.11 Government-Industry Relations

Many companies have called for a review and restructuring of government-industry relations to be able to provide an effective response to the integrated market.

Assessment of Indian Missions in EU:

- Many companies do not use Indian trade missions, while some believe that there cannot be a general opinion on Embassies and Missions in EU as some tend to be good and some tend to be ineffective depending on the personnel.

- Some companies find that Indian missions in EU are ineffective while some companies believe that all Indian missions in EU are effective and helpful provided the corporate sector knows how to use them.

There is no need for India to feel intimidated by the magnitude of the Single Market or its importance in world trade. Outside the developed world, India will remain one of the world's two or three largest and still expanding import market. India's principal needs are advanced technology and capital and the very size and range of India's requirements will command the competing attention of rival suppliers. This would give India sufficient bargaining strength.

If India has to expand its export market, then, as stated above, Indian firms must prepare themselves according to changes that have been brought about as a result of unification.

Notes

1. K.B. Lall, H.S. Chopra, Thomas Meyer (Eds): *"India, Germany and the European Community"* Radiant Publishers, New Delhi; 1993.

2. Report of Ambassador's Committee on 'The Single European Market 1992 and India', Printed in Belgium; 1993.

3. The Associated Chambers of Commerce and Industry of India; *"Restructuring Indian Industry to Meet the Challenges of EC 1992"* A Summary Report.

4. Report of the Ambassador's Committee on 'The Single European Market 1992 and India; Printed in Belgium, 1993.

5. Sundeep Waslekar, "*Response of Indian Firms to Meet the Challenges of the Single European Market*"; RIS Discussion papers, April, 1992.

6. The Hindustan Times, July, 18, 1995.

7. "*The European Union and India - Partnership in Progress*"; Delegation of the European Commission; March, 1995.

Chapter 6

Birth of Euro and its Impact on India's Trade with EU

6.1 Single Currency : Euro

Europe's dream of monetary union became a reality on Thursday midnight (31st December, 1998) when eleven countries swept away their monetary borders to launch a single currency throwing down a challenge to the mighty dollar. These 11 nations locked their currencies together to form the euro and create an economic giant whose boundaries stretch from beyond the Arctic circle to the shores of the Mediterranean.

The euro's birth is being hailed as a historic turning point in international finance and is arguably the greatest single step in the drive to create a united Europe from the ruins of World War II. "This December 31, 1998, will be one of the greatest dates in the history of the 20th century", said French Finance Minister Dominique Strausskahn.

At a ceremony in Brussels, European Union finance ministers unanimously adopted exchange rates at which 11 currencies were locked to the new money, the euro from January 1, 1999. The 11 euro zone members - Britain, Denmark, Sweden and Greece remain on the sidelines for now - are taking one of the most extraordinary steps in Europe's history, forging a common future as an integrated economic power when, little over 50 years ago, many were enemies on the battlefield.

Some 50 billion coins and 13 billion notes will be needed to replace existing currency and they will not be ready until 2002. The euro-zone - grouping Germany, France, Austria, Belgium, Finland, Ireland, Italy, Luxembourg, the Netherlands, Portugal and Spain - will account for nearly a fifth of world economic output and trade and its significance was immediately apparent.

Greece, which was deemed economically unfit to join the euro now, reconfirmed its desire to be ready in two years and said its drachma would be pegged to the euro. Denmark also announced a formal link between its crown and the new currency, as for their currencies did non-EU members from central Europe to West Africa.

Economic and monetary union has been a recurring ambition of the European Union since the late 1960's, because it promises both currency stability and a strong advance towards the integration of Europe.

The Madrid Council of December 1995 decided upon a three-phase scenario for the introduction of the single currency. Under the Treaty on European Union the third stage of economic and monetary union is to begin on January 1, 1999. Subsequently, the exchange rates among participating countries will be locked and a common currency, the EURO, will be gradually introduced in those member states which have qualified for EMU.

Originally, the EC Treaty called the new currency the 'ecu' (European Currency Unit). The *ecu* has served as the unit of account between the member states since the introduction of the European Monetary System.

ECU is a basket of currency made up of the weighted values of the currencies of the EU states. That is why, in recent years, the value of the ecu has declined against the stable currencies of some countries.

The new currency 'EURO' will not be a basket currency and will tend to take the value of the most stable currencies. It is also tended to be a symbol of European Identity. For these reasons, the Heads of State or Government agreed, in December 1995, that it should be called the 'Euro'. One advantage of the name is that it is short. It can also be written in the same way in all European languages. The 'EURO' is further divided into 100 cents.

The transition to the euro will be smooth. The two main reasons being: (1) The changeover is backed by solid legal guarantees and (2) The financial markets are carefully preparing for the creation of the euro.

In 1996, the Commission proposed legislation on the legal status of the euro. This was approved by the Heads of state or government at Dublin in December in the same year and was ratified by the Amsterdam European Council in June, 1997. It is based on two key principles:

- First principle: the euro will be the single currency of participating countries from January 1, 1999. National currencies in these countries will continue to be legal tender until 2002, but only as sub-units of the euro. During the transitional phase between 1999 and 2002, use of the euro will neither be obligatory, nor prohibited. But the euro will be heavily used from the start. Monetary policy and the financial markets will switch to the euro on that date. It will also be used by many large companies, especially those with substantial export business.

- Second principle: the continuity of contracts. The introduction of the euro will have no impact on contracts in force, whether they are denominated in national currency or in ecu. The only change will be in the reference currency unit. This principle naturally applies to contracts covered by legislation in an EU country.

6.1.1 Will Euro Be a Stable Currency ?

The stability of the euro will result from three factors:

- the conditions laid down for its creation are strict and will be respected;

- it will be managed by an independent central bank;

- strict regulations, with no equivalent anywhere in the world, will guarantee lasting, sound public finances in Europe.

A. The Conditions in the Maastricht Treaty will be strictly respected: The Maastricht Treaty set a number of conditions which the member states have to meet in order to take part in economic and monetary union.

And these are rules of economic good sense. Inflation, deficits and government debt have to be brought under control, interest rates must be similar and countries must have experienced a period of exchange rate stability.

The majority of countries in European Union will meet the conditions laid down by the Treaty. Inflation is under control and should not exceed 2.2 per cent in 1997 and 1998. Government deficits, which averaged 6.3 per cent of GDP in 1993 was 3 per cent or less in a large number of member states in 1997. Long term rates have converged towards the lowest level in the member states, to stand at an average of 6 per cent in 1997. Lastly, since 1995 Europe has enjoyed great exchange rate stability.

When it comes to recommending the initial participants in the euro, the Commission will examine whether economic convergence is sustainable. The decision will be taken on the basis of actual economic data for 1997, but also in the light of the 1998 budgets and future economic forecasts. To sum up, the euro will be under-pinned by sound fundamentals.

B. The euro will be managed by an independent central bank: The ECB will be totally independent. The members of its governing bodies will be appointed by the Heads of State or Government for a non-renewable eight year term of office. The Treaty requires the ECB to manage the euro with the primary objective of price stability.

C. The stability and growth pact: This is the key to the credibility and future stability of the euro. It will guarantee a policy of sound management of public finances within the euro area.

The main principles are:

- Members States should aim for balance in their public finances in the medium term. This balance is expected around 2002 if the present rate of budgetary consolidation is maintained.

- The stability and growth pact stipulates that any member State exceeding a public deficit ceiling of 3 per cent of GDP risks being penalised. It will have to lodge a deposit, which will be converted into a fine if corrective measures are not taken. The level of these fines - up to 0.5 per cent of GDP - will have a very dissuasive effect.

Respecting the conditions in the Maastricht Treaty, the creation of a large and liquid financial market, the independent European Central Bank and the implementation of the stability and growth pact will make the euro a stable, credible and therefore attractive currency.

6.1.1.1 Role of Euro: The role of the euro can be expected to develop as a reserve currency, an investment currency and a transaction currency:

- Firstly, the euro as a reserve currency. The composition of official foreign exchange assets has already become much more diverse since the beginning of the 1970s. The dollar accounted for 76 per cent of central bank reserves is 1973. That proportion is now 61 per cent. Over the same period, the share taken by European currencies (pound sterling, German mark, French franc and Dutch guilder) has increased sharply from 14 per cent to 20 per cent. The euro will account for a higher proportion of central banks' reserves than European currencies today.

- The euro as an international portfolio currency. The euro will benefit from both the substitution effect and a size effect:

Firstly, the substitution effect: it will replace currencies which are already being used increasingly for international financial deals. The European currencies' share of international bond portfolios rose from 20 per cent in 1981 to 37 per cent in 1995.

Secondly, the size effect: once it is set up, the bond market in euros should automatically become one of the two largest in the world. All new government debt issues by states belonging to economic and monetary union will be denominated in euros, and many states, including France and Germany, have announced that they will convert the bulk of their outstanding government debt into euros on January 1, 1999. The size and depth of the euro market will contribute to reducing the costs of using the euro to a level close to that of the dollar. This will reinforce the attractiveness of the European currency investors seeking to diversify their financial holdings.

Finally, the *euro as an international transaction currency:*

European companies will use the euro for invoicing trade in the euro-zone. First of all, it will be used in central and eastern European countries.

Most of these countries, which have applied for membership of the Union, have already tied their currencies to the German mark and are trading increasingly with the European Union. Secondly, the euro will be used in Africa where it will replace the French franc as the reference currency for the CFA area.

Finally, it will probably be used as an invoicing currency by Mediterranean countries given their close links with the European Union and the prospect of a Euro Mediterranean free trade area by 2010.

The euro is being introduced in four steps:

Step 1: On May 4, 1998, EU finance ministers fixed the exchange rates of 11 national currencies to one another. The Euro-zone members consist of 11 of the EU's 15 member countries. They are Germany, France, Italy, Luxembourg, Ireland, Netherlands, Finland, Austria, Belgium, Portugal and Spain.

The currencies translate into euros in the following manners:

U.S. Dollar	-	1.122
Deutsche mark	-	1.999
British Pound	-	0.687
French franc	-	6.702
Swiss franc	-	1.670
Italian lira	-	1.972
Dutch guilder	-	2.254
Yen	-	165.1
HK dollar	-	8.698
Singapore dollar	-	1.976

(Source: FTSE International Ltd; Euro rates as on August 12, 1998 calculated by applying GDP weights to euro-zone currencies).

Step 2: January 1, 1999: Exchange rates are set for the euro. European Central Bank takes charge of monetary policy. National currencies remain; stocks and government bonds are denominated in euros; companies can start accounting in euros.

Step 3: January 1, 2002: Euro bank notes are introduced. Retailers and service providers must display prices in euros and national currencies. Business may be done in either currency.

Step 4: July 1, 2002: Euro becomes the only legal tender inside 'Euroland'

For Asia, the effects of the euro will come at two levels. The first, and most immediate, will be at the micro level in trade and finance. Not only will Asian companies and governments have to start thinking and dealing in euros, but a giant new euro market will also present them with new funding choices. That could quickly erode the region's heavy reliance on the dollar.

The second impact will be more far-reaching but harder to gauge. The euro will inevitably change the world's currency mix; over the long term, Europe's new currency will blossom at the expense of both the dollar and the Yen. It will also help Europe grow and make it a more productive place. That means more demand and bigger markets for Asia and the rest of the world's exports- but it could also spark stiffer competition.

Beyond trade, the second near-term effect on Asia and Asian companies will be in finance. Theoretically, European markets should become an even more attractive destination for Asian portfolio investment. The reason being, all European government bonds and all European stocks will be priced in euros. For the first time ever, that will allow fund managers to compare investments across borders on a like for like basis.

Another attraction for Asian companies is Europe's low interest rates. Most economists expect interest rates for euro-denominated bonds to more or less mimic the yield curves of France and Germany- the two core euro countries. Currently, euro rates range from 4.16 per cent on maturities of one year to 5.1 per cent on maturities of 10 years. That's lower than even U.S. Treasury's. The U.S. 52-week bill is paying 5.22 per cent and the 10-years note 5.46 per cent.

The development of euro and dollar bond markets "will allow Asian borrowers to play the two markets off against each other."

6.1.1.2 Advantages of a Single Currency: The advantages of having a single currency are numerous.

- Firstly, a single currency means that travellers across the Community no longer have to change money, while losing money on every transaction, as is currently the case.

- Secondly, exchange margins and commission fees paid to banks will simply disappear. Small businesses in particular will benefit as payments and transfers between member states end up being quicker and more reliable, as well as cheaper.

- Thirdly, for business and consumers, a single currency will also take away the uncertainty about the price for which goods are sold.

- Fourthly, if goods and services are priced in one and the same currency the competitive effect of the single market will be strengthened considerably, much to the community's benefit as a whole. In this way, the single currency will also help stimulate growth and employment.

- Lastly, a move to a common currency will also mean that national governments will have greater influence over each others' economic policies, and therefore over each others' interest rate changes. A single currency will be able to withstand, far more confidently, the pressures which have been put very visibly on separate national currencies by speculators. This would also discourage uncertainty about interest rates.

6.2 Countdown to Euro : Impact of Euro on Global Business

The count down to the formation of European Monetary Union (EMU) and the introduction of a single European currency (Euro) on January 1, 1999 began in 1998. In May 1998, three important events towards formation of the EMU took place. First, the European Central Bank (ECB) came into existence replacing the European Monetary Institute (EMI). Second, the bilateral exchange rates among the "In Currencies" were decided and third, and most important, 11 countries ("In Countries") decided to participate in the EMU.

Europe's first XI Squad for the opening round of the EMU has been named. The line-up for the kick off include Austria, Belgium, Finland, France, Germany, Ireland, Italy, Luxembourg, Netherlands, Spain and Portugal. However, the fitness of some of the players is in question. Belgium and Italy, both still have accumulated government debt of more than twice the convergence limit of 60 per cent of GDP. There are four reserve players of which one is not fully fit (Greece) and three players are reluctant to play (U.K., Denmark and Sweden).

Greece is struggling to meet the exchange rate convergence criteria. The UK and Denmark have both opted out, and Sweden failed to meet the exchange rate fluctuation criteria and in any case said it does not want to play.

The two questions that are being intensely debated regarding the trends once the Euro is in place are : Will the Euro ease out the US Dollar in International trade and finance? Will the Euro be weak, strong, stable or unstable against the USD?

The USD is the king in International trade and finance accounting for 48 per cent of world's trade, 37 per cent of world's debt securities, 50 per cent of developing country debt, 55 per cent of global foreign exchange reserves, and 40 per cent of the foreign exchange market and is the most liquid and acceptable currency. However, it is not a stable currency. The new Euro-land (11 countries) will have nearly 300 million inhabitants accounting for 19.4 per cent of world's GDP and 18.6 per cent of world's trade compared with the US which has a population of 270 million accounting for 19.6 per cent of world's GDP and 16.6 per cent of world's trade, and Japan with a population of 125 million accounting for only 7.7 per cent world's GDP and 8.2 per cent of world's trade. Clearly, the single currency will create an economic block rivalling the US and could challenge the USD over a period of time as an international means of exchange.

Although, the USD has dominated international trade and finance during the past four decades, its share in these transactions has been steadily declining. For example, the USD's share in international private portfolios has declined from 67 per cent in 1981 to 40 per cent in 1996 while the share of European currencies has increased from 13 per cent to 37 per cent and that of Japan has increased from 2 per cent to 12 per cent during the same period. In the international bond market, the share of the USD has declined from 53 per cent in 1981 to 34 per cent in 1996 while the share of European currencies has increased from 20 per cent to 37 per cent and that of Japan has increased from 7 per cent to 16 per cent during the period.

The share of USD in foreign exchange reserves has declined from 80 per cent in 1975 to 50 per cent in the beginning of 1990s. However, its share increased marginally to 55 per cent in 1996 because of capital flight in favour of the USD on account of the German reunification and the road to EMU.

The euro may emerge as a preferred currency compared to the USD if it fulfils two major prerequisites; liquidity and stability. The Euro will be immediately an intervention and reserve currency by central banks. All central banks will have to build their foreign exchange reserves in Euro. Asian central banks may use the Euro as a reserve and intervention currency, and gradually sell off the USD. The key question is whether the Euro will be used in Asia as a trade invoicing currency. This will largely depend on the pattern of trade between Asian countries and European countries and on the stability of the Euro vis-a-vis the USD.

Will the Euro be strong, weak, stable or unstable? In the US, the growth rate was expected to contract to 1.6 per cent in the last quarter of 1998 from 3 per cent during the first half of the year whereas in Euroland, the GDP growth has increased to 2.5 per cent in 1997 compared to 1 per cent in the previous year. The upswing is becoming firmer. growth is picking up, unemployment is beginning to fall and budget deficits are under control. Furthermore, the DM and the Ff. have strengthened by about 65 per cent against the USD since the beginning of 1998. All these economic fundamentals suggest that the euro will be strong and a stable currency at the outset.

The long-term strength and stability of the euro will depend on three factors: the sustainability of the EMU and the credibility of the ECB, the macroeconomic policies and the relative cyclical position of the USA versus Europe and most importantly the policy of US towards the USD.

Global business dynamics indicate that monetary integration will place Euro at the centre of world business. The US economy is doing well, the

Far-East has taken a beating and it is in Europe that maximum opportunities will develop. In 1997, Euroland's combined population was 290 million, that of the United States 268 million and of Japan, 126 million.

If in the future, UK and the other remaining EU members join up to the Euro, then Euroland will be a formidable place for companies to operate from (In addition, the EU expansion includes Hungary, Poland, the Czech Republic, Estonia and Slovenia and also Cyprus). Corporate mergers in the last three years have risen from 100 worth $ 16.8 billion to 250 worth $ 250 billion. A prime example is the merger of two giants Daimler Benz and Chrysler. This is especially important for software exporters from India who after their success in the US are devising ways of increasing their presence in Europe.

Companies seeking to enter or consolidate their position in Europe, need to proactively strategise by identifying these developments and the new complex but rewarding scenarios they represent.

India is already a unified union with a single currency. No other country can be as diverse and unified as India and still remain one of the largest and most stable democracies in the world. Probably, Europe has a lot to learn from India in this context. Till now only the US has been the strongest and largest single currency area and now Europe proposes to challenge that.

Major banks such as UBS (Switzerland), ING and ABN-AMRO (The Netherlands), Barclays (UK), Deutsche Bank (Germany) and Stock exchanges like the London Stock Exchange (LSE) and the Deutsche Boerse are vying for the new business that corporates are expecting in the wake of the Euro. For example, the LSE currently has 531 companies from more than 60 different countries and trades in 35 different currencies. The Euro will be the 36th.

Out of 371 foreign banks in the European Union (EU), 82 are in Germany, 81 are in France, 53 in Luxembourg and the remaining in the other eight euroland states.

If the Euro-market is to be pursued, different categories of financial institutions that need to be targeted should be looked into. Radical orientation issues such as what was considered 'export' till yesterday becoming domestic sales from January 1, 1999 will impact IT systems. From an obvious supplier angle the financial industry will be the major user of IT services to offer new features arising out of the Euro.

Post-EMU, companies will not be able to hide behind national boundaries. With the eradication of monetary boundaries within the EMU, there will be strong tendencies for mergers in some cases and consolidation in others. Consequently, the need to review the merged company's IT systems.

It is a combination of many such mergers which determine the potential size of software development business in this segment.

Another industry which will be impacted greatly is the travel industry. Companies such as Eurostar which have train services from London to France, Belgium and the Netherlands via the English Channel have to eliminate cross-border price differences.

Euroland presents multi-dimensional opportunities for companies both within and outside Europe. It will force innovative thinking in both product and service companies. Mergers and acquisitions, extensive cross-cultural business alignments, paradigm shifts and constant change in business attitudes will prevail during the period when the Euro attempts to stabilise.

This will force change in systems within and outside organisations causing large scale modifications to IT systems world-wide. Indian companies need to closely monitor these vibrations in the evolving of new Euro-order and unshackle existing mindsets.

6.3 Effect of Euro on Indian Companies

Our trade relationship with the European Union indicates, as in 1998, that more than 80 per cent of India's exports and imports are invoiced in the dollar and the European Union currencies. India remains a marginal player in both the world trade and in trade with the European Union.

According to available statistics, India's share in the European Union imports from the world is about 0.40 per cent and European Union's share of exports to India in its exports to the world is about 0.47 per cent.

A recent study undertaken by the Reserve Bank of India's (RBI) Department of Economic Affairs and Policy states that there are several commercial policy constraints to trade between India and the European Union.

India currently enjoys the most favoured nation status with the European Union for many of its exports but the average tariffs are always 5-10 percentage points above average. The quantitative restrictions such as quotas force Indian exporters to the European Union. Though member states abolished quotas, the European Union wide quotas remain for some sensitive products exported from India. "Technical barriers in the form of product standards, certification requirements etc., greet many marine product exports to the European Union. And any attempt towards upgrading of products by the Indian exporters invites suspicious investigations of anti-dumping complaints from the European Union", states RBI study.

On the Indian side, plans are afoot to the complete removal of quantitative restrictions in about six years whereas the European Union wants that to be done within a three year period. India's fears that lifting of quantitative restrictions may hit about 180 million agricultural work force and 40 million in textile products industry justify the six years time frame.

European importers, however, perceive that Indian exporters fail to stick to quality standards, delivery time and compliance of contracts.

The German Ambassador to India stated that introduction of the "Euro" currency will benefit India and other countries of the third world considerably by way of reduced risk, lower interest rates, lower transaction costs and improved access to foreign capital.

RBI study further observed that Deutsche mark is actively traded in the Indian market against the US dollar, Japanese Yen and the British Pound. The volatility of the European Union currencies is generally high except Deutsche mark and pound.

One of the major advantages to Indian corporates would be lower borrowing costs (GDR, floating or fixed rate bonds) on account of reduction of multi-currency exposure and abolition of transaction costs.

As a result, Indian corporates are most likely to increase their borrowings in Euro-dominated debt as a broader, deeper and more liquid Euro-financial markets which are going to offer cheaper finances.

There is, however, an urgent need for the corporate to learn and get familiar with some of the technical aspects of Euro-conversions, securities settlements systems, accounting for forward-dated transactions, TARGET and SWIFT message standards, legal issues etc.

At the moment, European Union's share of direct investment flow to India is about 18-19 per cent. In fact, European Union is the largest source of foreign direct investment in terms of actual inflows. India is also one of the largest recipient of European Union's development grants. India is also the Asian country to have accessed the European Investment Bank for a ECU 55 million loan.

A major concern at the moment is India's external debt - whether the external debt will move up post-1999 or go down? The effect of Euro on the debt side depends on whether a strong or a weak euro comes into being.

6.4 Effect of Euro on MNC Subsidiaries Operating in India

The introduction of Euro on January 1, 1999 may lead some of the Indian subsidiaries of the European Union based multi-national corporations to redundancy.

According to an assessment made by the economic division of the External Affairs Ministry of the Government of India, the MNCs of the EU member countries will undergo restructuring and also mergers in the transitional phase of Euro in order to be more competitive and efficient.

This will require reorientation of their business focus and also rationalisation of their existing markets in the developing countries including India. This means that some of the traditional Indian subsidiaries of the European Companies will scale down their investments scheduled earlier and many of them will be postponing the new investments taking into account the likely impact of restructuring on a global scale. This development, according to their assessment, might lead to the withdrawal of some of the MNCs business operations from India as a part of the global adjustment. The External Affairs Ministry however says that it will be cheaper to import from EU after the introduction of Euro.

The Indian importers will have larger reach with lower operational and marketing costs. In the short term, the Indian software sector is expected to cash in on the huge demand for work relating to modification of software in the context of the introduction of Euro.

At the trade policy level, more efforts are on in the government to give a fresh edge to the Indo-EU trade in the coming period to take advantage of cheaper imports.

The Government hopes that the Euro will be a strong and stable currency and it has the potential to emerge as the leading currency by replacing the US dollar after some time.

The RBI which is monitoring the transitional phase to Euro is also equally optimistic about the benefits according to Indian companies as a result of the introduction of Euro. The RBI believes that Indian corporates are most likely to increase their borrowing in Euro denominated debt as a broader, deeper and more liquid euro financial markets which are going to offer cheaper finances. Borrowing through equity issues in GDRs will become more attractive after January 1999. However, the RBI has made some interesting analysis, about the impact of the euro on India's external debt.

Presently, the country's external debt is nearly $ 100 billion, out of which 13 per cent is denominated in EU currencies. The effect of Euro on the debt depends on whether a strong or weak Euro comes into being.

One scenario projected by the RBI is that if US dollar depreciates because of unleash of US dollar assets by the EU countries, India's external debt in terms of US dollar would move up. On the contrary, if Euro comes with congenital weaknesses, the debt in dollar terms would move down.

6.5 SBI-ABN Amro Deal

State Bank of India (SBI) and ABN Amro bank on Friday (January 1,1999) struck a five million euro-deal, probably the first inter-bank trade in the world, heralding the arrival of the single currency of the European Monetary Union.

The US dollar-euro deal was clinched at an exchange rate of US $ 1.1740 to an euro according to foreign exchange (Forex) dealers.

Engineering major Larsen & Toubro (L&T) on 31st December, 1998, became the first Indian corporate to borrow in the Europe's new currency.

Euro rates are as follows:

1.95582	German marks
6.55957	French francs
1936.27	Italian lira
166.386	Spanish pesetas
2.20371	Dutch guilders
40.3399	Belgian francs
13.7603	Austrian schillings
200.482	Portuguese escudos
5.94573	Finnish markka
0.787564	Irish pounds
40.3399	Luxembourg francs

Based on these rates, the euro is expected to start trading at $ 1.1665.

The Euro Time Table is:
From January 1, 1999

1. The new European single currency, the Euro will be launched replacing the European currency Unit (the ECU) on a one for one basis, and the ECU will cease to exist.

2. 1 Euro will comprise of 100 euro cents.

3. There will be no notes and coins until 2002.
4. Euro payments can be made by credit card, cheque or electric means.

5. The first 11 EU member states - Austria, Belgium, Finland, France, Germany, Ireland, Italy, Luxembourg, the Netherlands, Portugal and Spain - to join the Economic and Monetary Union (EMU) will have their exchange rates irrevocably fixed to the euro.

6. There will no longer be any exchange rate fluctuations between EMU member states.

7. The European Central Bank (ECB) will set a single interest rate for all the 11 member states.

8. A single monetary policy will be framed and implemented by the European System of Central Banks (ESCB), composed of the central banks of the participating countries and the ECB.

9. The 11 member states will denominate their new public debt issues in Euro.

From January 1, 2002,

1. Euro notes and coins will be introduced in the 11 EMU member countries. Notes will be issued in denominations of 5, 10, 20, 50, 100, and 500 euros. There will be eight different coins ranging from 1 cent to two euros, each of which will have a common face and a national face.

2. National currency notes and coins will start to be withdrawn from circulation.

3. In member states all prices will be converted into euros.

4. Dual pricing will exist in EMU member states with both local and euro payments accepted from July 1, 2002.

5. Local currencies in the 11 EMU member countries will cease to exist.

Impact of Euro on Indian Business

The European Monetary Union (EMU) represents one of the most important economic events of this country. The frontline event for the EMU is the euro, which has been fixed irrevocably against members (or 'in' or 'legacy') currencies. Some of the important issues for corporates in India are:

Invoicing and pricing: While one-fifth of India's foreign trade is with Euroland, less than 10 per cent is invoiced in the EMU currencies. The immediate impact of the EMU will therefore be muted, though, despite there being no compulsion, there may be pressure from counter parties and banks to move to the euro. Besides, it will be necessary to revisit one's pricing and marketing policy. As currency barriers vanish, transparency and efficiency gains for the markets will be tremendous. Euroland contributes roughly 17.5 per cent of world trade (the US is lower at 15.9 per cent) and synergies will only improve their share.

Effect on Rupee

There is not likely to be any immediate impact on the rupee. It is expected that the US dollar will retain the intervention currency for the forseeable future. However, as invoicing shifts to the euro and its importance increases, the euro-rupee rate will be looked at more closely.

Forecasting & Budgeting

It is important to understand the economic impact of the EMU to enable intelligent forecasting, and further to have a grip on the overall economic performance of the EMU 11 rather than individual nations. It bears keeping in mind that the European Central Bank's mandate is price stability and not an exchange target for the euro.

Re-conventioning & Re-denominating

Outstanding debt in the in-currencies need to be redenominated into euro only after 2002, but it will have to be re-conventioned in terms of floating rate indices, day count conventions, etc It has generally been agreed that the LIBOR (London Inter Bank Offer Rate) for in-currencies will be replaced by the euro-LIBOR and that PIBOR, FIBOR (Paris/Frankfurt) etc. will be replaced by the Euribor. The day count for bond is expected to be Act/Act. These details should be agreed with one's counterparties. This holds true for derivatives as well. For option players, historical volatility measures for risk analysis are available, obtained by creation of a synthetic euro tracked over time.

Funds Transfer and Trade Documentation

The Principle of 'No prohibition, no compulsion' ensures that remittances can be received or paid in either the legacy currency or the euro. However, settlement mechanisms for the Eurozone are changing-a fact that should be kept in mind. TARGET, which ensures instantaneous transfers in the Eurozone, is very expensive and will be used only for large value transactions. It has been clarified that the EMU shall not have the effect on altering, discharging or excising performance under any instrument subject to ICC rules. Documents may be submitted in either euro or the legacy currency.

The larger development is the emergence of a market to rival the United States in its size and depth, and a larger role for Euroland in world affairs. A case in point is the involvement of the US in resolving the Asian crisis, even though Europe's exposure to Asia was much higher. Once any teething problems are resolved, it is expected that investors and borrowers will look to Euroland as a viable market.

The EMU 11 have a combined GDP of $ 6.9 trillion compared to USA's $ 7.6 trillion (as in 1998), even though the US stock market capitalisation is $ 7.5 trillion compared to the EMU 11'States $ 3.6 trillion. Corporate bond issuance in the US is $ 800 billion compared to only $ 160 billion in Euroland. The European Monetary Union heralds the formation of a new trading bloc, a financial market and a potential reserve currency. Like all developments, it comes with new opportunities and new threats. How best the change is managed depends on how well it is prepared for it.

Conclusion on Impact of Euro on Indian Exporters

As mentioned earlier, switching over to the Euro would help Indian exporters to cut the expenses involved in carrying out trade with the European Union members. Currency fluctuation risks would be minimised, hedging cost eliminated and better banking services accessed on account of Euro.

Larger market and lower transaction costs would mean better prospects for Indian exporters. With a population of 375 million and a share of 18 per cent in global trade, EU was a much bigger market than the U.S. According to Mr. Samadria, President of Federation of Indian Export Organisation (FIEO), despite global recession, EU economy is growing at 2.5 per cent to emerge as the strongest in the world.

Indian businessmen will be able to reduce the cost of business with EU members and also benefit from harmonised tariff rates and interest costs.

The potential would expand as new and wider commercial markets and sectors within the EU emerge, especially in the field of telecom and software.

A forecast by the President of FIEO has been made about considerable gains for Indian exporters who would be dealing with 'a big expanse of a single market' with currency stability and other strengths.

Mr. M. B. McGeever, Ambassador and Head of the Delegation of the European Commission in India, stated that the Euro would emerge as a strong currency since EU had a current account surplus of around $ 110 billion. As compared to this, the US faces a current account deficit of $ 120 billion.

According to Mr. McGeever, there are strong and good chances of an increase in EU's trade with India and also investments in India. In the years to come, Euro would be the currency of choice due to better liquidity and improved investor interest. The transparency and competition would increase but at the same time there would be greater opportunities for exporters and importers.

<u>Preparation by Indian Banks and Exporters towards Europe's New Currency 'Euro'</u>

Indian banks were still not fully prepared to handle the new Euro currency when financial markets opened on January 4, 1999. Eleven EU countries moved to the new single currency for all financial transactions and wholesale trade.

Of the 15-member EU, Greece has been kept out for now while Britain, Denmark and Sweden have opted out. The currency is being powered largely by the strong economies of Germany, France and Italy.

The switch to the Euro has "immediate and extensive" significance for our trade with Europe but Indian banks are by and large still unprepared to handle all the implications of the new currency.

Coins and notes in the Euro will be issued only in 2002. But Indian Banks have been instructed to prepare themselves to build positions in the Euro, list exchange rates with the Euro and be prepared for making payments, processing letters of credit and making settlements in the Euro.

As is already known that a lot of our exports go to several European countries and while national currencies are still valid, European banks will increasingly demand the use of Euro. As of January 4, 1999 large scale exporters from India will have to process transactions in the Euro.

Since many such transactions are forwarded by Indian banks, Indian exporters need efficient banking services to handle the transactions. Indian exporters, however, are facing difficulties with Indian Banks.

The EU, as we all know, is India's largest trade partner, accounting for a third of India's exports. To the EU, India accounts for only 0.5 per cent of its total trade. The EU also has the largest direct investment in India.

But more than the immediate transaction issues, Indian exporters are still not fully alive to the new potential a Europe now without currency borders holds.

Exporters selling goods in several countries can have much to gain from the Euro. Price denomination in a single currency can add both ways. It can open up more markets, but it can also bring down prices of goods imported into Europe.

A "Partenariat" between India and the EU is due to be held in March 1999 to smooth out difficulties following introduction of the Euro. Indian banks need to move fast to give Indian exporters the competitive edge. The Indian trade basket to the EU is heavy with textiles, garments and leather goods and it faces stiff competition from China. The better prepared Indian banks are to conduct financial deals in the Euro, the more of a competitive edge Indian exporters will have.

In each field, Indian traders will need to make a careful examination of the consequences of dealing in the Euro, for which exporters need the support both of banks and of the Indian government.

Conclusion

The EU came into existence when six members of European Coal and Steel Community signed the Treaty of Rome in 1957. Since then the EU dream was a single currency. However, nothing happened till 1970 when Pierre Werner, the former Prime Minister of Luxembourg, was asked to prepare a plan for a single currency. He set a ten year deadline for himself.

But his plan could not materialise. The whole idea was buried for a while but revived in 1977 by Roy Jenkins, a former British European Commission President. France and Germany took initiative in 1978 to establish the exchange rate mechanism (ERM). But again, the pace of action slowed down.

A dynamic revival of the concept took ten years. In 1988, Jacques Delors, a Frenchman, conceptualised the Euro-currency and worked for it with the active support of the former German Chancellor Helmut Kohl. On January 1, 1999, the dream of a common currency became a reality.

The name euro was agreed upon in December 1995 by the EU leaders. Earlier, the Maastricht Treaty had accepted ecu as the EU currency. This name was not acceptable to Germany as ecu was also a French coin minted in the middle ages. Several names were considered like thaler (which America adopted for dollar), the crown, and the schilling. Someone from the Germany suggested Frankfort, as the European Central Bank was situated in Frankfort. Ultimately euro was agreed upon as it symbolised not only particular country but the entire Europe.

Euro will be the first common currency since Roman times for 290 million people in 11 countries of Europe. Euro coins and currencies will not be in circulation until the end of transition period in 2002. However, euro-denominated credit cards, traveller's cheques and even bank accounts will be available on demand. For the first three years, 1999 to 2002, euro will exist as a unit of value for stocks and bonds, electronic transactions, credit cards and checking. Banks machines will dispense marks, francs and pesetas but will electronically record deposits, transactions and withdrawals in euros. It will be a "book currency" till 2002 when 11 currencies will be replaced by euro bank notes.

The 11 national currencies have been permanently locked against the euro at 2300 GMT on 31 December, 1998. One euro will be equal to 1.6675 dollars and 49.586875 rupees.

The euro has been accepted by the EU mainly for three reasons. One, euro being the single acceptable currency will bring in smooth trade and investment within Europe. Two, it will integrate the European economies and would be a strong deterrent to another. Three, Europe will get a greater voice in the global economy. To become stronger than the United States has been a long cherished dream of Europe, particularly Western Europe. It is hoped that the euro will become the leading investment, transaction, reserve and anchor currency in the world. Already the total overseas trade of the current EU member states ·(ECU 757 billion) is greater than the volume of foreign trade conducted by the United States (607 in ECU billion).

But it is not all that rosy. There may be pitfalls too. The major one is the growth and stability pact undergone by the euro zone members. It ties the 11 countries to a budget deficit of less than three per cent of their GDP The implication is that in case of recession in a country, it will not be able to adopt an expansionary fiscal policy. Getting out of the slump will be a difficult task then.

India, unfortunately, has not taken the emergence of euro seriously. The EU is India's largest trade partner as one third of its exports are to EU, though India's share is just half per cent of its foreign trade. The EU's direct investment in India is the largest. However, Indian exporters and financial institutions have not prepared themselves to negotiate the implications of an EU currency, More serious is their inability to understand the potential of a huge common market. This, in fact, is the perception of the trade officials in EU. It is high time we should move fast to give our exporters the competitive edge in the euro market where we face a stiff competition from the Chinese. We must also prepare ourselves to use the euro as a reserve currency in place of the dollar. If it becomes a strong currency, India stands to benefit as the almighty dollar's domination will come to an end.

Chapter 7

Summary and Conclusions

The European integration, as in 1999, has reached a fairly advanced stage; but as the saying goes "Rome was not built in a day", this has been literally true in regard to the evolutionary process pursued in the formation of the European Union. Some term the pace of integration as "slow relying upon small steps"; others call it "a case of hastening slowly". The fact is that during the past forty five years, the strategy has all along been to keep the goal of unity and integration in the forefront and then take only such steps as appear, at the given stage, to be both feasible and sustainable. A fine balance has all through been maintained between "ideal to be achieved" and "realities to be faced:" and this has on the whole imparted the movement a high degree of sustainability [1].

7.1 Phases in Integration Process

As one looks back at the past forty nine years, one discerns five distinct phases in the European integration process. These are discussed below:

7.1.1 First Phase : Sectoral Integration (1950 - 58)

This is appropriately called 'the foundation laying phase'. During this phase, covering around nine years from 1950 to 1958, integration was attempted in selected sectors only, the start being with coal and steel. At a press conference held on May 9, 1950, a day which is celebrated as the birthday of the European Union, Robert Schuman, foreign minister of France, announced that it would further the cause of unity in Europe and would also benefit coal and steel producing countries in the region if Franco-German coal and steel production is placed under the control of a 'Common High Authority'. Later Belgium, Luxembourg, the Netherlands and Italy also decided to support the plan and a treaty establishing the European Coal and Steel Community was signed by the six in Paris in

April, 1951 and came into force in July, 1952. This treaty provided inter-alia for the establishment of two review institutions also: one, The Common Assembly and two, The Court. During this phase, the six attempted to work out common approach and unity in two other fields also: (i) political affairs, principally concerned with foreign relations and (ii) co-operation in defence. Two separate drafts, one dealing with "Treaty on European Political Community (EPC)" and another on "Treaty on European Defence Community (EDC)" were negotiated. However, the latter was rejected by the French Parliament in August 1954 and, therefore, it could not come into being.

Undaunted by the failure on the EDC front but enthused by the enlargement of the Brussels Treaty into WEU, the foreign ministers of the Six at their May 1955 meeting held in Messina, Sicily, pressed for a new effort to revive European ideals and to strengthen European institutions. In the declaration issued by them on June 2, 1955, they recommended (i) the founding of a common organisation to develop nuclear energy for peaceful purposes and (ii) the initiation of a common European market free from all custom duties and all quantitative restrictions. In May 1957, two separate treaties - one, establishing the European Economic Community (EEC) and the second, European Automatic Energy Community (EURATOM) - were formally signed in Rome and with effect from January 1, 1958, both these treaties came into force and in pursuance thereof EEC and EURATOM Commissions were set up in Rome.

7.1.2 Second Phase : Widening and Enlarging of Area of Integration (1959 - 73)

This phase covered the period from 1959 to 1973 and was characterised by widening and geographical enlargement of area of European integration. Once the institutional set up was put in place, the implementation of the EEC treaty proceeded exceedingly well, indeed initially at a faster rate than visualised in May 1957. For example, whereas the treaty had provided that internal import duties would be reduced by 10 percent in the first year (1958) and an additional 20 percent in the block of following three years (1959, 1960 and 1961), the internal duty cut to be implemented thus being 30 per cent by the end of 1961. In actual fact this order of cut was achieved one year before time viz. by 1960. The treaty had provided for two phases: the first phase was to cover 1958 to 1961 and the second one 1962 to 1968. Achievements in each of these phases were much more substantial in terms of internal duty reductions and also reductions in quotas. By July 1968, all custom duties in intra-Union trade in manufactured goods were abolished.

Once a measure of success started becoming visible in adoption of common policies and integration in these selected sectors - steel, coal, and atomic energy - the six decided to turn their attention to other areas, important ones in this respect being the following:

i) Agricultural Policy
ii) Foreign Policy
iii) Exchange Rate Regime and Monetary Policy
iv) Widening the coverage of European Integration: Denmark, Ireland, Norway and U.K. expressed their desire to join the EEC and in January 1972, a treaty on the accession of these countries was signed in Brussels. Later, Norway could not join in view of the national referendum going against its joining the EEC. However, with effect from January 1, 1973, the other three viz. Denmark, Ireland and U.K. became full-fledged members of the EEC. The Community, thus, became a Community of Nine.
v) Strengthening Resources Base of the Community.

7.1.3 Third Phase: Mixed Achievements and Emergence of a Blue Print for a Single Market (1974-86)

This is the phase in which two oil shocks occurred - the first one in 1973 and the second one in 1979. These had adverse effects on economies of all the oil-importing countries, including the nine member states of the Community. Recessionary conditions developed and the attention of the governments of member countries got diverted towards tackling them on priority basis with a view to limiting their fall-out on employment, exports and production. The work on strengthening Community's institutions, however, continued. In January 1985, Jacques Delors joined the European Commission and immediately on assumption of the charge, he and his colleagues in the Commission got busy with the preparation of a blueprint for converting the Community into a Single European Market - a market in which there would be no frontiers and no restrictions and would thus enable people, goods, services, and money to move unhindered throughout the Community. Their labour resulted in the signing of the Single European Act, in Luxembourg, on February 17-18, 1986, which came into force with effect from July 1, 1987. This was indeed the most outstanding achievement of this phase.

In the meeting of Heads of State/Governments, at Paris, on December 9-10, 1974, it was decided to convert the forum of heads of States/Governments into European Council and it was resolved that the Council would meet three times in a year. Two other decisions were also taken at this meeting: One related to agreement in principle that elections to European Parliament would be by direct universal suffrage and the second one was in respect of setting up the European Regional Fund. On the Parliamentary front, another development that took place during this phase was the signing of a treaty enhancing budgetary powers of the Parliament. The treaty came into force with effect from June, 1977. In addition to changes in budgetary powers of the Parliament, a Court of Auditors was also set up in 1977.

During this phase, there was further enlargement of the membership of the Community. Greece joined it on January 1, 1981 and Spain and Portugal five years later viz. with effect from January 1, 1986. Thus, the Community became a Community of Twelve.

On the monetary co-operation front, a significant development that took place during this phase was the establishment of European Monetary System (EMS), which came into operation from March 1979.

7.1.4 Fourth Phase: Putting the Single Market in Place (1988-92)

Main objectives set out in the Single European Act were :

- completion of the European Internal Market Monetary Union,
- enhanced economic and social cohesion,
- technological development and technical excellence,
- making the Community more effective and democratic,
- institutionalised co-operation in the area of foreign policy among the member states.

The single market formally came into being with effect from January 1, 1993. A large number of measures along the lines indicated below have already been taken:

- the liberalisation of public procurement, which involved making the rules on works and supplies contracts more transparent, stepping up checks and extending the rules to important new areas such as transport, energy and telecommunication;

- the harmonisation of taxation, which meant aligning national provisions on indirect taxes, VAT and excise duties;

- the liberalisation of capital markets and financial services;

- standardisation, thanks to a new approach to certification and testing, recognition of the equivalence of national standards, and some harmonisation of safety and environmental standards;

- the abolition of technical barriers (freedom to exercise an activity and recognition of the equivalence of training qualifications) and physical barriers (elimination of border checks) for the free movement of individuals;

- the creation of an environment which encourages business co-operation by harmonising company law and approximating legislation on intellectual and industrial property (trade marks and patents).

7.2 Achievements of the Single Market

The Single European Market completed six years on January 1, 1999. As has been pointed out earlier, 95 per cent of the legislative programme established in 1985 has now been completed, and on an average 87 per cent of these measures have been transposed into national legislation by the member states with Denmark (96 percent) in the lead followed by Spain (83 percent).

The four pillars of the Single Market are free movement of people, goods, services and capital. Two years after the deadline for the completion of the Single Market, the position is that it is possible for goods, services and capital to move freely across the entire Union.

As regards people, they now cross the EU's internal frontiers without custom checks, but checks on identity remain and there are problems with respect to right of residence and the mutual recognition of diplomas and professional qualifications.

The Commission is seeking to overcome these difficulties by pursuing its policy of developing mutual confidence and improving administrative co-operation.

The elimination of border checks on goods have been virtually achieved, though some sensitive goods, such as weapons and drugs, are still subject to spot checks. The Commission has used all the instruments provided by the law in order to ensure free movement of goods. The principle of mutual recognition has formed the basis for all that it has done to remove and prevent barriers to trade.

Regarding the free movement of services, the overall position is positive, though progress between different sectors has been uneven. In the field of transport, for example, the adoption of all the measures contained in the White Paper has been completed. The problems most commonly encountered by the Commission with regard to services relate to transposition and implementation.

Due to the introduction of the new VAT arrangements and the definitive rules on excise duties, there are no longer any tax formalities on crossing intra-Union frontiers. The freedom of the European consumer to purchase, inclusive of tax, the products he wishes to buy in the member states of his choice, irrespective of his country of residence, is thus protected.

The conditions required for the achievement of free movement of capital were established through the adoption of the directive providing for the complete liberalisation of all forms of capital movement between Union residents. The directive has been implemented by all the states.

The Union is adopting a pragmatic policy towards the increase in competition resulting from a number of factors including the completion of the Single Market, the globalisation of markets and rapid technological advance. The policy of dismantling monopolies has been pursued, particularly in the telecommunication sector where technological progress has removed the justification for them. The Commission is trying to minimise the administrative, legal and financial burden on SMEs resulting from Union legislation.

7.3 Fifth Phase: Maastricht Treaty and After

One of the objectives of the Single European Act was to prepare ground for the launching of a full-fledged European Union. As the steps taken during the years 1987 to 1990 started showing results, the European Council took the view that time had come to prepare a working programme that would speed up integration process further and would make it possible to take the Single market concept to its logical conclusion.

In view of the changed scenario, the then twelve member states decided to strengthen their political and monetary bonds and negotiated a new treaty at the meeting of Heads of States held in the Dutch city of Maastricht on December 9 and 10, 1991. The negotiated agreements, called Maastricht European Union Treaty (in short, Maastricht Treaty) was signed by foreign and finance ministers of the member states in February 1992.

Considered as a watershed for the Union, the Treaty laid the foundation for three principal tasks:

- Continued internal development from a Single market to Economic and Monetary Union with the ultimate objective of creating a European Union.

- Evolving a strategy for the future enlargement of the European Union.

- Expanding external responsibilities of the European Union by helping define a new post-cold war world order and by being a role model for the East European countries which are adopting market economies and democratic set-up.

The Maastricht Treaty has set numerous goals in regard to various issues, selected ones are discussed as follows:

7.4 Economic and Monetary Union

The Maastricht Treaty provided a legal and political framework and a three stage time table for the formation of the European Monetary Union (EMU), the ultimate goal being emergence of a single currency to be known as 'EURO'. The three stages spelt out in the Treaty were patterned along the lines proposed by the Delors' Report in 1989 and adopted by the inter-governmental conference on Economic and Monetary Union held in Rome in December 1990.

Stage I: It started in 1990 and covered the period upto the end of 1993. Efforts in this phase were directed at bringing about policy changes at the initiative of individual member states, so as to achieve better co-ordination in the policies of different member states with a view to working towards convergence of economic performance as measured by following criteria: inflation differentials, exchange rate stability, interest rate differentials, and sustainable fiscal deficits and public debt.

Stage II: Commenced from the beginning of 1994. In this phase, member states made determined efforts to achieve performance convergence. A European Monetary Institute was set up in January 1994, which among other functions, undertook surveillance of progress towards meeting performance criteria. The Institute replaced the Committee of Central Bank Governors and the European Monetary Cooperation Fund (EMCF) and consists of the National Central Bank Governors and a President appointed by the Heads of States and Governments. Its principal task was to monitor developments in the European Monetary System and in the matter of economic performance criteria and prepare the ground for the establishment of the European Central Bank in Stage III.

Stage III: The provision in the Treaty initially was that stage III would commence at the earliest from January 1, 1996. But, at the Madrid summit held on December 15-16, 1995, it was decided that the third stage would commence latest from January 1, 1999 as the requirement of majority of member states regarding fulfilling the convergence criteria was unlikely to be met by January 1, 1996. For Stage III to commence, it was necessary for the Council of Ministers to determine whether seven or more member states met the economic performance criteria indicated below:

Inflation Differentials: A member state's consumer price inflation not to exceed more than 1.5 percentage points of the inflation rates of the three best performing member states.

Exchange Rate Stability: The exchange rate to be held for two years within the narrow band of fluctuation margin of 2.25 percent of the Exchange Rate Mechanism (EMS) without a devaluation.

Interest Rate Differentials: Long term interest rate not to be more than 2 percentage points above those in three member states with the lowest inflation.

Government Deficit: Consolidated deficit of the central, state and local governments, and the social security funds not to surpass 3 percent of GDP.

Public Debt: Ratio of public debt to GDP not to exceed 60 percent of GDP.

The criteria for Stage-III to commence latest by January 1, 1999 was that seven or more member states met the economic performance criteria as indicated above. If no decision was taken, the countries meeting the performance of convergence criteria, irrespective of the number, would automatically progress to Stage-III on January 1, 1999.

Stage-III commenced in mid-1998, and a European Central Bank was set up at the beginning of it. This bank will be independent of national governments and will manage the monetary policies of the member states that have progressed to Stage-III.

There is a provision in the Treaty that on reaching Stage-III, the States qualified to join the European Monetary Union, will set up European System of Central Banks (ESCB), which will consist of ECB and National Central Banks.

The most important objective of the Monetary Union was to introduce a single currency six months after the establishment of the ECB.

Introduction of Euro on January 1, 1999: In an unwitting economic parallel to the nativity almost 2000 years ago, the arrival of the 'euro', single currency of Euroland is being described as a birth and a salvation. Europhoria has overtaken the 11 countries of the European Union (EU) that began the year 1999 by bartering away economic freedom on credit and europhilia is prompting Asian investors to put their money on the revolutionary symbol of irrevocable European integration.

Europe's first 11 squad for the opening round of the EMU includes Austria, Belgium, Finland, France, Germany, Ireland, Italy, Luxembourg, The Netherlands, Spain and Portugal. Greece is struggling to meet the exchange rate convergence criteria. U.K. and Denmark have opted out and Sweden failed to meet the criteria too.

Launching of euro is a good news for India. To exporter's advantage, the hydra-headed dragon of fluctuating exchange rates, repeated currency conversion fees and a fragmented European market has been decapitated in one fell swoop by the euro for the first time since the days of the Roman empire. Larger market and lower transaction costs would mean better prospects for Indian exporters.

The potential would expand as new and wider commercial markets and sectors within the EU emerge, especially in the field of telecom and software. There are strong and good chances of an increase in EU's trade with India and also investments. In the years to come, euro would be the currency of choice due to better liquidity and improved investor interest.

7.5 Europe after Maastricht

The Maastricht Treaty, which attracted unprecedented attention and strong emotions, amply demonstrated that the European Union believes in moving forward in small steps rather than in great leaps. Some quarters have shown concern regarding the Economic and Monetary Union. Of much anxiety was the decision on issuance of a single European currency [2].

It is argued that individual national currencies are not only a means of exchange but also a symbol of national identity and financial security. On the other hand, without the single currency, the internal market would remain distorted. The European Industry had to spend about 10 billion ECUs ($ 15 billion) in a year on currency conversion costs, in the past. The pressure was more on small and medium sized companies, as such costs had become one of the biggest obstacles to cross-border trade. The lack of a single currency also restricted free movement of labour and capital within the Union. However, the Maastricht summit also realised that national traditions, characterises and identities will have to be maintained and cannot be simply 'harmonised' out of existence.

Although U.K. has not participated in the implementation of the Monetary Union, it did exercise its right to vote on the issue of EMU and, indeed, voted in its favour. With respect to social policy, U.K. did not join its EU partners in signing the same. Thus, Maastricht has made EU somewhat more complicated even if it has strengthened the Union. It further implies that the Maastricht Text, which is more about ends than means, may be interpreted in other than the envisaged perspective and even negotiated in some cases before it fully accomplishes its goals.

The positive effects of the European Union, however, cannot be underplayed. The Single Market would lower enterprise costs due to abolition of formalities and cutting back of delays at the internal frontiers. Primarily, it is the elimination of numerous technical impediments that would accelerate economic momentum in the Union and would hopefully lead to better allocation of resources. Another important outcome of the European Union was the decision to introduce the single currency latest by 1999. The challenge, therefore, lied in restructuring the respective internal economies of the member states.

Undoubtedly, four decades of constant attempts at European Union has triggered development of the continent and the attitude of the people. Post-Maastricht message to Europe has been that the era of absolute sovereignty of national states is almost over. Though not very visible at present, the federalist approach has helped in constant balancing of national and common interests and in forging of a separate identity. However, the task of promoting harmonious development of economic activities, balanced expansion, increased stability and rapid rise in living standards of the European people cannot be attained at one stroke but has to evolve gradually. It is in this light that the Maastricht Treaty has to be evaluated. Austria, Finland and Sweden joined the European Union in 1995, raising the number of members to Fifteen. With this enlargement, the EU's population has gone up from 340 million to 375 million. The total GDP of the fifteen member states is now over 5.5 billion US $. Countries of Central and Eastern Europe and the Baltic states have expressed their desire to join the EU. The decision for further enlargement was taken in an inter-governmental conference held in March, 1996. Fresh round of negotiations with Cyprus, Malta etc. would begin in mid-1999.

After the Maastricht Treaty which came into force on November 1, 1993, the leaders of every member state of the European Union, on June 17, 1997 agreed on a new Treaty for Europe, the Treaty of Amsterdam.

The Treaty of Amsterdam has four main objectives:
- to place employment and citizens' right at the heart of the Union.
- to sweep away the last remaining obstacles to freedom of movement and to strengthen security.
- to give Europe a stronger voice in world affairs.
- to make the Union's institutional structure more efficient with a view to enlarging the Union, with new member states joining.

In other words, the Treaty of Amsterdam consolidates each of the three great pillars which have been the foundation of the Union's work since the Masstricht Treaty of November 1, 1993.

7.6 Impact of European Unification on India's Trade

7.6.1 Indo-EU Trade

Foreign trade makes an important contribution to economic growth in both the European Union and India. Bilateral trade has been the bedrock of the Indo-EU relationship.

European Union has been India's largest trading partner. EU accounted for 26 per cent of India's global exports and 25 per cent of imports in 1997-98. However, the converse does not hold true for India. India's share in EU as in 1997-98 was still less than 1 percent.

7.6.2 India's Exports to EU

India's exports to EU can be classified into following categories:

- Agricultural and Marine Products.

- Leather and its products including Footwear
- Chemicals and Allied Products.
- Textiles and Garments.
- Jute and Coir Products.
- Gems and Jewellery.
- Engineering and electronic goods.

Nearly 70 per cent of India's exports to EU comprises of commodities like leather, tea, diamonds, cotton fabrics, tobacco, precious and semi-precious stones and coffee. The residual exports of about 30 per cent comprise engineering goods, chemicals and software which form a dynamic area which still has a wider scope for exploitation.

It has been observed that from 1973-74 to 1997-98, within EU, U.K. Germany, Belgium, Italy, Netherlands and France have been India's major export partners. From 1973-74 to 1979-80, U.K. dominated the European Union by having a share of 29 per cent. In the 1980s, however, its share started declining. From 26.39 per cent in 1980-81, U.K.'s share fell down to 22.53 per cent in 1989-90 and share of Germany rose to 25 per cent in 1989-90. From 1994-95, however, U.K.'s share vis-a-vis Germany started rising. In 1997-98, U.K. had a share of 24 per cent followed by Germany with a share of 22 per cent. Share of other major trading partners, i.e. Italy, the Netherlands and France maintained an almost constant mark over the years i.e., from 1973-74 to 1997-98. Belgium, however, showed a rising trend till 1989-90, its share falling slightly to 13 per cent in 1992-93. In 1997-98, its share increased to 14 per cent.

Greece, Luxembourg, Portugal, Denmark, Ireland, Spain and the newly joined member states of Finland, Austria and Sweden are small partners. Share of Portugal, Greece and Ireland together was even less than 1 per cent of India's total exports to EU over the years.

7.6.3 India's Imports from EU

India imports almost 25 per cent of its total imports from EU. Imports of India from the EU, from 1973-74 to 1985-86, were in the range of 24 per cent to 28 per cent of the total imports from the world. From 1986-87 to 1989-89, they grew to the extent of 34 per cent. However, share of India's imports from EU fell in the early 90s; in 1993-94 its share was 30 per cent.

In 1997-98, however, India's share of imports fell down to 25 per cent. India's major imports from EU are:

- Iron and Steel
- Gems and jewellery, particularly rough diamonds.
- Capital goods, particularly machinery and transport equipment.
- Organic Chemicals.
- Inorganic Chemicals.
- Chemical material and products.
- Non-ferrous metals.
- Professional and Scientific instruments.

Together, they accounted for 74.5 per cent of total imports in 1997-98. Imports of capital goods was 46 per cent of total imports in 1973-74 and was 39 per cent in 1986-87 but, fell down to 19 per cent in 1992-93. Its share started rising again and in 1997-98 it was 25 per cent. Share of Gems and jewellery, however, rose from 8 per cent approximately in 1973-74 to 31 per cent in 1997-98.

Within EU, in 1997-98, major import sources were U.K. (21 per cent), Germany (19 per cent), Belgium (12 per cent), followed by France (7.5 per cent) and Italy (11 per cent).

Thus, imports are highly concentrated in countries like Germany, U.K., France, Italy and Belgium. Greece, Luxembourg, Ireland, Denmark, Portugal, Spain and the newly joined member countries of Finland, Austria and Sweden are very small partners.

7.6.4 Impact of European Unification on India's Exports

A major outcome of Single European Market is wide market catering to over 375 million people in 1999 under a unified system. The integration is likely to lead to an increased production level and thus increased GDR. This might require more imports from within the Union and without.

Hence, India's exports to the European Union was considered to be a function of these three important factors and an attempt was made to establish the relationship through a multiple regression analysis of the following form:

$$\text{Ln Exp} = \text{Lnb}_o + b_1 \text{Ln Imp} + b_2 \text{Ln GDP} + b_3 \text{Ln Pop} + u.$$

where

Ln Exp = Indian Exports to EU in log natural form.

b_o = constant

Ln Imp = European Union's Imports from rest of the world in log natural form.

Ln GDP= European Union's combined GDP in log natural form.

Ln Pop = European Union's combined Population in log natural form

u = Error term.

b_1, b_2 and b_3 are the constant elasticities of India's exports to EU with respect to the respective variable.

A log linear relationship was obtained. Though the results were in desired direction, the problem of multicollinearity was faced and the following results were obtained.

$$\text{Ln Exp} = 131.99 + 0.1284 \text{ Ln Imp} + 0.0159 \text{ Ln GDP} + 23.93 \text{ Ln pop}$$

$$(-2.38) \quad (1.74) \quad (0.04) \quad (2.36)$$

$R^2 = 0.9049$ $R^2 = 0.8870$ F = 50.7376 D.W. = 1.41

As there were a lot of fluctuations in the imports, a two stage least square method was adopted using the fitted values of imports regressed against GDP. Because of high correlation amongst these three variables, no statistically significant results could be obtained. Hence, the Ln values of India's exports were regressed against each individual variable separately. Following results were obtained:

Ln Exp is the dependent variable.

C	Ln Imp	Ln Imp F	Ln GDP	Ln Pop	R^2	F Value
-8729	-	0.9504	-	0.8391		93.8826
(-3.69)		(9.68)				
-0.1770	-	-	1.0185	0.8426		96.34
(-0.2145)			(9.81)			
-150.46	-	-	-	27.45	0.8868	140.95
(27.45)				(11.87)		
-148.76	-	-	0.0122	27.14	0.88	66.56
(-2.57)			(0.0304)	(12.57)		
					Time	
6.99	-	-	-	-	(0.0866)	0.86
(73.68)					(10.92)	
-1.17	0.1600		0.8748	-		0.87 57.73
(-1.27)	(1.96)		(7.22)			(1.16)

A number of salient features emerge from these results:

1. The impact of EU's income on India's exports is significant.

2. The impact of EU's imports from world is also significant on India's exports to EU.

3. The impact of increase in EU's Population on India's exports is also significant.

Regressions were also run to see the impact of European unification on India's exports of major commodity groups to EU and it can be concluded from them that:

1. Impact of increase in EU-12's imports, from rest of the world, on India's exports of Gems and Jewellery, Cotton, Fish, Agro-based goods, Leather, Carpets and Ready-made Garments to EU is very significant.

2. Increase in Gross Domestic Product of EU has a positive impact on all the India's major export commodity groups to EU.

3. Increase in EU's population on India's major export commodity groups is also significant.

7.7 Measures for Enhancing India's Trade With EU

It is clear from our earlier analysis that India has not been able to make a dent into the Union and India's deficit with the Union continues to be high.

India has been facing increasing difficulty in gaining market access due to the protectionist policies of the Union in areas like clothing, where India has comparative advantage. On the other hand, import liberalisation in India has provided a fast growing market for European industry. Besides, composition of India's exports to the Union is not well diversified. Leather and its products, textiles and its articles and pearls and precious stones account for two-thirds of India's total exports to the Union. India must try to diversify its exports to the Union of commodities which have a greater demand.

India must particularly concentrate on markets like Denmark, Germany, Italy, U.K. and Spain where intra-Union imports are relatively of lesser magnitude. In certain products like apparel and clothing, knitted and crocheted goods, carpets, tobacco, animal feeds, pearls and precious and semi-precious stones, India has better price and competitiveness with non-Union suppliers. Whereas, in other major products like marine, edible fruits and nuts, oilmeals and leather goods, India's competitiveness is very much behind the non-Union suppliers. It is, therefore, important to improve the productivity and competitiveness of these major export products.

Development of large monopolies and cartels in the Union, however, would reduce India's bargaining leverage. It is, however, possible to develop long-term production and trade relations with major European companies.

Since the services sector has expanded, Indian banks must enter the area of investment banking so as to utilise the increasing opportunities. India can also gain a foothold in foreign travel, which is likely to increase in the years to come.

Certain recommendations have also been made in this regard in our previous chapter. The broad strategies, are for firms, industries and some policies that the country can adopt.

For Indian firms, it is recommended that they should establish an organic presence in the EU. This will help them to be a part of EEIG and, consequently a part of new European corporate culture. Apart from the advantage by gaining an organic presence in the Union, they will be in a position to take advantage of the European Company Statute. Another recommendation is to give priority to Quality Assurance and Standards. Already, under the scheme of Harmonisation of Standards, more than 142 Indian Standards have been harmonised with European Standards. Other sets of recommendations to Indian firms include strengthening of marketing capability, establishing links with European SMEs and to maximise use of official schemes.

Another set of strategies suggested to Indian industries, which can be adopted by the Industry Associations and Exporters' Associations of India include:

a) Promoting Indian presence in the EU.
b) Promoting Cooperation on Standards.
c) Encouraging Technology Absorption.
d) Undertaking Aggressive Marketing.

Country-specific strategies fall within the realm of official policy. Important areas of policy support have been pinpointed which can improve trade relationships with the EU. These include:

a) Promoting greater Indian presence in the EU.
b) Providing marketing support.
c) Sponsoring a Standards 'Offensive'.
d) Promoting SMEs for Export and Joint Ventures.

These recommendations are by no means exhaustive. These guidelines are fairly general in nature. More work and attention is needed at the micro-level to identify specific actions for taking on the challenge of the European Market. As pointed out earlier, strategies at all the three levels should go hand in hand and should be undertaken without delay.

7.8 Conclusions

European unification implies increase in Gross Domestic Product, increase in European Union's imports and an increase in Union's combined population. In more specific terms, according to estimates, it will result in one time addition of 200 billion ECUs in the Union's GDP and an all round reduction in prices to the tune of 6 per cent.

The implications for India could be an increase in the exports to EU. Over 70 per cent of India's exports to the EU comprise of consumer goods which have a great potential for expansion with the predicted higher economic growth of the Union finding reflection in higher rate of consumption.

Restructuring of industry, formation of larger trading companies through mergers and acquisitions and progressive harmonisation of technical standards could also result in an expansion of Indian exports to the Union.

Hence, it can be concluded that the unification has a very high potential of increasing India's trade relations with the European Union.

Also, the pessimism of declining Indian exports to European countries seems to have no validity. It has been observed that after unification, India's exports to the Union, in absolute terms, have not declined, but on the other hand have increased, albeit at a lower rate. This seems to be the initial impact and over a period the growth rate is likely to pick up.

There seems to be bright chances in future for an expansion in India's exports to EU. Enhanced global competition and the imperative of increased cost efficiency could lead to a search for production/servicing facilities even outside the Union, particularly, in labour-intensive section. On a selective basis, India's opportunities could be explored in the fields of textiles and clothing, automobile components, gems and jewellery, electronic goods and components, software development etc.

India is capable of conforming to the high quality of exports expected by the Union. Different technical standards in different member states had proved to be big obstacles of Indian goods in the past. The EU 1992 process had assigned prime importance to technical harmonisation and standards. The introduction of ISO-9000 standards has been an important step for India which is meant to assess manufacturing processes and not merely the specifications of the final product.

Under the harmonisation scheme, more than 142 Indian standards have already been harmonised with European standards. More than 300 Indian companies have already been awarded ISO-9000 certificates which shows that India is equally capable of conforming to the high quality of exports expected by the Union.

The Single European Market would also have some impact on India's import from the Union. It may, on the one hand, become more competitive vis-a-vis other suppliers, namely, the USA, Japan and the EFTA countries. On the other hand, the development of large monopolies and cartels in the Union could reduce our bargaining leverage. Also, with an increase in liberalisation in imports and move towards globalisation, imports from EU are likely to go up; but, at the same time increase in demand in Indian goods would offset the fear of negative trade balance.

India's exports to EU, after unification, has been increasing at a faster rate than India's imports from EU. In 1993-94 and 1994-95, India's exports to EU increased by 19.78 per cent in 1993-94 whereas India's imports from EU rose by 14.50 per cent over the previous year. Similarly, India's exports to EU increased by 11.56 per cent in 1994-95, whereas, India's imports from EU increased only by 2 per cent over the previous year. In 1997-98,

India's exports to EU increased by 7.5 per cent, whereas imports rose by 2.6 per cent over the previous year. Negative trade balance also fell down as a result of a higher increase in exports to EU as compared to the imports from the European Union in these years. From the recent experience, it can be concluded that though imports of India from EU, as a result of liberalisation and globalisation, have gone up, the increase in India's exports to EU has offset the fear of increased negative trade balance.

India must concentrate on countries like Spain, Portugal, Denmark, Luxembourg, Greece, Ireland and also the newly joined member countries of Austria, Finland and Sweden which have not been significant partners in the past. Markets for exports should be explored in these countries so that trade with EU is enhanced.

Alternatively, now that the members of the EU have become more or less one market, an attempt should be made to increase our exports of commodities/products, which have the potential to enter these neglected markets, to the already known companies in the Union with which our exporters have established long term relationship so that these surplus imports by our well known partners find their way to the unexplored markets. This strategy fits very well into the recent government strategy of country-commodity matrix, if it is possible for us to trade with some members of the Union, it should not be difficult for us to trade with others of the same Union.

Hence, it can be concluded that there is no need for India to feel intimidated by the magnitude of the Single Market or its importance in world trade. Outside the developed world, India will remain one of the world's two or three largest and still expanding import market. India's principal needs are advanced technology and capital and the very size and range of India's requirements will command the competing attention of rival suppliers. This would give India sufficient bargaining strength.

If India has to expand its export market, then as stated earlier, Indian firms must prepare themselves according to changes that have been brought about as a result of unification.

Hence, the so called Unified Europe is likely to have greater advantages than the disadvantages for India if the Indian exporters are capable of providing quality goods which are competitive in nature; further they should always look out for cheaper sources of imports from the world.

Notes

1. National Conference on "European Union : Now and Beyond - A Backgrounder": PHD Chamber of Commerce and Industry; February 9, 1995.

2. National Conference on "European Union : Now and Beyond - A Backgrounder": PHD Chamber of Commerce and Industry, February 9, 1995.

Statistical Tables

Table 4.1: India's Imports, Exports and Trade Balance: 1950-51 to 1996-97

(Rs. crore)

Years	Imports	Exports	Trade Balance	Per cent increase	
				Imports	Exports
1950-51	608	606	- 2	-	-
1960-61	1,122	642	- 480	84.5	5.9
1970-71	1,634	1,535	- 99	45.6	139.0
1976-77	5,074	5,142	+ 68	210.5	235.0
1980-81	12,549	6,711	- 5,838	147.3	30.5
1990-91	43,193	32,553	- 10,640	244.0	385.0
1994-95	89,971	82,674	- 7,297	108.0	154.0
1995-96	1,22,678	1,06,353	- 16,325	36.0	29.0
1996-97	1,38,919	1,18,817	- 20,102	13.0	12.0

Source: Government of India, *Economic Survey*, 1997-98

Table 4.2 Exports, Imports and Trade Balance

(US $ million)

Year	Exports (inclusive re-exports)	Imports	Trade Balance
1950-51	1269	1273	- 4
1960-61	1346	2353	-1007
1970-71	2031	2162	-131
1980-81	8486	15869	-7383
1990-91	18143	24075	-5932
1994-95	26330	28654	-2324
1995-96	31797	36678	-4881
1996-97	33470	39133	-5663
1997-98 (P) (April-Feb)	30585	36983	-6398

Source: Government of India, *Economic Survey*, 1997-98.

Table 4.3 :Balance of Payments Position of India:1991-92 to 1996-97

(Rs. crore)

	1991-92	1992-93	1993-94	1994-95	1995-96	1996-97
1. Imports (cif)	51417	72000	83869	112748	146542	170646
2. Exports (fob)	44923	54762	71146	84329	108481	119876
3. Trade Balance (2-1)	-64950	-17238	-12723	-28420	-38061	-50770
4. Invisibles						
a) Receipts	23449	27038	35500	48838	59482	75537
b) Payments (of which interest and service payments on loans and credits)	19191	22564	26414	31001	41027	37702
c) Net	4258	4474	9087	17837	18455	37835
5. Current A/c (net)	-2237	-12764	-3636	-10583	-19607	-12935

Contd...

6. Capital Account						
i. Foreign Investment (net)	340	1700	13282	15087	15624	20721
ii. Loans (net)	7381	5739	5949	4773	3302	3970
iii. Banking (net)	1351	12156	7099	- 1058	4672	6540
iv. Rupee debt service	- 2785	-2335	- 3302	-3090	- 3106	- 2542
v. Other capital (net)	980	- 841	5141	6211	- 8666	2046
vi. Errors and Omissions	- 301	- 246	2510	2049	1287	-2114
7. Total capital (i to vi)	9511	11881	30415	28742	15558	37155
8. Overall Balance (5±7)	7274	- 883	26779	18160	-4049	24220
9. Monetary movement						
a) IMF Transactions (net)	2078	3363	587	-3585	- 5749	- 3461
b) Increase(-)/Decrease (+) in Reserves	- 9351	-2481	-27366	-14575	9798	-20759
10. Total (a+b)	-7274	883	-26779	-18160	4049	- 24220

Source: Government of India, *Economic Survey*, 1997-98.

Table 4.4: India's Exports by Commodity Groups: 1960-61 to 1996-97

(Rs. crore)

Commodity	1960-61	1970-71	1980-81	1990-91	1994-95	1995-96	1996-97
I. Agricultural & allied goods	284	487	2057	6317	13712	21138	25040
Coffee	7	25	214	252	1053	1503	1426
Tea & mate	124	148	426	1070	975	1171	1037
Oil cakes	14	55	125	609	1798	2349	3495
Tobacco	16	33	141	263	255	447	757
Cashews	19	57	140	447	1247	1237	1288
Spices	17	39	11	239	612	794	1202
Sugar	3	29	40	38	62	506	1078
Raw cotton	12	14	165	846	140	204	1575
Rice	-	5	224	462	1206	4568	3172

Contd...

Fish & fish preparations	5	31	217	960	3537	3381	4008
Meat, etc.	1	3	56	140	403	627	709
Fruits & vegetables	6	12	80	213	606	802	828
Misce. food items	1	4	36	213	282	745	974
II. Ores & minerals	52	164	414	1497	2538	3061	3185
Mica	-	16	18	35	22	27	25
Iron ore	17	117	303	1049	1297	1721	1706
III. Manufactured goods	291	772	3747	23736	64688	80219	88528
Textiles	73	145	933	6832	19945.	24149	27793
Cotton yarn	65	142	408	2100	7014	8619	11082
Ready-made garments	1	29	550	4012	10305	12295	13324
Coir yarn	6	13	17	48	173	210	217
Jute manufactures	135	190	330	298	473	621	552
Leather etc.	28	80	390	2600	5057	5790	5609

Contd...

Handicrafts	11	73	952	6167	16730	20501	20110
Gems & Jewellery	1	45	618	5247	14131	17644	16872
Chemicals & Allied Products	7	29	225	2111	7642	9849	11463
Machinery, transport equip.	22	198	827	3872	10947	14578	17431
IV. Mineral fuels & lubricants	7	13	28	948	1610	1761	1832
V. Others	8	100	466	55	126	174	232
Total	642	1535	6711	32559	82674	106353	118817

Source: Government of India, *Economic Survey*, 1997-98.

Table 4.5: India's Exports by Commodity Group: 1992-93 to 1996-97

(US $ million)

	1992-93	1993-94	1994-95	1995-96	1996-97
I. Agricultural and Allied Products	3265	4151	4367	6320	7054
Coffee	130	174	335	449	402
Tea and Mate	337	338	311	350	292
Oil Cakes	534	741	573	702	985
Tobacco	164	147	81	134	213
Cashew Kernals	258	334	397	370	363
Spices	136	181	195	237	339
Sugar & Molasses	122	57	20	151	304
Raw Cotton	63	209	45	61	444
Rice	337	410	384	1366	894
Fish and its Preparations	602	814	1126	1011	1129

Contd...

Meat and Meat Preparations	89	78	128	187	200
Fruits, Vegetables and Pulses	126	156	193	240	233
Miscellaneous Processed foods	129	150	90	223	274
II Ores and Minerals, of which	626	756	808	915	897
Mica	8	9	7	8	7
Iron Ore (million tonnes)	381	438	413	515	481
III Manufactured Goods of which	14099	16803	20602	23984	24938
Textile, Fabrics and Manufactures	4315	4739	6352	7220	7829
Cotton yarn fabrics	1350	1537	2234	2577	3122
Readymade Garments	2393	2586	3282	3676	3753
Coir Yarn	31	41	55	63	61
Jute Manufactures	123	124	151	186	155
Leather and Its Manufactures	12277	1300	1611	1731	1580

Contd...

Handicrafts of which	3783	4768	5328	6129	5665
Gems and Jewellery	3072	3996	4501	5275	4753
Chemicals & Allied Prod.	1378	1813	2434	2945	3229
Machinery, Transport & metal manufactures including iron & steel	2458	3024	3486	4358	4910
IV Mineral fuels & Lubricants	525	495	513	526	516
Others	21	33	40	52	65
Total	18537	22238	26330	31797	33470

Source: Government of India, *Economic Survey*, 1997-98

Table 4.6: Composition of India's Exports: 1960-61 to 1993-94

(per cent shares)

Commodity group	1960-61	1970-71	1980-81	1990-91	1991-92	1993-94
I. Agricultural & allied goods	44.24	31.72	30.65	19.40	18.68	18.0
Tea	19.31	9.64	6.35	3.28	2.75	1.5
Coffee	1.09	1.63	3.19	0.77	0.75	0.8
Tobacco	2.49	2.15	2.10	0.81	0.86	0.5
Spices	2.65	2.54	0.16	0.73	0.89	0.8
Cashew	2.96	3.71	2.01	1.37	1.53	1.5
Marine products	0.78	2.02	3.23	2.95	3.28	3.7
Raw cotton	1.87	0.91	2.46	2.60	0.69	0.9
II. Ores & minerals	8.10	10.68	6.17	4.60	4.61	4.0
III. Manufactured goods	45.33	50.29	55.83	72.90	74.23	75.5
Leather	19.47	5.21	5.81	7.98	7.10	6.0

Contd...

Gem & jewellery	0.16	2.93	9.21	16.11	15.33	18.0
Ready-made garments	0.16	1.89	8.19	12.32	12.31	11.6
Machinery & Electronic goods	3.42	12.90	12.32	11.89	12.51	9.8
IV. Minerals & lubricants	1.09	0.85	0.42	2.91	2.36	2.9
V. Others	1.24	6.51	6.94	0.17	0.12	0.7
Total	100.00	100.00	100.00	100.00	100.00	100.0

Source: Government of India, *Economic Survey*, 1995-96.

Table 4.7: Composition of India's Exports: 1994-95 to 1997-98

(per cent share)

	1994-95	1995-96	1996-97	1997-98 (April-January)
I Agriculture and allied products, of which	16.0	19.2	20.3	18.8
a. Tea	1.2	1.1	0.8	1.2
b. Coffee	1.3	1.4	1.2	1.2
c. Cereals	1.5	4.7	3.3	2.4
d. Unmanufactured tobacco	0.2	0.4	0.4	0.7
e. Spices	0.7	0.7	1.0	1.1
f. Cashew	1.5	1.2	1.1	1.1
g. Oil Mills	2.2	2.2	3.0	2.6
h. Fruits and vegetables	0.7	0.7	0.6	0.6
i. Marine products	4.3	3.2	3.4	3.7
j. Raw cotton	0.2	0.2	1.4	0.8

Contd...

II. Ores and minerals of which	3.8	3.7	3.4	3.1
k. Iron ore	1.6	1.6	1.4	1.4
l. Processed minerals	1.0	1.0	1.0	1.0
m. Others ores and minerals	1.0	0.9	0.9	0.6
III Manufactured goods, of which	78.1	75.4	74.1	75.7
n. Leather and manufactures	4.0	3.6	2.9	2.8
o. Leather footwear	2.1	1.8	1.7	0.8
p. Gems and Jewellery	17.1	16.6	14.3	14.3
q. Drugs chemicals etc.	3.0	3.2	3.6	4.0
r. Dyes/Coal tar	1.8	1.5	1.7	1.8
s. Manufactures of metals	2.7	2.6	2.8	3.3
t. Machinery & instruments	2.8	2.6	3.2	3.4
u. Transport equipment	2.9	2.9	2.8	2.5

Contd...

v. Primary & semi-finished iron and steel	1.6	1.6	1.7	1.9
w. Electronic goods	1.6	2.1	2.4	2.1
x. Cotton yarn fabrics	8.5	8.1	9.4	9.5
y. Readymade garments	12.5	11.6	11.3	11.1
z. Handicrafts	3.9	3.5	3.3	3.4
IV Crude and petroleum products	1.6	1.4	1.5	1.5
V Other and unclassified items	0.6	0.4	0.7	1.3
Grand Total	100.0	100.0	100.0	100.0

Source: Government of India, *Economic Survey*, 1997-98.

Table 4.8: India's Imports by Commodity Groups: 1960-61 to 1996-97

(Rs. crore)

Commodity group	1960-61	1970-71	1980-81	1990-91	1993-94	1994-95	1995-96	1996-97
I. Food & live animals, of which:	214	242	380	n.a	n.a	n.a	n.a	n.a
Cereals & preparations	181	213	100	182	290	92	80	488
II. Raw materials & intermediate manufactures	527	889	9760	n.a	n.a	n.a	n.a	n.a
1. Cashewnuts	-	29	9	134	483	691	760	688
2. Crude rubber	11	4	32	226	342	371	719	630
III. Fibres, of which:	101	127	164	n.a	n.a	n.a	n.a	n.a
1. Synthetic	-	9	97	56	126	444	502	423
2. Raw wool	1	15	43	182	372	351	486	581

Contd...

3. Raw cotton	82	99	-	1	18	507	521	31
4. Raw jute	8	0	1	20	33	62	48	76
IV. Petroleum, oil & lubricants	69	136	5264	10816	18046	18613	25173	35629
1. Animal and vegetable oils	5	39	709	n.a	n.a	n.a	n.a	n.a
2. Edible oils	4	23	677	326	167	624	2260	2929
V. Fertilizers & chemical products	88	217	1490	n.a	n.a	n.a	n.a	n.a
1. Fertilizer & fertilizer material	13	86	818	1766	2591	3304	5628	3235
2. Chemicals & compounds	39	68	358	2289	4823	7344	9403	10382
3. Dyeing, tanning & colouring	1	9	21	168	287	439	509	600
4. Medical & pharma. products	10	24	85	468	807	937	1358	1089
5. Plastic material	9	8	121	1095	1363	1903	2687	2826
6. Pulp & waste paper	7	12	18	458	497	635	921	823
7. Paper & paper board	12	25	187	456	696	773	1583	1770
8. Non-metallic minerals	6	33	555	n.a	n.a	n.a	n.a	n.a
9. Pearls & precious stones	1	25	417	3738	8263	5116	7045	10384

Contd...

VI. Iron & steel	123	147	852	2113	2494	3653	4838	5866
10. Non-ferrous metals	47	119	477	1102	1503	2954	3024	3925
11. Capital goods	356	404	1910	10466	16663	19990	28289	29868
Manufactures of metals	23	9	90	302	559	648	930	1123
Non-electrical machinery	203	258	1089	4240	6388	9236	14376	14801
Electrical machinery	57	70	260	170	640	789	1292	1155
Transport equipment	72	67	472	1670	3985	3497	3697	5269
VII. Others	25	99	499	n.a	n.a	n.a	n.a	n.a
Total	1122	1634	12549	43198	73101	89971	122678	138919

Source: Government of India, *Economic Survey*, 1997-98.

Table 4.9: India's Imports by Commodity Groups: 1992-93 to 1996-97

(US $ million)

Commodities	1992-93	1993-94	1994-95	1995-96	1996-97
I Food and Allied Products, of which:	721.0	550.4	1658.7	1317.8	650.6
1. Cereals	333.5	84.9	29.4	24.0	11.0
2. Pulses	115.5	180.9	188.8	205.0	92.7
3. Cashewnuts	129.9	153.9	220.1	227.2	64.1
4. Edible oils	57.6	52.2	198.8	676.3	440.7
II Fuel, of which:	6396.1	6221.5	6636.2	8451.9	5031.1
5. Coal	477.6	465.0	708.4	925.6	448.7
6. POL	5918.6	5756.5	5927.8	7526.3	4582.4
III Fertilisers	977.7	831.2	1052.4	1682.8	368.4
IV Paper board, manufactures & Newsprint	177.2	222.1	246.2	473.4	264.0
V Capital goods, of which:	4531.0	6040.0	7594.6	10210.1	4480.0
7. Machinery & machine tools	1652.6	2190.7	2727.8	3924.6	1907.8

Contd...

8. Electrical machinery and electronic goods	826.2	794.4	1479.7	2138.9	828.6
9. Transport Equipments	461.8	1266.8	1113.6	1105.2	485.3
10 Project Goods	1218.5	1401.0	1853.6	2391.2	914.0
VI Others, of which:	8067.0	6377.5	6866.6	8633.7	4455.6
11 Chemicals	2017.5	1956.3	2945.3	3614.7	1745.0
12 Pearls, semi-precious stones	2441.9	2641.2	1629.5	2106.2	1241.9
13 Iron and Steel	711.4	781.6	1082.1	1339.7	683.0
14 Non-Ferrous metals	394.8	474.9	717.9	904.0	521.0
15 Professional Instruments	501.4	493.4	491.8	669.1	264.7
VII Unclassified Items	3011.5	3064.0	4599.7	5908.3	2703.6
Grand Total	21881.6	23308.7	28654.4	36677.9	17953.2

Source: Government of India, *Economic Survey*, 1997-98.

Table 4.10: India's Imports by Commodity Groups: 1960-61 to 1991-92

(per cent share)

Commodity group	1960-61	1970-71	1980-81	1990-91	1991-92
I. Cereals & its preparations	16.13	13.04	0.79	0.42	0.36
II. POL	6.15	8.32	41.95	25.04	27.43
III. Chemical materials & products	6.42	11.93	4.66	9.31	11.53
IV. Paper & paper board	1.07	1.53	1.49	1.06	1.02
V. Pearls & precious stones	0.09	1.52	3.32	8.65	10.08
VI. Iron & steel	10.96	8.99	6.79	4.89	4.12
VII. Non-ferrous metals	4.19	7.28	3.80	2.55	1.76
VIII. Capital goods	31.72	24.72	15.22	24.23	21.81
IX. Others	23.27	22.67	21.98	23.85	21.89
Total	100.00	100.00	100.00	100.00	100.00

Source: Government of India, *Economic Survey*, 1994-95.

Table 4.11: India's Imports by Commodity Groups: 1992-93 to 1997-98

(per cent share)

	1992-93	1993-94	1994-95	1995-96	1996-97	1997-98 (April-Jan.)
I Food and Allied Products	3.3	2.4	5.8	3.6	3.8	4.3
1. Cereals	1.5	0.4	0.1	0.1	0.4	0.7
2. Pulses	0.5	0.8	0.7	0.6	0.5	0.7
3. Cashewnuts	0.6	0.7	0.8	0.6	0.5	0.5
4. Edible oils	0.6	0.7	0.7	1.8	2.1	2.0
II Fuel, of which:	29.0	26.7	23.2	23.0	21.5	28.0
5. Coal	2.2	2.0	2.5	2.5	2.3	2.5
6. POL	27.0	24.7	20.7	20.5	19.2	25.5
III Fertilisers	4.5	3.6	3.7	4.6	5.0	2.1

Contd...

IV Paper board, manufactures & Newsprint	0.8	1.0	0.9	1.3	1.4	1.5
V Capital goods, of which:	20.7	25.9	26.5	27.8	27.7	25.0
7. Machinery & machine tools	7.6	9.4	9.5	10.7	10.3	10.6
8. Electrical machinery and electronic goods	3.8	3.4	5.2	5.8	5.5	4.6
9. Transport Equipments	2.1	5.4	3.9	3.0	3.0	2.7
10 Project Goods	5.8	6.0	6.5	6.5	7.2	5.1
VI Others, of which:	27.7	27.4	24.0	23.5	24.1	24.8
11 Chemicals	9.2	8.5	10.3	9.9	10.4	9.7
12 Pearls, scmi-precious stones	11.2	11.3	5.7	5.7	5.7	6.9
13 Iron and Steel	3.3	3.4	3.8	3.7	3.5	3.8

Contd...

14 Non-Ferrous metals	1.8	2.0	2.5	2.5	2.5	2.9
15 Professional Instruments	2.3	2.1	1.7	1.8	1.9	1.5
VII Unclassified Items	13.8	13.1	16.1	16.1	16.6	15.5
Grand Total	100.0	100.0	100.0	100.0	100.0	100.0

Source: Government of India, *Economic Survey*, 1997-98.

Table 4.12: Direction of India's Trade with the World (A) Exports

(Rs. crore)

Counry	1980-81	1990-91	1993-94	1994-95	1995-96	1996-97
I. OECD of which:	3126	17428	39672	48491	59223	65487
a. EU, of which:	1447	8951	18182	22075	28157	29352
i. Belgium	145	1259	2644	3104	3748	3825
ii. France	147	766	1582	1828	2499	2525
iii. Germany	385	2549	4828	5488	6614	6627
iv.Netherlands	152	644	1604	1838	2572	2989
v. U.K.	395	2128	4326	5305	6726	7208
b. North America	806	5077	13256	16602	19487	24470
i. Canada	62	281	715	838	1022	1235
ii. U.S.A.	743	4797	12542	15764	18466	23234

Contd...

c.Other OECD, of which:	708	3401	6336	7623	8870	8654
i. Australia	92	321	769	1088	1257	1356
ii. Japan	598	3039	5460	6363	7411	7068
II. OPEC, of which:	745	1831	7473	7631	10300	11365
i. Iran	123	141	501	492	514	689
ii. Iraq	52	44	12	1	2	8
iii. Kuwait	97	74	332	420	453	546
iv. Saudi Arabia	165	419	1602	1368	1613	2002
III. Eastern Europe of which:	1486	5819	2657	2983	4092	3366
i. G.D.R.	49	-	-	-	-	-
ii. Romania	58	96	70	51	100	69
iii. Russia	1226	5255	2037	2534	3495	2766

Contd...

IV. Other LDC's,	1286	5465	16902	19726	27324	31648
of which:						
i. Africa	350	668	1816	2074	3584	3438
ii. Asia	900	4665	14430	16610	22613	26641
iii. Latin America and Carribean	36	132	655	1044	1127	1569
V. Others:	68	2010	3048	3841	5414	5659
Total	6711	32553	69751	82674	106353	117525

Source: Government of India, *Economic Survey*, 1997-98

Table 4.13: Direction of India's Trade with the World (B) Imports

(Rs. crore)

Country	1980-81	1990-91	1993-94	1994-95	1995-96	1996-97
I. OECD, of which:	5740	23310	41037	46255	64254	67385
a. EU, of which:	2639	12680	21962	22339	32691	34983
i. Belgium	296	2718	5881	3789	5693	8614
ii. France	280	1304	1860	1933	2812	2694
iii. Germany	694	3473	5615	6867	10520	9811
iv. Netherlands	215	793	1205	1212	1907	1735
v. U.K.	731	2894	4818	4895	6415	7402
b. North America	1851	5804	9319	9957	14191	13080
i. Canada	332	559	736	834	1275	1102
ii. U.S.A.	1619	5245	8584	9124	12916	11977

Contd...

c. Other OECD, of which:	932	4326	7075	9517	11881	12402
i. Australia	170	1464	2068	2873	3418	4361
ii. Japan	749	3245	4774	6405	8254	7758
II. OPEC of which:	3488	7041	16377	19002	25586	36188
i. Iran	1339	1018	1191	1685	2001	3090
ii. Iraq	753	496	0	0	0	88
iii. Kuwait	338	363	3532	4648	6590	8474
iv. Saudi Arabia	540	2899	4836	4928	6773	9931
III. Eastern Europe of which:	1296	3377	1288	2129	4217	3257
i. G.D.R.	44	-	-	-	-	-
ii. Romania	97	50	79	151	496	545
iii. Russia	1014	2548	806	1584	2864	2230

Contd...

IV. Other LDC's,	1966	7965	11246	18160	22509	23175
of which:						
i. Africa	205	959	1608	2615	2763	3272
ii. Asia	1431	6033	8875	13092	17723	18119
iii. Latin America and Carribean	313	873	764	2454	2022	1784
V. Others:	60	1765	3152	4424	6112	6840
Total	12549	43198	63375	89971	122678	136844

Source: Government of India, *Economic Survey*, 1996-97

Table 4.14: Direction of India's Trade with Selected East Asian Countries

(per cent share)

Country	Exports			Imports		
	1993-94 (Apr-Mar)	1994-95 (Apr-Mar)	1995-96 (Apr-Sept)	1993-94 (Apr-Mar)	1994-95 (Apr-Mar)	1995-96 (Apr-Sep)
Indonesia	1.00	1.1	1.6	0.50	1.1	1.2
Malaysia	1.10	1.1	1.2	1.10	1.7	2.6
Hong Kong	5.60	5.8	6.0	0.80	1.0	1.0
South Korea	0.90	1.3	1.3	2.40	2.2	2.1
Singapore	3.40	2.9	2.6	2.70	3.1	3.2
Thailand	1.60	1.5	1.5	0.20	0.6	0.5
Chinese Taipei	1.20	1.0	1.0	0.70	1.0	1.0
Total (SEASC)	14.80	14.6	15.0	8.40	10.8	11.7

Source: Government of India, *Economic Survey*, 1995-96.

Table 4.15: Direction of India's Trade with World (A) Exports

(per cent share)

Counry	1980-81	1990-91	1993-94	1994-95	1995-96	1996-97
I. OECD, of which:	46.6	53.5	56.9	58.7	55.7	55.7
a. EU of which	21.6	27.5	26.1	26.7	26.5	25.0
i. Belgium	2.2	3.9	3.8	3.8	3.5	3.3
ii. France	2.2	2.4	2.3	2.2	2.3	2.2
iii. Germany	5.7	7.8	6.9	6.6	6.2	5.6
iv. Netherlands	2.3	2.0	2.3	2.2	2.4	2.5
v. U.K.	5.9	6.5	6.2	6.4	6.3	6.1
b. North America	12.0	15.6	19.0	20.1	18.3	20.8
i. Canada	0.9	0.9	1.0	1.0	1.0	1.1
ii. U.S.A.	11.1	14.7	18.0	19.1	17.4	19.8

Contd...

c. Other OECD, of which:	10.6	10.4	9.1	9.2	8.3	7.4
i. Australia	1.4	1.0	1.1	1.3	1.2	1.2
ii. Japan	8.9	9.3	7.8	7.7	7.0	6.0
II. OPEC of which:	11.1	5.6	10.7	9.2	9.7	9.7
i. Iran	1.8	0.4	0.7	0.6	0.5	0.6
ii. Iraq	0.8	0.1	0.0	0.0	0.0	0.0
iii. Kuwait	1.4	0.2	0.5	0.5.	0.4	0.5
iv. Saudi Arabia	2.5	1.3	2.3	1.7	1.5	1.7
III. Eastern Europe, of which:	22.1	17.9	3.8	3.6	3.8	2.9
i. G.D.R.	3.7	-	-	-	-	-
ii. Romania	0.9	0.3	0.1	0.1	0.1	0.1
iii. Russia	18.3	16.1	2.9	3.1	3.3	2.4

Contd...

IV. Other LDC's, of which:	19.2	16.8	24.2	23.9	25.7	26.9
i. Africa	5.2	2.1	2.6	2.5	3.4	2.9
ii. Asia	13.4	14.3	20.7	20.1	21.1	22.7
iii. Latin America and Carribean	0.5	0.4	0.9	1.3	1.1	1.3
V. Others:	1.0	6.2	4.4	4.6	5.1	4.8
Total	100.0	100.0	100.0	100.0	100.0	100.0

Source: Government of India, *Economic Survey*, 1997-98

Table 4.16 : Direction of India's Trade with World (B) Imports

(per cent share)

Counry	1980-81	1990-91	1993-94	1994-95	1995-96	1996-97
I. OECD, of which:	45.7	54.0	56.1	51.4	52.4	49.2
a. EU of which	21.0	27.4	30.0	24.8	26.7	25.6
i. Belgium	2.4	6.3	8.0	4.2	4.6	6.3
ii. France	2.2	3.0	2.5	2.1	2.3	2.0
iii. Germany	5.5	8.0	7.7	7.6	8.6	7.2
iv. Netherlands	1.7	1.8	1.6	1.3	1.6	1.3
v. U.K.	5.8	6.7	6.6	5.4	5.2	5.4
b. North America	14.7	13.4	12.7	11.1	11.6	9.6
i. Canada	2.6	1.3	1.0	0.9	1.0	0.8
ii. U.S.A.	12.9	12.1	11.7	10.1	10.5	8.8

Contd...

c. Other OECD, of which:	7.4	11.2	9.7	10.6	9.7	9.1
i. Australia	1.4	3.4	2.8	3.2	2.8	3.2
ii. Japan	6.0	7.5	6.5	7.1	6.7	5.7
II. OPEC, of which:	27.8	19.9	22.4	21.1	20.9	26.4
i. Iran	10.7	2.4	1.6	1.9	1.6	2.3
ii. Iraq	6.0	1.1	0.0	0.0	0.0	0.1
iii.·Kuwait	2.7	0.8	4.8	5.2	5.4	6.2
iv. Saudi Arabia	4.3	6.7	6.6	5.5	5.5	7.3
III. Eastern Europe of which:	10.3	7.8	1.8	2.4	3.4	2.4
i. G.D.R.	0.4	-	-	-	-	-
ii. Romania	0.8	0.1	0.1	0.2	0.4	0.4
iii. Russia	8.1	5.9	1.1	1.8	2.3	1.6

Contd...

IV. Other LDC's, of which	15.7	18.4	15.4	20.2	18.3	16.9
i. Africa	5.6	2.7	2.2	2.9	2.3	2.2
ii. Asia	11.4	17.1	12.1	14.6	14.4	13.2
iii. Latin America and Carribean	2.5	2.8	1.0	2.7	1.6	1.3
V. Others	0.5	3.5	4.3	4.9	.5.0	5.0
Total	100.0	100.0	100.0	100.0	100.0	100.0

Source: Government of India, *Economic Survey*, 1997-98

Table 4.17 :Direction of India's Trade with the World

(per cent share)

Country	Exports				Imports			
	1993-94	1994-95	1995-96	1996-97	1993-94	1994-95	1995-96	1996-97
A. U.K.	6.20	6.42	6.31	6.48	6.60	5.44	5.29	5.74
B.Germany	6.90	6.64	6.23	5.66	7.70	7.63	8.63	7.63
C. Other EU Countries	12.90	13.65	13.89	12.91	15.70	11.75	12.90	12.56
D. U.S.A.	18.00	19.07	17.34	19.98	11.70	10.14	10.53	8.98
E. Japan	7.80	7.70	6.96	6.11	6.60	7.12	6.63	5.74
F. Russia	2.90	3.07	3.29	2.46	1.10	1.76	2.35	1.72
G. East Europe	0.90	0.54	0.56	0.56	0.60	0.61	1.09	0.94
H. OPEC	10.70	9.23	9.64	9.54	22.40	21.12	20.09	24.75
I. LDC's	24.10	23.66	25.90	25.89	15.30	19.84	18.32	17.20

Contd...

J. Others	9.70	9.83	9.87	10.41	12.40	14.59	13.30	14.73
Total	100.00	100.00	100.00	100.00	100.00	100.00	100.00	100.00

Source: Government of India, *Economic Survey*, 1997-98.

Table 4.18: Number of Approvals of Foreign Collaborations with EU Member Countries for 1991, 1992 and 1993

Country	1991	1992	1993
Belgium	7	11	8
Denmark	11	16	15
France	39	59	49
Germany	154	196	170
Greece	--	---	--
Italy	60	67	54
Ireland	6	1	5
Luxembourg	-	-	-
Netherlands	52	59	55
Portugal	3	3	1
Spain	5	8	9

Contd...

U.K.	136	184	172
Total	473	604	540

Source: *Indo-EC Business Pulse*. Official Publication of European Community, October, 1994.

Table 4.19: Top 10 Country Sources of Foreign Collaborations (Cumulative total of approvals by RBI and FIPB fromAugust 1991 to September 1995)

Rank No.	Country/Category	Number of Approvals (Total)	Foreign Investment	
			Value (Rs. Million)	Per cent of total
1.	U.S.A.	1434	116128.1	30.0
2.	U.K.	805	37564.9	9.7
3.	Japan	473	14944.6	3.9
4.	Switzerland	294	13091.2	3.4
5.	Germany	875	11988.1	3.1
6.	Mauritius	57	11727.3	3.0
7.	Thailand	46	10815.3	2.8
8.	Netherlands	348	8219.5	2.1

Contd...

9.	Singapore	196	8117.9	2.1
10.	Australia	149	6188.7	1.6
Excluding following special categories:				
i.	Euro issues	24	59403.1	15.3
ii.	Non-Resident Indian (from all countries)	458	24314.0	6.3
	Total (All countries and Categories)	7201	387537.8	100.0

Source: Computed from data from the Government of India, Ministry of Industry as reproduced in the Centre for Monitoring Indian Economy, *Monthly Review of the Indian Economy*, June 1996.

Table 4.20: Sector-Wise Break-up of FDI (August 1991 to February 1996)

S.No.	Name of Industry	Value of FDI Approved (cumulative)	Per Cent of Total Value approved
1.	Metallurgical Industries	42157.0	6.8
2.	Power (Fuel)	64296.9	10.3
3.	Oil Refinery(Fuel)	47423.5	7.8
4.	Electrical Equipments beilers and prime movers (other than electrical)	31962.4	5.1
5.	Telecommunications	187572.9	30.0
6.	Transportation Industry (mainly automobiles)	34535.9	5.6
7.	All other Industries (including food processing)	38082.9	6.1
8.	Services Sector (Including hotels, restaurants and tourism)	55231.0	8.9

Contd...

9.	Grand Total (including miscellaneous)	624774.5	100.0

Sources: 1. Computed from the Government of India, SIA, Newsletter, March 1996, pp. 7-9.
2. Compiled by the Government of India, Indian Investment Centre on the basis of official data collected by the RBI and the Secretariat of Industrial Approvals (including approvals by the Foreign Investment Promotion Board).

Table 4.21: Selected States Attracting Approved FDI in India (from January 1993 to April 1995)

State	Number of FDI/ Approvals	Investment approved (Rs. million)	% of total FDI approved
1. Maharashtra	387	56281	19.6
2. Delhi	209	33814	11.8
3. Gujarat	109	18601	6.5
4. Tamil Nadu	214	22459	7.8
5. West Bengal	81	36434	12.7
6. Andhra Pradesh	135	11531	4.0
7. Orissa	19	11134	3.9
8. Total	1154	190254	66.3

Source: Compiled from the Government of India, *SIA Newsletter*, May 1995.

Table 4.22: Indo-EU Bilateral Trade

(Rs. crore)

Year	Exports	Imports	Trade-Balance
1973-74	642.54	709.83	-67.39
1978-79	1658.06	2130.67	-472.61
1983-84	1815.01	4022.54	-2207.53
1988-89	4986.18	9523.96	-4537.78
1989-90	7088.57	12112.94	-5024.36
1990-91	8951.62	12681.30	-3729.68
1991-92	11898.09	13966.30	-2068.21
1992-93	15151.38	19123.90	-3972.52
1993-94	18148.90	21897.00	-3748.10
1994-95	22075.26	22338.71	-263.45

Contd...

1995-96	28075.32	32691.04	-4615.72
1996-97	29574.17	35192.10	-5617.93
1997-98	31793.74	36194.09	-4400.35

Sources: 1. *India's Exports by Countries-Commodities*; Government of India Publication; Ministry of Commerce; Various issues from March 1974-98.

2. *India's Imports by Countries - Commodities*; Government of India Publication, Ministry of Commerce; Various issues from March 1974-98.

Table 4.23: Indo-EU Bilateral Trade

Year	Exports (Rs. crore)	Percentage change over previous year/ decade	Imports (Rs. crore)	Percentage change over previous year/decade
1973-74	642.54	-	709.83	-
1983-84	1815.00	+ 182.47	4022.54	+ 466.69
1993-94	18148.90	+ 899.93	21897.00	+ 444.35
1994-95	22075.26	+21.63	22338.71	+ 2.01
1995-96	28075.32	+27.26	32691.04	+46.34
1996-97	29574.17	+ 5.33	35192.10	+ 7.65
1997-98	31793.74	+ 7.51	36194.09	+ 2.84

Note: For comparative purposes, EU as from 1973-74 onwards has been taken as comprising of 12 member countries.

Table 4.24: EU's Share in India's Exports

(Rs. crore)

Year	India's Exports to EU	India's Exports to World	% Share of EU
1973-74	642.54	2523.34	25.46
1983-84	1815.01	9771.52	18.57
1993-94	18148.90	69547.12	26.01
1994-95	22060.88	82673.39	26.71
1995-96	28075.32	10646.86	26.43
1996-97	29574.17	118817.32	24.89
1997-98	31793.74	126285.76	25.18

Source: *India's Exports by Countries-Commodities*; Government of India, Ministry of Commerce; Various issues from March 1974 - March 1998.

Table 4.25: EU's Share in India's Imports

(Rs. crore)

Year	India's Imports from EU	India's Imports from World	% Share of EU
1973-74	709.84	2955.37	24.02
1983-84	4022.54	15831.46	25.41
1993-94	21897.02	72806.01	30.07
1994-95	22338.71	89970.66	24.83
1995-96	32691.04	122678.14	26.65
1996-97	35192.10	138919.68	25.33
1997-98	36194.09	151553.52	23.88

Source: *India's Imports by Countries-Commodities*; Government of India, Ministry of Commerce; various issues from March 1974-March 1998.

Table 4.26: India's Exports to EU

(Rs. crore)

Country	1973-74	1983-84	1993-94	1994-95	1995-96	1996-97	1997-98
Belgium	44.38	214.31	2641.77	3099.29	3727.14	3839.98	4426.45
Denmark	13.05	37.81	280.95	406.19	487.03	528.00	567.04
France	48.57	160.28	1578.19	1827.49	2487.29	2540.51	2750.56
Germany	108.36	477.45	4803.19	5480.48	6600.35	6703.83	6891.95
Greece	2.31	9.24	169.58	230.79	330.15	332.09	330.53
Ireland	9.07	9.17	73.12	109.55	164.44	210.67	244.09
Italy	69.32	163.76	1890.02	2693.61	3391.42	3313.67	4081.98
Luxembourg	0.01	0.05	2.85	12.70	8.69	11.43	11.56
Netherlands	73.26	203.12	1603.00	1838.15	2567.38	3022.41	2903.68
Portugal	0.00	12.03	169.97	213.89	306.63	311.96	409.75

Cond...

Spain	11.47	35.88	607.57	845.45	1307.62	1508.76	1598.28
U.K.	262.74	491.88	4319.79	5303.24	6697.16	7250.86	7577.86
EU Total	642.54	1815.01	18148.90	22060.88	28075.32	29574.17	31793.73

Source: *India's Exports by Countries-Commodities*; Government of India, Ministry of Commerce; various issues from March 1974-March 1998.

Table 4.27: Break-up of India's Exports to EU - Percentage Share of Member Countries

Country	1973-74	1983-84	1993-94	1994-95	1995-96	1996-97	1997-98
Belgium	6.91	11.81	14.56	14.05	13.27	12.98	13.92
Denmark	2.03	2.08	1.55	1.84	1.73	1.78	1.78
France	7.56	8.83	8.70	8.28	8.86	8.59	8.65
Germany	16.86	26.30	26.48	24.84	23.51	22.67	21.68
Greece	0.36	0.51	0.93	1.05	1.76	1.12	1.04
Ireland	1.41	0.50	0.40	0.49	0.58	0.71	0.77
Italy	10.79	9.02	10.42	12.21	12.08	11.20	12.84
Luxembourg	0.00	0.00	0.01	0.05	0.03	0.04	0.04
Netherlands	11.40	11.19	8.84	8.33	9.14	10.22	9.13

Contd...

Portugal	0.00	0.66	0.94	0.97	1.09	1.05	1.29
Spain	1.78	1.98	3.35	3.83	4.66	5.10	5.03
U.K.	40.89	27.10	23.81	24.04	23.85	24.52	23.83

Source: *India's Exports by Countries-Commodities*; Government of India, Ministry of Commerce; various issues from March 1974-March 1998.

Table 4.28: Share of India's Export Basket to EU

(Rs. crore)

Commodities	1973-74	1983-84	1993-94	1994-95	1995-96	1996-97	1997-98
Gems & Jewellery	36.54	231.32	2270.73	2450.31	3068.22	3111.57	3601.03
Percentage	**5.69**	**12.74**	**12.51**	**11.10**	**10.92**	**10.52**	**11.33**
Agrobased goods	117.64	291.17	1138.03	1402.78	1576.53	2164.18	3117.53
Percentage	**18.31**	**16.04**	**6.27**	**6.35**	**5.62**	**7.32**	**9.80**
Leather, its mfrs.	89.67	222.59	2401.90	2969.10	3512.06	3375.64	3342.73
Percentage	**13.95**	**12.26**	**13.23**	**13.45**	**12.51**	**11.54**	**10.51**
Carpets & other floor coverings	16.61	125.59	855.17	776.22	1904.56	950.64	842.21
Percentage	**2.58**	**6.92**	**4.71**	**3.52**	**6.78**	**3.21**	**2.65**
Cotton	24.27	35.77	22.29	44.03	59.40	166.62	121.56
Percentage	**0.38**	**1.97**	**0.12**	**0.20**	**0.21**	**0.56**	**0.38**

Contd...

Readymade Garments	31.74	237.73	2815.68	3445.41	4323.28	4499.49	4164.09
Percentage	**4.95**	**13.10**	**15.51**	**15.61**	**15.40**	**15.21**	**13.10**
Engg. Goods	21.27	65.05	689.93	927.41	1231.07	1431.37	1718.73
Percentage	**3.31**	**3.58**	**3.80**	**4.20**	**4.38**	**4.84**	**5.41**
Fish etc.	6.70	35.16	630.46	683.11	836.79	726.87	385.99
Percentage	**1.04**	**1.94**	**3.47**	**3.09**	**2.98**	**2.46**	**1.21**
Chemical material.	8.06	64.93	1081.22	1419.06	1895.27	2276.34	2289.68
Percentage	**1.25**	**3.58**	**5.96**	**6.43**	**6.75**	**7.70**	**7.20**
Others	311.88	505.68	6243.49	7957.83	9668.14	10871.45	12210.19
Percentage	**48.54**	**27.86**	**34.40**	**36.05**	**34.44**	**36.76**	**38.40**
Total	642.54	1815.00	18148.90	22075.26	28075.32	29574.17	31793.74

Source: *India's Exports by Countries-Commodities*; Government of India, Ministry of Commerce; various issues from March 1974-March 1998.

Table 4.29: India's Exports to Belgium

(Rs. crore)

Commodities	1973-74	1983-84	1993-94	1994-95	1995-96	1996-97	1997-98
Gems and Jewellery	18.68	168.39	1812.04	1947.12	2391.52	2382.39	2757.14
Products of Chemicals	0.41	0.83	86.15	115.78	138.85	176.28	165.01
Ready-made Garments	0.49	3.26	112.68	106.80	146.30	145.95	140.02
Cotton	0.44	5.92	4.87	8.87	10.17	18.93	6.93
Tobacco and its Substitutes	0.34	2.17	17.78	13.18	23.54	48.59	101.87
Carpets and other Floor Coverings	0.78	3.24	30.44	36.54	28.48	54.28	41.61
Leather, its articles and Footwear	5.92	3.17	27.58	37.04	36.81	42.60	23.39
Engineering Goods	0.19	0.73	12.91	22.82	29.15	47.15	56.22
Fish and its products	0.98	3.46	63.26	79.73	69.05	76.88	33.04

Contd...

Sugar	0.00	2.64	0.00	0.03	0.00	0.03	0.02
Rice	0.00	0.13	2.56	5.86	8.20	2.95	20.42
Tea and Mate	0.20	0.39	1.33	1.48	0.99	0.73	18.33
Spices	0.08	0.27	1.42	1.53	2.41	3.06	8.24
Coffee and its substitutes	1.77	1.91	5.45	13.56	26.43	33.59	58.99
Cashew-Kernels	0.14	0.02	0.00	0.00	0.60	1.46	3.55
Others	13.88	19.71	470.38	712.49	814.56	787.29	801.32
Total	44.38	214.30	2648.91	3102.89	3727.13	3822.19	4236.18

Source: *India's Exports by Countries-Commodities*; Government of India, Ministry of Commerce; various issues from March 1974-March 1998.

Table 4.30: India's Exports to France

(Rs. crore)

Commodities	1973-74	1983-84	1993-94	1994-95	1995-96	1996-97	1997-98
Gems and Jewellery	3.86	16.30	63.37	74.59	77.79	88.10	87.89
Products of Chemicals	0.26	8.32	65.96	89.70	112.75	159.50	166.97
Ready-made Garments	6.25	35.46	493.23	545.55	764.67	792.54	869.86
Cotton	0.76	0.14	2.68	4.75	0.65	9.57	1.05
Tobacco and its Substitutes	0.22	1.01	4:27	1.68	2.73	5.46	8.73
Carpets and other Floor Coverings	0.52	5.88	27.55	35.15	50.88	74.99	63.59
Leather, its articles and Footwear	9.11	22.61	191.74	269.02	287.21	267.00	212.91
Engineering Goods	6.64	7.05	81.76	88.32	85.00	91.35	155.51
Fish and its products	0.90	4.47	44.94	47.68	44.42	43.81	20.66

Contd...

Sugar	0.00	0.44	23.65	0.04	78.90	37.64	27.79
Rice	0.00	0.01	9.10	13.58	25.49	10.47	31.08
Tea and Mate	0.14	1.22	3.68	5.35	3.83	5.19	4.25
Spices	0.79	1.64	14.76	17.87	19.69	13.33	38.90
Coffee and its substitutes	1.18	2.10	7.95	10.45	16.13	12.63	20.14
Cashew-Kernels	0.09	0.11	6.58	8.12	11.50	17.94	37.01
Others	17.79	53.45	536.88	615.58	905.59	910.90	1004.15
Total	24.62	81.56	1578.19	1827.49	2487.28	2540.51	2750.56

Source: *India's Exports by Countries-Commodities*; Government of India, Ministry of Commerce; various issues from March 1974-March 1998.

Table 4.31: India's Exports to Germany

(Rs. crore)

Commodities	1973-74	1983-84	1993-94	1994-95	1995-96	1996-97	1997-98
Gems and Jewellery	2.20	20.78	174.84	164.10	222.57	219.73	209.16
Products of Chemicals	1.61	10.67	346.63	458.82	569,90	607.03	752.11
Ready-made Garments	5.78	80.59	870.09	1169.22	1269.19	1313.48	1171.31
Cotton	0.79	6.51	2.85	3.42	1.79	10.26	9.84
Tobacco and its Substitutes	0.14	0.66	22.43	4.63	14.87	73.06	88.90
Carpets and other Floor Coverings	10.18	86.86	618.50	537.58	588.77	627.25	490.15
Leather, its articles and Footwear	12.38	81.75	1004.61	1160.14	1355.44	130.00	896.85
Engineering Goods	3.52	16.38	161.58	201.98	280.33	306.36	424.05
Fish and its products	0.99	0.71	18.01	25.32	23.80	37.37	19.56

Contd...

Sugar	0.00	2.62	0.32	0.12	4.84	0.73	0.03
Rice	0.00	0.17	5.03	6.33	16.26	12.69	13.95
Tea and Mate	6.36	13.40	57.01	72.00	74.91	63.33	79.65
Spices	1.22	4.93	23.29	22.64	27.99	38.14	65.05
Coffee and its substitutes	3.39	19.76	130.78	199.11	142.65	180.41	277.93
Cashew-Kernels	1.57	1.69	19.91	32.01	1.88	28.90	23.44
Others	58.15	124.79.	1347.31	1422.99	1988.09	1890.93	2369.89
Total	108.34	473.42	4803.19	5480.47	6600.35	6703.83	6891.95

Source: *India's Exports by Countries-Commodities*; Government of India, Ministry of Commerce; various issues from March 1974-March 1998.

Table 4.32: India's Exports to Italy

(Rs. crore)

Commodities	1973-74	1983-84	1993-94	1994-95	1995-96	1996-97	1997-98
Gems and Jewellery	0.56	5.33	22.17	22.56	28.00	31.02	37.43
Products of Chemicals	1.47	4.47	110.90	152.99	196.48	236.89	317.85
Ready-made Garments	4.24	28.97	235.89	325.21	368.31	337.76	375.46
Cotton	0.15	4.38	5.16	5.68	18.64	73.28	49.23
Tobacco and its Substitutes	0.00	0.00	0.00	0.57	3.70	6.28	5.67
Carpets and other Floor Coverings	0.30	7.02	58.85	58.59	51.84	42.84	46.74
Leather, its articles and Footwear	25.42	53.04	405.89	610.73	741.90	651.49	578.75
Engineering Goods	0.60	3.30	61.53	79.95	131.15	178.82	263.05
Fish and its products	0.00	0.12	115.20	111.50	179.85	111.60	62.74

Contd...

Sugar	0.00	1.39	2.61	0.00	10.47	20.14	0.01
Rice	0.00	0.00	0.86	1.12	6.63	8.62	6.43
Tea and Mate	0.62	0.39	3.31	1.98	3.05	2.71	4.10
Spices	2.24	2.47	9.43	17.16	23.25	22.88	37.94
Coffee and its substitutes	4.59	10.75	60.79	176.34	197.79	184.85	222.08
Cashew-Kernels	0.14	0.14	1.11	1.65	4.25	7.23	17.14
Others	28.92	41.94..	796.76	1127.51	1426.03	1397.18	2057.27
Total	69.32	163.76	1890.02	2693.61	3391.41	3313.67	4081.98

Source: *India's Exports by Countries-Commodities*; Government of India, Ministry of Commerce; various issues from March 1974-March 1998.

Table 4.33: India's Exports to The Netherlands

(Rs. crore)

Commodities	1973-74	1983-84	1993-94	1994-95	1995-96	1996-97	1997-98
Gems and Jewellery	5.24	4.52	22.88	17.07	33.59	18.32	23.72
Products of Chemicals	1.89	31.23	134.43	197,01	311.34	399.28	471.80
Ready-made Garments	2.30	15.43	324.04	376.13	473.77	490.97	427.93
Cotton	0.01	0.00	0.00	0.00	1.23	6.35	2.99
Tobacco and its Substitutes	0.31	·2.99	7.24	7.24	6.85	7.89	12.58
Carpets and other Floor Coverings	1.28	7.05	32.68	32.81	38.28	34.45	38.50
Leather, its articles and Footwear	2.69	3.82	84.22	89.49	120.92	124.25	107.03
Engineering Goods	0.46	8.19	80.29	141.22	151.58	191.37	158.29
Fish and its products	0.32	5.07	78.78	61.30	85.32	84.46	27.78

Contd...

Sugar	0.00	5.38	0.06	0.00	56.90	125.39	5.92
Rice	0.00	0.00	3.06	1.26	11.18	2.90	23.60
Tea and Mate	10.07	3.29	14.78	20.58	20.35	18.85	24.97
Spices	0.26	1.16	12.75	13.02	15.36	38.45	32.53
Coffee and its substitutes	1.65	6.15	8.76	11.33	14.34	32.91	58.63
Cashew-Kernels	1.08	12.56	217.08	213.69	209.22	321.49	328.74
Others	45.64	96.22	581.91	655.92	1017.08	1125.02	1158.58
Total	64.81	131.86	1603.01	1838.15	2567.38	3022.41	2903.67

Source: *India's Exports by Countries-Commodities*; Government of India, Ministry of Commerce; various issues from March 1974-March 1998.

Table 4.34: India's Exports to Spain

(Rs. crore)

Commodities	1973-74	1983-84	1993-94	1994-95	1995-96	1996-97	1997-98
Gems and Jewellery	0.93	6.84	5.37	11.24	16.73	26.80	29.98
Products of Chemicals	0.06	0.66	60.53	84.56	133.25	168.23	221.34
Ready-made Garments	0.16	1.87	67.28	98.03	136.62	163.68	138.41
Cotton	0.00	8.93	1.61	0.76	0.00	7.31	1.70
Tobacco and its Substitutes	0.00	0.00	0.15	0.03	3.11	1.62	23.32
Carpets and other Floor Coverings	0.00	0.19	9.20	11.87	15.09	30.94	32.17
Leather, its articles and Footwear	1.07	4.28	79.07	115.94	167.81	169.29	167.66
Engineering Goods	0.16	0.35	29.73	47.73	134.26	157.68	132.18
Fish and its products	0.01	0.49	121.66	109.51	155.96	107.84	79.97

Contd...

Sugar	0.00	0.00	1.40	0.00	12.42	36.38	1.63
Rice	0.00	0.00	0.31	0.17	0.62	0.62	0.50
Tea and Mate	0.00	0.06	0.00	0.02	0.13	0.03	0.77
Spices	0.21	0.29	4.60	5.65	12.44	31.73	26.97
Coffee and its substitutes	0.01	5.98	8.65	16.12	17.97	32.07	50.00
Cashew-Kernels	0.01	0.00	4.56	3.72	9.63	7.68	13.59
Others	8.80	5.87	213.37	340.05	491.50	566.78	678.01
Total	11.46	35.88	607.57	845.47	1307.62	1508.76	1598.28

Source: *India's Exports by Countries-Commodities*; Government of India, Ministry of Commerce; various issues from March 1974-March 1998.

Table 4.35: India's Exports to U.K.

(Rs. crore)

Commodities	1973-74	1983-84	1993-94	1994-95	1995-96	1996-97	1997-98
Gems and Jewellery	4.98	11.09	167.39	217.12	282.54	294.59	439.50
Products of Chemicals	2.25	8.22	220.55	255.42	354.90	420.99	499.34
Ready-made Garments	8.06	61.05	639.48	843.14	1102.90	1066.00	863.30
Cotton	0.24	7.05	2.52	20.36	22.18	34.65	30.99
Tobacco and its Substitutes	31.55	34.12	46.21	58.29	72.28	145.02	138.12
Carpets and other Floor Coverings	2.80	11.25	48.82	69.84	82.53	101.09	78.33
Leather, its articles and Footwear	32.55	40.36	488.44	598.90	648.22	740.50	519.59
Engineering Goods	9.47	27.10	222.34	299.05	403.16	403.75	467.13
Fish and its products	3.40	19.91	123.88	164.39	182.23	180.46	79.00

Contd...

Sugar	2.80	7.71	0.96	0.65	7.75	15.56	1.33
Rice	0.40	7.81	98.67	84.34	119.79	100.14	169.46
Tea and Mate	35.61	94.20	138.84	162.03	125.59	144.98	197.76
Spices	1.28	15.32	37.05	37.46	46.27	69.55	87.43
Coffee and its substitutes	0.47	1.42	7.78	19.81	14.21	7.24	9.33
Cashew-Kernels	1.64	4.56	70.25	66.12	42.30	79.83	91.36
Others	125.17	140.65	2006.54	2406.23	3190.22	3481.41	3905.81
Total	262.74	491.88	4319.79	5303.23	6697.16	7250.86	7577.85

Source: *India's Exports by Countries-Commodities*; Government of India, Ministry of Commerce; various issues from March 1974-March 1998.

Table 4.36: India's Exports and Imports of Gems and Jewellery to EU

(Rs. crore)

Year	Exports to EU	Imports from EU	Trade Balance	Exports as % of Imports
1973-74	36.53	56.00	-19.46	65.18
1978-79	302.52	448.48	-145.96	67.45
1983-84	231.32	920.23	-688.91	25.14
1988-89	951.35	2901.72	-1950.37	32.79
1993-94	2270.73	7782.12	-5511.39	29.18
1994-95	2450.31	4728.54	-2278.23	51.82
1995-96	3068.22	6312.27	-3244.05	48.61
1996-97	3111.57	9112.78	-6001.21	34.14
1997-98	3601.03	11240.86	-7639.83	32.03

Table 4.37: India's Exports to EU - 12

Year	In Million Rupees	In Million US Dollar
1973	6425.42	1018.83
1975	8659.68	1564.74
1977	14489.90	2048.69
1979	17226.33	2515.57
1981	14961.47	2576.05
1983	18150.06	2339.89
1985	20147.09	2347.64
1987	40614.42	3905.33
1989	70885.71	5818.09

Contd...

1991	118,980.96	6261.37
1992	151,513.83	6784.91

Source: *International Trade Statistics*, UN Publication; various issues from 1974-94.
Government of India, Ministry of Commerce; India's Exports by countries-Commodities, various issues from March 1974 to 1994.
For comparison purposes EU has been taken as consisting of all existing members (i.e. 12 countries from 1974 - 1993).

Table 4.38: Index Numbers

(US dollar million)

Year	India's Exports to EU	EU's Imports from world	GDP of EU	Population of EU (in million)	Index of India's Exports	Index of EU's Imports from world	Index of GDP of EU	Index of Population of EU
1973-74	1019	317009	1115	310	100.00	100.00	100.00	100.00
1978-79	2509	638726	2009	316	246.22	201.49	180.18	101.94
1983-84	2339	629995	3125	320	229.54	198.73	280.26	103.23
1988-89	4651	1158375	4433	324	456.43	365.41	397.58	104.51
1991-92	6261	1514807	5322	330	614.43	477.84	477.31	106.45
1992-93	6785	1296383	5353	332	665.84	408.95	480.08	107.09

Table 4.39: Break-Up of India's Imports from Leading Trading Partners of EU and Their Percentage Share

(Rs. crore)

Year	Belgium	France	Germany	Italy	Netherlands	Spain	U.K.
1973-74	65.52	69.75	220.56	49.07	54.32	1.80	244.81
Percent share	**9.23**	**9.83**	**29.07**	**6.91**	**7.65**	**0.25**	**34.49**
1983-84	648.58	289.33	1183.86	282.99	278.70	143.06	1152.71
Percent share	**16.12**	**7.19**	**29.43**	**7.03**	**6.93**	**3.55**	**28.65**
1993-94	2648.91	1578.19	4803.19	1890.03	1603.01	607.57	4319.79
Percent share	**12.09**	**7.20**	**21.93**	**8.63**	**7.32**	**2.77**	**19.72**
1994-95	3102.89	1827.49	5480.47	2693.61	1838.15	845.47	5303.23
Percent share	**13.89**	**8.18**	**24.53**	**12.05**	**8.22**	**3.78**	**23.74**
1995-96	3727.14	2487.28	6600.35	3391.41	2567.38	1307.62	6697.16
Percent share	**11.40**	**7.61**	**20.19**	**10.37**	**7.85**	**3.99**	**20.48**

Contd...

1996-97	3822.19	2540.51	6703.83	3313.67	3022.41	1508.76	7250.86
Percent share	**10.86**	**7.22**	**19.05**	**9.41**	**8.59**	**4.28**	**20.60**
1997-98	4236.18	2750.56	6891.96	4081.98	2903.67	1598.28	7577.85
Percent share	**11.70**	**7.59**	**19.04**	**11.28**	**8.02**	**4.41**	**20.94**

Table 4.40: Share of India's Imports of Major Commodity Groups from EU - 12

(Rs. crore)

Commodities	1973-74	1983-84	1993-94	1994-95	1995-96	1996-97	1997-98
Gems and Jewellery	56.00	920.23	7617.12	4709.55	6298.77	9079.78	11144.86
Percentage	**7.89**	**22.88**	**34.78**	**21.08**	**19.27**	**25.80**	**30.79**
Capital Goods	329.06	1341.62	4886.47	6013.15	9514.97	8738.04	9136.07
Percentage	**46.35**	**33.35**	**22.31**	**26.91**	**29.10**	**24.83**	**25.24**
Iron and Steel	84.79	411.61	1377.26	1598.22	1911.25	2001.46	1754.57
Percentage	**·11.95**	**10.23**	**6.29**	**·7.15**	**5.84**	**5.68**	**4.85**
Organic Chemicals	38.14	265.14	1007.71	1306.83	1629.07	1458.92	1369.97
Percentage	**5.37**	**6.09**	**4.60**	**5.85**	**4.98**	**4.14**	**3.78**
Chemical Mater.	92.83	308.49	1286.44	1403.16	1969.69	1948.05	2018.73
Percentage	**13.07**	**7.67**	**5.87**	**6.28**	**6.02**	**5.53**	**5.57**

Contd...

Professional & Scien. Instrument	13.16	128.15	483.43	477.68	724.38	604.96	871.98
Percentage	**1.85**	**3.18**	**2.21**	**2.13**	**2.21**	**1.72**	**2.40**
Non-ferrous metals	16.26	91.89	246.33	425.92	594.52	590.10	463.80
Percentage	**2.29**	**2.28**	**1.12**	**1.90**	**1.81**	**1.67**	**1.28**
Inorganic Chem.	10.10	49.13	148.35	141.73	169.79	188.36	223.97
Percentage	**1.42**	**1.22**	**0.68**	**0.63**	**0.51**	**0.53**	**0.61**
Others	69.46	526.23	4843.89	6262.47	9878.60	10582.44	9210.14
Percentage	**9.78**	**·13.08**	**22.12**	**28.03**	**30.21**	**30.07**	**25.45**
Total	709.83	4022.54	21897.00	22338.71	32691.04	35192.10	36194.09

Table 4.41: India's Imports from Belgium (Rs. crore)

Commodities	1973-74	1983-84	1993-94	1994-95	1995-96	1996-97	1997-98
Gems and Jewellery	20.66	485.50	5168.46	2917.95	4467.86	6698.15	7751.53
Inorganic Chemicals	0.56	4.32	10.51	14.39	15.51	26.27	28.94
Organic Chemicals	3.97	31.07	81.01	75.51	92.59	85.51	103.57
Chemical Material and Products	6.54	6.96	25.41	112.14	150.57	169.43	181.05
Iron and Steel	12.03	38.67	138.22	155.69	243.37	218.47	165.17
Non-ferrous Metals	2.36	5.29	24.42	46.58	43.26	94.17	81.74
Capital Goods	8.57	31.97	92.53	143.92	290.74	267.66	312.12
Professional and Scientific Instruments	0.84	9.16	43.30	48.71	59.51	62.55	73.58
Others	9.67	30.67	296.60	165.16	308.92	371.23	370.68
Total	65.52	648.58	5880.49	3680.09	5672.26	7993.48	907.44

Source: *India's Exports by Countries-Commodities*; Government of India, Ministry of Commerce; various issues from March 1974-March 1998.

Table 4.42: India's Imports from France

(Rs. crore)

Commodities	1973-74	1983-84	993-94	1994-95	1995-96	1996-97	1997-98
Gems and Jewellery	0.00	0.11	0.32	16.98	17.51	16.76	1.37
Inorganic Chemicals	0.37	4.69	34.32	12.39	13.40	20.20	29.89
Organic Chemicals	1.35	17.45	92.08	105.84	136.57	170.67	175.61
Chemical Material and Products	4.08	29.33	27.87	153.40	183.15	190.43	253.65
Iron and Steel	5.00	40.07	136.91	128.73	114.33	296.14	132.87
Non-ferrous Metals	0.34	10.57	21.24	29.79	30.39	32.07	31.07
Capital Goods	53.02	140.10	898.24	846.16	856.98	837.25	989.78
Professional and Scientific Instruments	0.46	6.74	35.84	32.76	47.23	53.78	70.70
Others	3.97	38.17	613.29	568.96	1412.68	1110.03	1238.49
Total	69.75	289.33	1860.15	1895.04	2812.28	2726.76	2923.46

Source: *India's Exports by Countries-Commodities*; Government of India, Ministry of Commerce; various issues from March 1974-March 1998.

Table 4.43: India's Imports from Germany

(Rs. crore)

Commodities	1973-74	1983-84	1993-94	1994-95	1995-96	1996-97	1997-98
Gems and Jewellery	0.12	0.38	11.95	21.74	29.80	75.21	45.78
Inorganic Chemicals	2.32	19.87	48.19	62.09	70.93	92.04	81.62
Organic Chemicals	12.45	86.79	315.18	395.46	452.17	434.72	470.75
Chemical Material and Products	43.27	103.40	50.26	538.21	799.04	615.40	625.99
Iron and Steel	36.04	156.58	602.12	665.48	797.56	719.59	687.91
Non-ferrous Metals	6.37	14.93	52.29	91.17	131.25	135.48	149.90
Capital Goods	100.23	612.76	2177.81	2781.75	4818.89	4375.53	4040.31
Professional and Scientific Instruments	6.88	64.29	170.76	197.36	324.81	223.03	313.85
Others	10.11	113.51	2180.76	1978.07	3095.65	3379.26	2878.48
Total	210.45	1070.34	5609.35	6731.37	10520.14	10050.31	9294.63

Source: *India's Exports by Countries-Commodities*; Government of India, Ministry of Commerce; various issues from March 1974-March 1998.

Table 4.44: India's Imports from Italy

(Rs. crore)

Commodities	1973-74	1983-84	1993-94	1994-95	1995-96	1996-97	1997-98
Gems and Jewellery	0.13	0.10	0.15	3.75	2.41	4.25	12.66
Inorganic Chemicals	1.17	2.20	18.01	4.69	4.94	5.51	9.15
Organic Chemicals	4.97	23.12	69.26	147.18	256.44	218.69	152.63
Chemical Material and Products	9.56	40.05	15.44	157.95	205.84	210.11	189.47
Iron and Steel	3.45	40.81	141.38	236.74	261.50	169.10	251.62
Non-ferrous Metals	0.66	2.55	12.44	16.27	23.06	18.27	18.35
Capital Goods	22.77	153.81	578.86	839.45	1182.92	1294.05	1490.68
Professional and Scientific Instruments	0.26	8.12	17.06	28.05	38.10	31.94	61.00
Others	5.97	11.43	833.74	868.59	1584.80	1553.22	1231.52
Total	49.07	282.99	1686.37	2302.71	3560.06	3505.18	3417.12

Source: *India's Imports by Countries-Commodities*; Government of India, Ministry of Commerce; various issues from March 1974-March 1998.

Table 4.45: India's Imports from Netherlands (Rs. crore)

Commodities	1973-74	1983-84	1993-94	1994-95	1995-96	1996-97	1997-98
Gems and Jewellery	0.02	0.00	0.00	0.32	4.52	3.22	4.50
Inorganic Chemicals	0.56	2.82	11.01	5.54	20.68	13.19	10.04
Organic Chemicals	4.10	32.84	207.37	272.51	386.32	182.17	181.37
Chemical Material and Products	15.71	73.73	24.60	172.60	219.59	193.78	218.65
Iron and Steel	2.43	18.81	14.30	219.17	127.98	68.73	75.79
Non-ferrous Metals	1:18	17.79	49.25	62.64	98.05	102.11	62.40
Capital Goods	16.04	50.20	284.91	264.48	580.51	313.81	403.78
Professional and Scientific Instruments	0.70	6.83	68.79	14.52	22.23	29.54	50.38
Others	13.45	74.76	524.15	363.00	447.47	847.02	600.99
Total	54.32	278.70	1184.41	1177.55	1907.40	1753.61	1607.94

Source: *India's Imports by Countries-Commodities*; Government of India, Ministry of Commerce; various issues from March 1974-March 1998.

Table 4.46: India's Imports from Spain

(Rs. crore)

Commodities	1973-74	1983-84	1993-94	1994-95	1995-96	1996-97	1997-98
Gems and Jewellery	0.00	0.02	0.05	0.06	0.47	4.43	0.00
Inorganic Chemicals	0.85	4.63	2.95	4.68	4.02	2.97	5.40
Organic Chemicals	0.97	20.38	112.48	155.45	136.19	151.17	86.09
Chemical Material and Products	0.46	12.14	2.40	46.20	57.00	49.98	56.77
Iron and Steel	0.03	31.29	65.36	117.92	79.03	148.23	130.66
Non-ferrous Metals	0.00	14.50	0.51	1.54	11.52	31.15	15.42
Capital Goods	0.07	9.07	38.01	73.97	109.74	159.59	101.74
Professional and Scientific Instruments	0.00	0.44	5.74	6.79	7.87	10.14	15.81
Others	0.37	50.50	154.69	155.97	202.99	189.92	193.73
Total	1.80	143.06	382.22	562.62	608.86	747.63	605.67

Source: *India's Imports by Countries-Commodities*; Government of India, Ministry of Commerce; various issues from March 1974-March 1998.

Table 4.47: India's Imports from U.K. (Rs. crore)

Commodities	1973-74	1983-84	1993-94	1994-95	1995-96	1996-97	1997-98
Gems and Jewellery	35.04	434.02	2375.17	1714.72	1770.16	2270.73	3319.01
Inorganic Chemicals	4.25	10.26	15.32	17.89	36.16	23.15	56.87
Organic Chemicals	11.07	31.60	77.30	129.91	162.76	202.91	196.92
Chemical Material and Products	12.18	38.28	70.44	209.63	346.45	499.90	541.89
Iron and Steel	25.57	81.59	208.95	183.64	284.55	376.17	306.52
Non-ferrous Metals	5.32	26.07	103.58	178.07	150.59	176.64	94.16
Capital Goods	126.82	327.56	748.62	1037.48	1665.17	1753.78	1795.62
Professional and Scientific Instruments	3.78	30.00	112.22	148.48	216.51	187.93	284.64
Others	17.43	168.43	1106.60	1216.70	1782.43	2086.82	2100.82
Total	245.92	1153.10	4818.25	4836.57	6414.82	7578.08	8696.48

Source: *India's Imports by Countries-Commodities*; Government of India, Ministry of Commerce; various issues from March 1974-March 1998.

Table 4.48: UK's Share in India's Exports to the World

(Rs. crore)

Commodity	1993-94	1994-95	1995-96	1996-97	1997-98
Tea & Mate					
World	1059.16	975.48	1171.65	1037.08	1505.07
U.K.	133.48	162.03	125.60	144.09	197.76
U.K.'s percentage share	13.11	16.61	10.72	13.98	13.14
Cotton					
World	653.59	139.76	206.10	1574.51	839.93
U.K.	25.27	20.37	22.19	34.66	30.99
U.K.'s percentage share	3.87	14.57	10.77	2.20	3.69
Spices					
World	568.91	612.24	785.89	1202.14	1407.70
U.K.	37.06	37.46	46.28	69.55	87.43
U.K.'s percentage share	6.51	6.12	5.89	5.79	6.21

Contd...

Rice					
World	1286.71	1205.79	4553.01	3172.35	3274.73
U.K.	98.68	84.35	119.79	100.15	169.46
U.K.'s percentage share	7.67	6.70	2.63	3.16	5.17
Leather					
World	4076.02	5057.15	5762.16	4539.71	4294.14
U.K.	488.45	598.91	648.29	740.50	519.59
U.K.'s percentage share	11.98	11.84	11.25	16.31	12.10
Ready-made Garments					
World	6891.13	8869.14	10603.44	11443.12	11720.32
U.K.	639.49	843.14	1102.90	1066.00	863.31
U.K.'s percentage share	9.28	9.51	10.40	9.31	7.36

Contd...

Cashew-Kernels					
World	1045.31	1244.65	1231.07	1285.48	1383.93
U.K.	70.26	66.13	42.31	79.83	91.36
U.K.'s percentage share	6.72	5.31	3.44	6.21	6.60
Tobacco etc.					
World	461.20	254.75	365.81	756.77	1058.51
U.K.	46.21	58.29	72.29	145.03	138.12
U.K.'s percentage share	10.02	22.88	19.76	19.16	13.05
Carpets					
World	1782.19	1758.19	1867.01	2096.29	1983.43
U.K.	48.82	69.84	82.54	101.09	78.33
U.K.'s percentage share	2.74	3.97	4.42	4.82	3.95

Contd...

Gems & Jewellery					
World	12532.36	14130.54	17644.97	16872.09	19013.55
U.K.	167.39	217.13	282.55	294.59	439.51
U.K.'s percentage share	1.34	1.53	1.60	1.75	2.31
Fish, Molluscs etc					
World	2551.89	3536.64	3384.25	4007.63	4312.71
U.K.	123.89	164.40	182.24	180.47	79.00
U.K.'s percentage share	4.85	4.65	5.38	4.50	1.83
Engg. Goods					
World	4040.35	4929.22	6212.67	7473.66	7790.84
U.K.	222.35	299.05	403.16	403.76	467.14
U.K.'s percentage share	5.50	6.07	6.49	5.40	5.99

Contd...

Sugar					
World	178.08	62.16	503.55	1077.89	248.22
U.K.	9.63	0.66	7.75	15.27	1.37
U.K.'s percentage share	5.41	1.06	1.54	1.42	0.55
Chemical Products					
World	3885.05	5024.22	6644.54	8308.11	9651.70
U.K.	220.55	255.43	354.90	420.99	499.35
U.K.'s percentage share	5.67	5.08	5.34	5.07	5.17
Coffee etc.					
World	545.60	1052.93	1509.17	1426.59	1621.68
U.K.	7.78	19.82	14.21	7.24	9.33
U.K.'s percentage share	1.42	1.88	0.94	0.51	0.58

Source: *Foreign Trade Statistics of India*; Government of India, Ministry of Commerce; March 1974-March 1998.

Table 5.1: India's Exports to EU

(Rs. crore)

Commodity	1993-94	1994-95	1995-96	1996-97	1997-98
1. Gems & Jewellery	2270.73	2450.31	3068.22	3111.57	3601.03
2. Agro-based goods	1138.03	1402.78	1576.58	2164.18	3117.53
3. Ldather, its articles & footwear	2401.90	2969.10	3512.06	3375.64	3342.73
4. Carpet	855.17	776.22	1904.56	950.74	842.21
5. Cotton	22.29	44.03	59.40	166.62	121.56
6. Readymade garments	2815.68	3445.41	4323.28	4499.49	4164.09
7. Engineering goods	689.93	927.41	1231.07	1431.37	1718.73
8. Fish and its preparation	630.46	683.79	836.79	726.87	385.99
9. Chemical material & its products	1071.22	1419.06	1895.27	2276.34	2289.68
10. Others	6243.49	7957.83	9668.14	10871.45	12210.13
Total	18148.90	22075.26	28075.32	29514.17	31793.74

Select Bibliography

Agraa, Ali-Mei; 'The Economics of the European Community'; Heritage Publishers; 1981.

Anwar S.A.; 'The European Community and Indo-British Trade Relations'; Gower Publishing Company Ltd.; England, 1983.

Balassa, B.; 'European Economics Integration'; North Holland Publishing Company; 1975.

Bhagwati, Jagdish N. and Desai, Padma; 'India: Planning for Industrialisation'; London; 1970.

Bhagwati, Jagdish N. and Srinivasan, T.N.; 'Foreign Trade Regimes and Economic Development'; New Delhi; 1976.

Ceccini, Paolo; 'The European challenge 1992 - The Benefits of a Single Market' Aldershot; 1988.

Cooney, John; 'A United States of Europe'; Dublin University Press; 1980.

Drew, John; 'Doing Business in the European Community;' Butterworth and Company Publishers Ltd.; 1983.

Dharma Kumar; 'India and the EEC'; Asia Publishing House, 1966.

E'Mile Noel; 'Working Together - The Institutions of the European Community'; European Documentation Series; printed in Germany; 1991.

Hallsteins Walter; 'The European Community - A New Path to Peaceful Union'; Allied Publishers Pvt. Ltd.; 1963.

Hopekins Michel; 'Policy Formation in the European Community'; Mansell Publishing; Great Britain; 1981.

Hans A. Schmitt;'The Path to European Union' Louisiana State University Press (Baton Rouge); 1962.

Kitzinger U.W.; 'The Politics and Economics of European Integration'; Fredrich A. Praeger Publishers; 1965.

Kerz Anthony J.C.; 'The Common Market and How it Works'; Pergamonn Press, Great Britain; 1984.

K.Venkatagiri Gowda Rao and Raghavan Publishers; 'The European Common Market and India'; 1962.

Lall K.B. and Chopra H.S. (Editors); 'EEC and the Third World'; Radiant Publishers; 1981.

Lall K.B. Ernest W. and Chopra H. S. (Editors); 'The EEC in the Global System'; Allied Publishers Pvt. Ltd.; 1984.

Lipgens Walter; 'A History of European Integration'; Clareudon Press; 1982.

Lipstein K.; 'The Law of the European Economic Community'; Butterworth and Company Ltd.; 1974.

Lucas, Robert E.B. and Gustav F.Papanek (Editors); 'India's Economy - Recent Development and Future Prospects'; Delhi; 1988.

Lodge Juliet (Editors); 'Institutions and Policies of the European Community'; Frances Puiter Publishers; 1983.

Mayne Richard; 'The Community of Europe'; Victor Gollancz Ltd., London; 1962.

Singh Manmohan; 'India's Export Trends'; London; 1964.

Sijthoff, Janoszita A.W.; 'Perspectives for All European Economic Cooperation'; London; 1977.

Uppal J.S. (Editor); 'India's Economic Problems'; New Delhi; 1987.

Reports, Articles and Papers

'A Guide to Working in Europe Without Frontiers'; Official Publication of European Community; 1988.

Analysis and Evaluation of Databases on Business and Management Training Schemes for Small and Medium-sized Enterprises in the European Community; Official Publication of European Community; 1991.

A Young People's Europe; Leaflet, Europe on the Move Series; 1991; official publication of European Community.

A Practical Guide to Cross-border Cooperation: Enterprise policy; A European Documentation; 1992.

Agreement for Commercial and Economic Cooperation between the European Economic Community and India; Official Journal of the European Community, No. L328/7.

Basic Statistics of the Community; Bulletin of the European Community; Luxembourg; Office for Official Publications; 1992.

Bakhoven A.F.; 'The Completion of the Common Market in 1992: Macroeconomic Consequences for the European Community'; Research Memorandum No. 56, Central Planning Bureau, the Hague; March, 1989.

'Building the Future Together'; Proceedings of the Symposium Organised by the European Commission to mark the 40th anniversary of the Declaration of May 9, 1950; Brussels; May 8, 1990.

Bieber R. Jacque, Jean Paul and Weifer H.H.; An Ever Closer Union; The European Perspective Series; Brussels; 1985.

Briefing Note; Completing the Internal Market Programme; 20th January, 1990; EEC Document.

Bulletin of the European Communities Supplement 1/87; The Single Act; A New Frontier Programme of the Commission for 1987; Office for Official Publication of the European Community; Belgium, 1987.

'Battling for the Union'; Bulletin of the European Communities; Luxembourg; 1988.

Calingaert M.; "The 1992 Challenge of the European Community's Internal Market"; National Planning Association Report, Washington D.C.; 1988.

'Completing the Internal Market: An area without internal frontiers'; Sixth Report of the Commission concerning the implementation of the Internal Market; official publication of the European Community; 1991.

Callewaert W.N. and Kumar Rajiv; EEC-India: Towards a Common Perspective; Proceedings of the EC-India Seminar, Leuves, 11-12 November, 1984; Petters-Leuvin; 1985.

Commission of the European Communities; The Economics of 1992; An assessment of the Potential Economics effects of completing the I Internal Market of the European Community; European Economy; March 1988.

Commission of the European Communities; "National Implementing Measures to give effect to the White Paper of the Commission on the completion of the Internal Market"; April, 1992.

Commission of the European Communities; "Completing the Internal Market : The Elimination of Frontier Controls"; Vol. 2; January, 1992.

Commission of the European Communities; Seventh Report to the Council and the European Parliament concerning the implementation of the White Paper on the completion of the internal market; COM (92) 33 Final Community.

Commission of the European Communities; "From the Signle Act to Maastricht and Beyond: The Means to Match Our Ambitions"; COM (92) 2000 Final; Brussels' February, 1992.

Committee for the study of Economic and Monetary Union; Report on 'Economic and Monetary Union in the European Community"; office for official publications of the E.C.; 1989.

'The European Community in 1992 and Beyond"; Speech given to the Federation of Indo-German Societies in India by Mr. Robert Houliston, Head of the Delegation of the Commission of the European Communities; March 9, 1989.

Indian Institute of Foreign Trade; 'Foreign Trade in India's Development: Performance and Prospects', 1988.

Indo-EC Business Pulse - Opportunity; The Council of EEC Chambers of Commerce in India; November 1993, December 1994.

International Trade Statistics; UN Publication, various issues from 1973 to 1993.

Neven D. J. (1990); 'EEC Integration Towards 1992: Some Distributional Aspects'; Economic Policy.

Noel Emile; "Working Together : The Institutions of the European Community' European Documentation, Catalogue Number cb-52-88-897-EN-C, Germany; 1991.

Panorama of EC Industry (1991-92); European Commission publication; 1990.

PHD Chamber of Commerce and Industry; Workshop on 'EEC 1992: Opportunities and Challenges - A Backgrounder'; May 2, 1989; March, 1995.

Rau M.V.B.' "Access to Single European Market 1992: Implications for India"; The Associated Chambers of Commerce and Industry of India.

Robsonn peter (Editor); 'Europe 1992 and the Developing Countries"; Special issue of Journal of Common Market Studies.

Report of the Ambassador's Committee on 'The Single European Market 1992 and India'; Ministry of Commerce, Government of India.

Sawaikar S.N.; "European Economic Integration 1992"; State Bank of India Economic Research Department.

Shobha Ahuja; 'Access to European Markets - EEC 1992: An assessment'; The Associated Chanbers of Commerce and Industry of India; 1989.

Council of the European Communities and Commission of the European Communities; 'Treaty on European Union'; Maastricht; February, 1992.

Das Amit; "Strategy for Promotion of India's Engineering Exports to EEC", Export-Import Bank of India; Occasional paper No. 6; June, 1989.

'Deadline 1992: Putting Europe to work'; official publication of the European Community; 1990.

DGCI & S. Calcutta; Ministry of Commerce, Government of India publication on 'India's Exports by Countries-Commodities' and 'India's Imports by Countries-Commodities'; various issues from March 1974 to March 1994.

'EC-India: Perspectives in a changing International Order'; Proceedings of a CEPS-ICRIER seminar; Centre for European Policy Studies, Brussels; 1989.

Economic Survey; Government of India publication, various issues.

'EC-India: Partners in Progress'; Commission of the European Communities, Directorate General for External Relation; Brussels; various editions - June 1988 December 1993, March 1995, December 1994 and March 1995.

European Documentation; 'Europe without Frontiers: Completing the Internal market' Periodical 2/198; Germany, 1989.

'Europe in ten lessons'; European Documentation, 1992.

'European Unification: The Origin and Growth of the European Community'; European Documentation No. 1/1989, 1990.

'Europe-A Fresh Start'; European Documentation No 3/90. 33. European Union News; Newsletter of the Delegation of the European Commission in India; various issues - December 94, March 94, December 95 and March 95.

'Economic and Monetary Union'; official publication of the European Community; May, 1991.

'From Single Market to European Union'; European Bulletin Series, official publication of the Community; 1992.

Swaminathan S., Anklesaria Aiyar; 'Europe in Transition: The Impact on India'.

The Associated Chambers of Commerce and Industry of India; "Restructuring Indian Industry to meet the challenges of EC 1992"; Summary Report of proceedings and Background paper; 1992.

'The Challenge of Enlargement'; Commission's opinion on Norway's application for membership, Bulletin of the European Communities, Supplement 2/93.

'The European Community: 1992 and Beyond'; Europe on the move series; 1991.

Target 1992: Newsletter on the Single Internal Market; Monthly Journal, 1991.

'The Impact of German Unification on the European Community; EC Research and Documentation Papers; 1990.

Waslekar Sundeep; 'Response of Indian Firms to the Challenges of the Single European Market"; RIS Discussion papers DP#92-02, April 1992.

Wiemann Jurgen; "Economic Developments in Europe and their Implications for India"; German Development Institute, Berlin.

Index

Duplicate

Uppal 945

10.09.01

Rs. 480/-